Advance Praise for *My Life in the NYPD: Jimmy the Wags*

"Jimmy Wagner was a cop in New York's Ninth Precinct. The Ninth is a high crime precinct, a mix of blacks, whites, Hispanics, hippies, runaways, revolutionaries, derelicts—and murdered cops. This is his portrait of his life and times. The detail is intimate, sometimes funny, and almost always frightening. His story gripped me from beginning to end."
—Robert Daley

"A memoir told from the heart while journeying through hell."
—Victoria Gotti

More praise for *Jimmy the Wags:*
Street Stories of a Private Eye

"If Bruce Willis wrote like Mario Puzo and hung out with John Gotti, the result would be this tough, hilarious, and consummately streetwise book. Jimmy the Wags knows."
—Jack Newfield

"James Wagner is one tough, street-smart hombre. . . . But for my money, the main attraction of this brutally honest book is that it is consistently laugh-out-loud funny."
—Nicholas Pileggi, author of *Wiseguy* and *Casino*

"Stocked with a stellar cast of swells and skells . . . rarely anything but fun."
—*New York Post*

"These streetwise recollections have the sound of tales told from a barstool . . . engaging."—*Publishers Weekly*

"Beneath the swagger and wisecracks, Wagner's embellished yarns of his post-NYPD career as a P.I. ring true. . . . An entertaining glimpse into an on-the-edge lifestyle."
—*Booklist*

"As cops privately will, Wagner crudely skewers most everyone in his way: inept FBI agents, Mafia goombahs, stool pigeons and their harridan wives. Yet his capacity to note the subtle absurdities of situations both banal and dangerous elevates this above the level of mere dreary war stories. . . . more than just entertainment."
—*Kirkus Reviews*

"Action-packed."
—*Star*

"A gritty, outrageous memoir."—*Staten Island Advance*

My Life in the NYPD

Jimmy the Wags

James Wagner

with Patrick Picciarelli

AN ONYX BOOK

ONYX
Published by New American Library, a division of
Penguin Putnam Inc., 375 Hudson Street,
New York, New York 10014, U.S.A.
Penguin Books Ltd, 80 Strand,
London WC2R 0RL, England
Penguin Books Australia Ltd, Ringwood,
Victoria, Australia
Penguin Books Canada Ltd, 10 Alcorn Avenue,
Toronto, Ontario, Canada M4V 3B2
Penguin Books (N.Z.) Ltd, 182–190 Wairau Road,
Auckland 10, New Zealand

Penguin Books Ltd, Registered Offices:
Harmondsworth, Middlesex, England

First published by Onyx, an imprint of New American Library,
a division of Penguin Putnam Inc.

First Printing, March 2002
10 9 8 7 6 5 4 3 2 1

This book is dedicated to the men and women of the Ninth Precinct—to those who survived and to those who didn't.

ACKNOWLEDGMENTS

Because I dug back to the 1970s to write this book, I relied on many other people's memories to help refresh mine. Instrumental in supplying an oral history of the Ninth Precinct and environs were Robert Kress, Jim Liedy, Steve Toth, and Donny Muldoon. To the men who so ably watched my back: Richie Innes, Tommy Dowd, and Vinny D'Adamo. Listen to these men relate their experiences for a few hours, and the wildest episode of *NYPD Blue* will leave you yawning.

To the professionals who guided me: my editor at New American Library, Ellen Edwards; novelist Randall Silvis; and manuscript genie Tanya Martin. A special thank-you to my agent, Frank Weimann, who fits into the world of the streetwise cop as easily as he does the literary world.

Most certainly to Don Imus, who has guided me masterfully through the beginnings of my writing career and was gracious enough to contribute his wit and wisdom to this book. It was Don who so humbly said, "Alright already; stop bugging me, I'll write the damn introduction."

Introduction
by Don Imus

I can't remember when I actually met Jimmy the Wags. Probably sometime during the 1980s. A decade I spent either drunk, coked up, or both. He says he never arrested me. I don't have a record so that's probably true.

Jimmy was a cop in a neighborhood not far from where I lived in New York City's East Village. Greenwich Village. Yes, "The Village," but no, I wasn't down there fixing hair, rearranging furniture, or licking dicks. Let me be clear. There are two Greenwich Villages: East, where I lived, and West, where the homos lived. In those days the gays were all mincing around in cowboy boots and hats, showing up at The Lone Star Cafe, where accommodating patrons would "push their stools in" for them. I was also wearing a cowboy hat and boots and showing up at The Lone Star. But while my aforementioned friends were getting butt fucked at the bar I was on the roof with Kinky Friedman and a giant iguana, industriously snorting enough cocaine to be eligible to run for president.

I don't want to give the impression that I was, or am, some kind of homophobic Nazi. In my view, pointing out who lived where and did what is not making a value judgment about sexual preference or lifestyle. It's just a statement of historical fact and residential patterns crudely embellished, in this case, by my unproductive observations regarding a few queers' anal compulsions. If I sound a little defensive, hysterical even, that may be an issue I need to work on. None of this, though, makes me a bad person.

Back to meeting Wags. As you can see, it's clear I was breaking the law about every twenty seconds during the '80s. So, managing to *not* get arrested is further evidence that the baby Jesus does take care of back-slid hopeless assholes. Even if I had not actually met Jimmy yet, Jimmy does admit he "heard things."

Like back around 1982. I'm living in the penthouse apartment at One Astor Place. It's three o'clock in the morning and I've been up, at that point, maybe four days, snorting cocaine and drinking vodka. I'm looking out the window, sixteen stories down, when two guys come running around the corner off Broadway, one chasing the other. They stop in front of my building where the one creep chasing the other creep pulls out a gun, shoots the poor bastard in the head, and kills him. Without thinking, I call the cops. Had I *been* thinking I might have given at least a passing thought to the pile of cocaine Edmund fucking Hillary couldn't have climbed that I had out on the coffee table. Before I can even think of hiding the dope three cops are at the door. I casually flipped open a newspaper on top of the coke and told my new best friends what I'd just witnessed. I could have sworn one of those cops was Jimmy the Wags. He says no. Anyway, they took a few notes and advised me to get some rest—a lot of rest—and left. It might not have been Jimmy, but it sounds like the kind of slack Wags might cut somebody who was not a cop-hating hippie shithead with green hair and enough body piercings to look like a colander. *They* did live in the Village. Both Villages.

So it's now 2001 and Jimmy's my security consultant. He discourages people from running up to me and saying things that might offend me, like "Hello." Or, "How are you?" Whatever.

Anyway, whether he remembers ever having met me or not, what's most disturbing about the stuff Jimmy does recall in here is that it's all probably true. Jimmy is also someone I would not fuck with. You probably shouldn't either. Do the right thing. Buy the book.

Don Imus
New York

Author's Foreword

Street police work is a world of mundane, yawn-inducing tedium that can change to heart-pounding, adrenaline-surging highs in a nanosecond. Such a dichotomy is the norm for a cop on patrol.

My name is James Wagner; my friends call me Wags. I was on patrol for twenty-two years, first as a radio-car cop, then as a sergeant. There was no glory here, no detectives wearing thousand-dollar suits, no headline-grabbing cases solved, no *Daily News* Hero of the Month accolades, certainly no praise from the politically connected in 1 Police Plaza. Just a group of men and women whose sole purpose in life was to make it to the end of their tour, attempting to find humor where it did not exist.

A street cop gets by on humor, tight friendships, and the occasional six-pack. Ours was a world of episodic paranoia, always on the lookout for danger, real or imagined—coping with the deaths of friends who fell in the line of duty, grieving with their families as though we were part of them, but guiltily glad we survived.

I joined the NYPD in the sixties, that decade of craziness, which sailed into the seventies with little or no urging from the folks who didn't want to let it go.

What you will read here is the reality of the street for the cop on patrol. Some of the stories don't have happy endings. Hell, some have no endings at all. Tell me a "war story" that has a happy ending and I'll show you fiction. The following is the truth, with all its grittiness, black humor, and grace. Just like in real street police work, you may be shocked when you least expect it.

Prologue
Under the Influence

Sunday, June 3, 1953

"**G**entlemen, the story you are about to hear is true; only the names have been changed to protect the innocent. Dragnet . . . The documented drama of an actual crime, investigated and solved by the men who unrelentingly stand watch on the security of your home, your family, and your life. For the next thirty minutes, in cooperation with the Los Angeles Police Department, you will travel step by step on the side of the law through an actual case from official police files, from beginning to end, from crime to punishment. This is the story of your police force in action.*"

My father and I were sitting shoulder-to-shoulder on our overstuffed couch in the living room, three feet from a Crosley floor-model radio that was bigger than a depth charge. Duffel bag–size bolsters cradled me on one side; my father's beefy arm sandwiched me on the other.

I lived for Sunday nights at nine-thirty. When I was nine years old, this was the only night I was permitted to stay up past nine. *Dragnet* was on, and Joe Friday wrote the rules. Besides, my father was a cop and he liked to have me around so he could tell me what was going on "between the lines."

"*It was Tuesday, March 25th; it was cold in Los Angeles. We were working the night watch out of Homi-*

*cide. Detectives in Los Angeles work in pairs. My part-
ner's Ben Romero; he's a sergeant; so am I. My name's
Friday. The boss is Ed Backstrand, Chief of Detectives."*

Television was just a rumor at our house, being a relatively new invention, and in the words of my parents,
"not perfected yet." We wouldn't see one for another
year, and that would be an oval-shaped, black-and-white
Du Mont that would last us until everybody on welfare
had a color set. Until then it was radio. I didn't know
any better, and when I closed my eyes I saw a picture
anyway. Spending time with my father and talking "cop
talk" was what made it fun. I also thought Sergeant Friday was the coolest guy since Hopalong Cassidy.

*"I was on the way back from the Record Bureau and
it was thirteen minutes past eleven."*

"You hear the way he's walking, Jimmy?" my father
said, the ice tinkling in his third—and last—highball of
the evening. "You counting the steps?"

I'd heard this before but still I asked, "Whaddaya
mean, Daddy?"

"The walking—he took fourteen steps, ya see? It's actually fourteen steps in real life down the stairs from the
Record Bureau in headquarters. I read it somewhere.
The rest of the building has thirteen steps to a landing,
but not the stairs leading from the Record Bureau; that's
got fourteen. Jack Webb loves a cop, wants to get it
right."

"Neat." I also knew that when Sergeant Friday read
from a police report he would have to flip a page or two
to get to certain information, just like on the actual reports. Sergeant Friday reads the names of witnesses;
that's on page three. Flip, flip.

We sat there staring at an inanimate boxy radio for
half an hour, my father chuckling and commenting on
police procedure and me planning my future. Yeah, at
nine I knew what I wanted to be: a cop, just like my
daddy and Joe Friday.

Most cops bring home their uniforms, gun belts and
all, the night before election day, because if they had the
detail to guard the polls (and almost everyone did) they

would save some time by leaving their homes before sunrise and driving straight to the polls, rather than stopping by the precinct to change. It was after my father went to bed the night before election duty that I would sneak downstairs to the basement and try on his uniform. He'd lock his four-inch Smith & Wesson Model Ten revolver in a fireproof metal box, but I had everything else to play with.

Within minutes I'd be enveloped in heavy blue wool, sleeves dragging on the floor, wearing a hat both me and my brother could fit in, and standing in front of a full-length mirror puffing out my chest. His shield gleamed, illuminated by the overhead fluorescent light, and looked more like a chest protector on my scrawny frame. I'd stare at myself for what seemed like hours, holding up his gun belt around my waist, heavy despite the lack of lethal iron, and wish the years would fly by so I could be a cop like my daddy.

My father spent his entire career in uniform in the One-Two-Oh Precinct on the north shore of Staten Island. We lived on the island, too, only on the other end where the cops and firemen lived, in a postwar single-family home with a minuscule mortgage.

The north shore encompassed Stapleton, Park Hill, and Saint George. In the fifties, and even part of the sixties, the north shore was peaceful and serene—think of the entire population of Santa Barbara on quaaludes—a cluster of quiet communities bonded together by a strong family ethic and consisting mostly of native Staten Islanders who rarely, if ever, ventured to "the mainland." This was pre–Verrazano Narrows Bridge, and World War II veterans were happy they survived the Big One and wanted only to raise their kids in the relative utopia of the closest thing they could afford to a suburban community.

In those days, my father didn't enforce the law so much as keep the peace. There's a difference. Lawbreakers consisted mostly of kids boosting cars, or the occasional burglar or stickup artist. Where's the holdup guy going to go after he makes his big score at the local mom-and-pop candy store? He'd be island-locked unless he carried around a ferry schedule with him, and the cops always had a presence at the ferry terminal. The local cops preceded *Hawaii Five-O*'s McGarrett with their own version of "sealing off the island."

These were the types of bad guys who needed "enforcing." Keeping the peace consisted of knowing every family in your sector (which could run for miles), knowing which kids needed "special attention," and having at least one snitch per block. Talking got the job done, and rarely did my father have to get physical with anyone.

Cops were respected. A family having problems with one of their kids would call my father, sometimes at home. Everyone had his number. The next time my father was working, he'd seek out the kid in question and give him a talking-to. If the kid wised off to my father to impress his friends, he'd get a slap in the mouth. Later the parents would call my house to thank my father for cuffing their son. Even the local wiseguys vacated the street when my father and his partner, Dave Ballantine, rolled onto the block. Crap games folded, street-corner betting took a recess. Respect. It made the neighborhood run cohesively. Then came the seventies.

The projects, which had sprung up after the war as inexpensive places to house families, now turned into war zones. Drugs had a hand in it; so did rampant poverty and the war in Vietnam. The Stapleton and Park Hill projects had the highest per-capita homicide rate in the city. These depressed neighborhoods were drug central for the entire island. My father went from being Bishop Sheen to Paladin almost overnight.

He'd still come straight home from work, sometimes with Dave, for an early dinner with my mom, my kid brother Ned, my sister Regina, and me, then have a few highballs in front of the TV or a game of catch with me, if he was up to it. But as time went by and I entered my teens I saw the subtle change in him. He became less communicative, less likely to brag about "The Job." My dad was no longer making a difference in the neighborhood. All the "communicating" did no good, and was replaced by violence, which became the only means of communication. His sources dried up as the neighborhoods changed ethnically. No one trusted the white cop anymore.

He took to carrying two guns. My father never drew his revolver until he was in the twilight of his career, and then almost on an hourly basis. His trusty nippers (a medieval device consisting of a six-inch length of chain supported by two pieces of steel, which when twisted around a suspect's wrist would garner instant compliance—some cops called them "come-alongs") were replaced by a cocobolo-wood nightstick that was tougher than iron and made of the only wood I know of that doesn't float. Nippers required that you got up close and personal with a suspect; a twenty-four-inch nightstick gave you some distance from the possibility of that all-too-unpleasant kick in the balls.

But people have a habit of remembering the good things, the "good old days." I recall actually being able to smell my father's scent when he came home for lunch. A pungent odor of leather, gun oil, and shoe polish would follow him into the kitchen, where I would be waiting for my hug. He'd drive the radio car right into the driveway, and he and Dave would chow down on hero sandwiches like they didn't have a care in the world. If a cop drove his radio car home for lunch today he'd be fired before he had a chance to burp. (Of course, the firing would occur *after* the cop was committed for psychological observation.) Dave would pick me up and swing me around the room. My mom would cluck, "Be careful, Dave; you'll hurt the boy."

"Lock up any bad guys, Daddy?" I would ask, a pre-pubescent innocence widening my eyes.

"Not today, Jimmy," he'd say, "but me 'n' Dave here are hot on the trail of the Mad Bomber. Gonna get him any day now." Dave would go along with the game. When George Matefsky, the Mad Bomber, was finally captured I told everyone in school that my dad had caught him. I think I believed it until I was around seventeen.

Even when I saw the harsh realities of police work—
my father's three-drink-a-night ritual gradually peaked
out at six or seven—along with the cynicism that arrived
late in his career, I still wanted to be a cop.

Just like my father.

And I would have a helluva career.

So we begin, for my father and Sergeant Joe Friday.

*The story you are about to read is true; only the names
have been changed to protect the innocent.* Well, some
have been changed. You'll see why.

1
The Class of '68:
Nuts, Sluts, and Butts

I got out of the navy in October 1967. After spending two years seeing the world, I was eager to get back to "the block." The world was interesting, but it wasn't New York.

I was twenty-one years old and eligible to take the New York City Police Department entrance exam. While I still maintained my dream of being a cop, I had other priorities as well, not the least of which was getting laid and having a good time. This is what young guys do. So for the next six months I partied and then partied some more.

My father, who by this time was a living legend among Staten Island cops, along with his partner, Dave, didn't press me to settle down. He knew that when I got bored with being George Hamilton I'd become responsible and take the police test.

Oh, I worked, all right. My first job was with the phone company. I fixed coin boxes. That lasted all of a month, until one day I got disgusted with a stubborn pay phone and walked off the job. Didn't even take my lunch hour. The following summer I was a lifeguard at a local beach. I liked that better (doesn't take a genius to figure out why).

During that time, Mayor John Lindsay, who had gotten into office by promising a slew of new cops, was getting pressured by the opposition party to appoint the three thousand probationary patrolmen to the force he had promised. The mayor, however, was having a hard time finding anyone who wanted to be a member of the NYPD. The sixties was the Decade of the Pig, and the Vietnam War turned most people under thirty against every form of authority. Being a cop just wasn't "in."

To boost interest in The Job, the mayor ordered a series of "walk-in" tests, where city high schools would throw open their doors and test applicants for the NYPD right off the street, no preapplication necessary.

Traditionally, applying for any city job required submitting a ton of paperwork in order to be considered for a position. The NYPD, because its members were supposed to be the cream of the crop (it turned out that the candidates recruited during this period were the cream of the *crap*), required even more paper and scrutiny than the average city job. Lindsay figured that people would be more likely to take a walk-in test because the paperwork (or most of it) had been eliminated. Sort of like impulse buying. I know it worked for me.

Thinking back, I visualize the following scene: Two guys on their way to stick up a liquor store pass a high school where five thousand guys are milling around.

"Yo, Angelo," the first mutt remarks, "what's this shit?"

"Fucked if I know," Angelo says, but being the brighter of the two (his lobotomy wasn't scheduled until next Tuesday), he investigates. "Police test or some shit," he reports back. "You wanna be a cop, Frankie?"

Frankie contemplates. "We get to pack?"

"Fuckin' A. All cops carry guns."

Frankie pulls a gravity knife from his pocket. "Great, we can get rid of these friggin' things. Let's do it."

And so two of New York's Finest are born. Believe me, at the time this scenario wasn't too far from the truth.

I was on my way to yet another party when I passed a similar scene. There were literally thousands of guys (and a handful of women) hanging around a high school waiting for the doors to open. It was a Friday night, and I bet most, if not all, of the budding Dick Tracys were on their way somewhere else when they figured, What the hell; I'll take the test. Mayor Lindsay's tactic worked. He was able to get huge numbers to take the entrance exam.

Of course, getting large numbers of applicants doesn't guarantee that they're going to pass the test. Therefore, the exam was so simple a moron could have passed it (and many did). I recall a few of the questions:

1. If it's 9:30 now, what time will it be in 33 minutes? (There was no A.M. or P.M. designation so as not to confuse the test takers.)
2. The Brooklyn Bridge goes from Manhattan to——?

These were multiple-choice questions, by the way. With my veterans' preference I scored a hundred and five percent, as did most of the other applicants, who were also veterans. And so, out of the turbulent sixties, the infamous Police Academy class of October 1968 was formed.

There was no background check for the successful applicants. To this day, thirty-four years later, I'm still waiting for my investigator to call me down to headquarters for my intake interview. I don't expect a call anytime soon. We were fingerprinted, but my class was appointed before the prints cleared. A complete round-robin print check usually took from two to three months. And that was a rush job.

It wasn't rare to be waiting on the biweekly pay line outside the Academy's sixth-floor administration office, when the rookie cop behind you was wrestled to the floor and cuffed by Internal Affairs detectives because his fingerprint check indicated he was wanted for something like sodomy in Wyoming. Some guys in my class made the Manson family look like the College of Cardinals.

During this time we were all running around with guns, those days being before a rookie had to complete the six-month Academy course *prior* to being issued a revolver. With us it was, "Raise your right hand, and swear you'll be a good guy and you won't shoot anyone unless you're reasonably sure they deserve it." Then they handed us guns and shields (badges to you civilians). All this was accomplished on the first day in the Academy. Armed and dangerous, that was us.

On our first day as new rookies we were lined up on the roof of the Police Academy building and inspected by three guys wearing the same gray suits. They pulled out about six young-looking guys from our ranks and left with them. We never saw the rookies or the suits again. Later we learned that the "chosen few" would be working undercover, most likely in Narcotics, and were pulled out of the class before they were tainted with police jargon that might get them killed. It was the fast track to getting the gold shield in those days (becoming a detective). Civil-service law dictated, however, that when their undercover careers were over, they would be mandated to return to the Academy to complete the six-month recruit course. Could you imagine some battle-weary undercover cop having to learn the proper way to address a member of some minority group after getting down and dirty with street junkies for a couple of years?

The two classes prior to mine, April and June '68 (they overlapped) were tossed out onto the street within days of being sworn in because of the riots caused by the Bobby Kennedy and Martin Luther King, Jr., assassinations. More than half of these rookies weren't even issued shields because the Personnel Bureau ran out of them. The cops without the shields carried a form letter explaining that they were indeed members of New York's Finest. I envisioned one of these guys getting involved in an off-duty arrest and having to resort to unfolding a piece of paper to ID himself: "Halt, police! Uh, I've got my letter here somewhere to prove it. Now where is that damn letter? Could you hold your fire for a second, please?"

New York City was one big bonfire, with insurrections

in Harlem and Brownsville, and the extra police presence was needed. Unfortunately the virgin cops received virtually no training, and were fed to the wolves wearing gray recruit uniforms, issued three hundred rounds of ammo, and told, "Go get 'em."

It was like Dodge City. Cops shot up entire city blocks, and many civilians were wounded. No one was held accountable. To be fair, many of the rookies were seriously hurt, too. Months later, when things settled down, the combat veterans were returned to the Police Academy for training. I remember their first day back.

I was entering the building in my grays for a day tour of classes. There must have been two hundred cops, also in grays, milling around in front of the building. They looked like they'd been on the ground during the Battle of Britain, sullen, hollow-eyed, not a smile anywhere. Most, as in my class, were ex-military, a lot of them Vietnam combat vets.

A pressed-out lieutenant, who hadn't been on the street since the Lindbergh kidnapping, strutted out of the building in a Smokey the Bear hat, blew a whistle, and shouted, "Fall in!" In unison, most of the rookies shouted back, "Fuck you!" From there it was all downhill.

After what these guys had seen, both in the military and on the mean streets of ghetto New York, no one was going to tell them they had to go back to the Academy. They didn't want to learn how to properly address a minority group member after they had seen a lot of residents of our poorer neighborhoods mugging priests.

There was a standoff for a while, but the rookies won. They were whisked back onto the street with little additional instruction, this time with blue uniforms, and assimilated into precincts. It's not surprising that these classes had the highest number of cops going to jail for everything from taking bribes to committing murder. One cop who's still on The Job from this era is rumored to be a contract hitter. Many are still out there, a few in supervisory positions. Now, don't you feel safe?

*   *   *

We were assigned to classes alphabetically. There were thirty-five men in my class, three women. Most of the rookies were Vietnam vets, used to taking orders. Our instructor was a hardened, streetwise lieutenant named Kurtz.

We were required to maintain a grade of seventy percent to graduate. No one flunked out. The only rookies who didn't graduate were those who got arrested. We had a few certifiably brain-damaged cops in my class, but their grades miraculously went from failing to passing as the written tests were carried from the classroom to the administrative office for posting. Every warm body counted toward the mayor's magic number of three thousand additional cops on the street.

While I had little problem with the written exams, the gym was a bitch. Those were the days when physical fitness was a term that applied only to Jack LaLanne. I was in reasonably good shape, but I smoked at the time, and the NYPD was nuts for running.

We'd run in circles around the interior of the gym for hours. Not only was it boring, but the pace was a killer. To break up the monotony, we started running around the neighborhood, but it didn't work out. Those residents who didn't complain about us snarling traffic threw garbage cans and bricks at us from rooftops.

I thought I was going to die by the end of the second week. My lungs were on fire. Then I discovered a way to beat the system. After my first lap I'd veer off to the right and down a stairwell, where I would remain until the troops were on their last lap; then I'd rejoin the run. The other rookies knew what I was doing, but kept quiet about it. My first exposure to the Blue Wall of Silence. This worked out well, until the day I was ambushed.

One of the gym instructors, Al Gotay, was a legend in the NYPD. It was rumored he was assigned to the Academy after he stuffed a junkie down a sewer and made him swim to jail. Gotay was in phenomenal shape and expected everyone else to be, too. Well, one morning he spotted my little bug-out and lay in wait for me on the stairwell.

I peeled off as usual, now ballsy enough to smoke a cigarette while my classmates ran their asses off. I puffed contentedly, not a care in the world. Then from behind me I heard, "Hey, Wags, got another smoke?"

My testicles dropped to my ankles. I knew I'd been nabbed by Gotay. Now what? I turned with a sheepish grin on my mug.

"Okay, Officer Gotay, you got me." I ground out the cigarette and waited.

"Feel like going for a run, Officer?"

And I ran; boy, did I ever run. I ran for the remainder of the day, missing my academic classes, stopping only to throw up. I learned my lesson: There were some people out there slicker than me.

I cut back on the smoking; I had to. After that the gym wasn't so bad; in fact, I actually looked forward to it, and I was getting into dynamite shape. On one particularly warm day we were standing in loose formation watching Gotay go through a handcuffing drill when I got a sudden pain in my ass. Normally the only pain in my ass was Gotay, but this time it was different. This was serious pain. I jumped and screamed. Whirling, I came face-to-face with the infamous Ruthie.

Ruthie was notorious in the NYPD. A woman in her fifties, with psoriasis-covered legs and a head of greasy, matted hair that made her look like she was dipped in the Gowanus Canal, and crazy as a bedbug, Ruthie's sole mission in life was to see how many cops she could grab by the ass or the testicles. Her turf was Manhattan South, and such was her reputation that she was known, if not by appearance, by her iron grip. She traveled with a dog she called Shep, who always had a signature red bandanna around his neck. It was said that you weren't truly a cop until Ruthie grabbed you by the gonads. I was about to become a real cop.

As soon as I turned she grabbed my balls in a viselike grip that brought tears to my eyes. She wouldn't let go. Apparently she had gained entrance to the gym because Gotay, in his infinite wisdom, had left the door to Twentieth Street open to increase ventilation. I seem to recall now that he had me stand in the rear of the formation that day, closest to the door. I think he ambushed me once again.

Ruthie let out a cackle and squeezed harder. All the rookies cracked up as I howled like a wolf and fought to get her hand from its death grip on my jewels. Finally she released me and ran after some of the other rookies. Eventually Gotay shooed her outside, but not before she lifted her skirt and mooned us. She had Xs and Os tattooed all over her ample ass. To this day I double over and my voice rises an octave when I recall the incident.

Eventually I saw the light at the end of the tunnel. I had completed about five months of training and was about to become a real cop. One of the last qualifying areas was swimming.

Our instructor was Officer Jimmy Smith, a.k.a. Mr. Clean. Smith looked exactly like the Mr. Clean of TV commercial fame. He also taught the boxing class and at one time had been legendary fighter Billy Conn's sparring partner. Mr. Clean was ageless.

Long after I'd retired and become a private investigator, I struck up a conversation with an ancient retired detective living in Miami. The old guy had to be ninety years old. *He* was trained by Mr. Clean. A kid who lives around the corner from me just graduated from the Academy. I don't think he shaves yet. He, too, was trained by Mr. Clean.

I ran into Mr. Clean one day at a police racket in Chinatown, once again long after I had retired. He was doing one-armed push-ups in the bathroom while he waited for a stall. He actually looked younger than when I knew him in the Academy. A regular Dorian friggin' Gray.

Anyway, we were standing around in our bathing suits, realizing that the three women in our class looked pretty good in their one-piece suits.

I had given little thought to the females in my class and, in fact, had little social interaction with any of my classmates. The hours and the work involved during the six-month course hindered getting involved socially with my fellow rookies. Everyone else kept pretty much to themselves as well, but one day I discovered that this social isolation didn't extend to the instructors.

I had realized, several hours after a swimming class, that I had forgotten my watch in the locker room. I had to wait until the academic day ended before I was permitted to get it.

The watch was still there, much to my amazement. As I was leaving the darkened locker room, I heard splashing sounds coming from the pool. I peeked through the door and saw eight naked people, sexes equally divided, frolicking in the water. The males were the instructors; the females were recruits from other classes.

There was a strict rule against instructors fraternizing with the recruits, but obviously no one paid attention to it. I eased out of the locker room and got the hell out of the building, believing that since I hadn't been spotted I hadn't seen anything.

Apparently the Venice Beach crowd couldn't stay away from their late-afternoon romps and were caught in the act by a janitor, who turned them in. The commanding officer of the Academy had to call in every favor owed him to put a lid on the scandal. It would be the first of many involving male and female cops, both in- and outside of the Academy.

After I graduated, I heard that instructors were passing certain female rookies for "sexual favors." You'll never hear about this stuff during recruitment drives.

2

Sex and the Single Cop

Every rookie cop dreams about his first arrest. I used to fantasize about locking up a bank robber after driving my car through the plate-glass window of the bank, freeing hostages, and capturing Willie Sutton, Jr., all without firing a shot. What actually happened was a little less spectacular.

While still in the Academy, rookies weren't permitted to drive to classes, the rationale being that if we took the limited amount of parking spaces in the crowded Lower East Side neighborhood it would further piss off the locals, who weren't crazy about cops to begin with. So it was the bus, the ferry, and a subway every day for me.

Most of my time was spent commuting, but I really didn't mind, because I was sure I'd make that big collar on the way to classes and be catapulted to detective without ever having to wear a uniform for my entire career.

I usually got to work a half hour early, slow trains being no excuse for being late. My daily routine consisted of stopping in a coffee shop on Twenty-first Street, picking up a bagel with a "shmear" and a coffee light to go, and then walking the block to the Academy.

Every morning I'd see Margaret Hamilton, the actress who played the Wicked Witch in *The Wizard of Oz,* at the same table in the coffee shop. She was in her late seventies by then, lived close by in Gramercy Park, and was a fixture in the neighborhood. A real nice lady who went out of her way to be friendly. And she loved a cop, even a rookie. We had our morning ritual.

"Good morning, Wags," she'd say. "Where're you going?"

"I'm off to see the Wizard, Margaret," I'd say; she'd laugh, and off I'd go. A nice way to start a day.

On the day of the big arrest I was looking forward to my bagel and coffee, cooling my heels on the uptown IRT, when I felt a hand wrap itself around my genitals. My first thought was of Ruthie, but the grasp didn't bring tears to my eyes. I think by that time I could have spotted Ruthie with a bag over my head. My second thought was that cops get grabbed by the balls a lot. If Mayor Lindsay had mentioned *that* was a perk of being in the NYPD, he would have gotten more applicants than he could handle.

Now, normally a hand on my dick would be a good thing. There were any number of gorgeous women going to work in the crowded subway, three of whom were jammed up against me. My assumption was that one of these lovely ladies liked men in uniform.

I began to get more than a little aroused. I looked at the three suspects, trying to pick out the future Mrs. Wagner. All three had angelic expressions on their faces and were engaged in the New York sport of not making eye contact with any of the three hundred people crammed into the two-hundred-person car.

I was perplexed, but being the sharp future detective that I thought I was, I placed my hand upon the hand that was now caressing my dick. The plan was to follow the hand to its owner, propose marriage, and ride off into the sunset. Instead of stroking a soft, feminine hand, I grabbed a mitt that made King Kong's paw seem like it belonged to Shirley Temple. In short, a guy had me by the Johnson.

Not only was I horrified, I was pissed. My love lance shrank to Lilliputian size as I followed the hairy append-age to its owner, a fifty-something fat guy dressed in an expensive suit and bow tie. I twisted his arm and shouted, "You're under arrest!"

The people standing around me parted like the Red Sea as I slapped handcuffs on my first prisoner, not the bank robber I had envisioned, but a Madison Avenue advertising executive with a penchant for young guys.

I was mortified as I dragged him off the train. In retrospect, I should have given him a swift kick in the ass or twisted his arm off, but the harm was already done. I had announced an arrest and now was obligated to see it through.

The booking experience was humiliating. I took a lot of abuse, and it was from the cops in the precinct, not the perp. It was all good-natured ribbing, but a little hard to take, particularly after I was repeatedly referred to as Officer Lance Rockhard by everyone from the desk officer to the precinct janitor.

I had had my eye on one of the clerical staff in the Academy for quite a while. Her name was Cora, and she was a cute little thing, about five-three, with short dark hair and a tight body. We flirted with each other all the time, and I had every intention of waiting until I graduated before asking her out, not wanting to break the rule I was certain existed against secretaries named Cora going out with cops named Wagner.

Anyway, fresh off my first big arrest and visualizing Cora's hand wrapped around my dick instead of Mr. Madison Avenue's, I cornered her one day coming into the building and asked her for a date. She accepted and gave me her address on the East Side in Midtown.

"See you Friday at eight," she said, giving me a coy sideways glance as she made her way to the elevator.

We saw each other practically every night for weeks. It was love brought on by lust and her apartment's close proximity to the Academy. I no longer had to make the trek to Staten Island every day. After work we'd go to dinner somewhere, to a movie, or just back to her place. She was into everything from Jell-O baths to "toys." I was in heaven. Until the first phone call.

It was a Saturday morning. Cora and I had gone to dinner the previous night at my favorite Italian restaurant, Ciro's, in Croton-on-Hudson. It was a bit of a ride, about fifty miles upstate, but we loved the place and we were comforted in knowing that no one we knew would see us together. I was a few weeks away from graduation, but we both thought it unwise to broadcast our relationship.

Cora was making breakfast; I was still in bed. Life was good. I heard her pick up the phone, gasp, and say, "Oh, my God." I rushed into the kitchen, which was about three steps away in Cora's average-size New York studio apartment.

"What happened?"

Cora was holding the phone at arm's length, staring at it.

"Some woman, someone I don't know, was screeching about me being a whore and fucking cops." She was shaken. I cradled the phone and had her sit down.

"That's it; that's all she said?"

She shook her head slowly. "No. When I said, 'Excuse me?' she said, 'You're fucking James Wagner. We know; we've been following you.' "

We had been very careful to avoid the rumor mill, and I always checked for a tail wherever we went. We were two single people, but we wanted to keep a low profile.

Before the weekend was over, we got another call. I assumed we were dealing with more than one stalker, because the caller made reference to "we" on two occasions during the first call. I listened in on this one.

"Cora?" the woman said. Whoever it was sounded like she was disguising her voice.

"Yes."

"We followed you, you know."

I felt Cora stiffen. "Followed us where?"

"To Ciro's, you fucking slut."

I was incredulous. The last leg of the trip was along a single-lane road that ran parallel to the Croton Reservoir. I tried to think back to whether there was a car on the road with us, but drew a blank. There was obviously a tail; whoever this was had to stay fairly close or risk

losing us at any one of dozens of secluded turnoffs. This
had to be a cop. I urged Cora to keep the stalker talking.

"Uh, I don't know what you're talking about," Cora
said. A real ad-libber, Cora.

"You think we're stupid, you cunt? I know your lover
Wagner's there. He's telling you what to say, isn't he?"

I got dressed in a flash and raced out of the apartment
in shirtsleeves, gun stuck in my waistband, no coat. It
was the first week in April, but spring hadn't yet arrived.
I started to shiver as soon as I hit the street.

East Thirty-sixth Street was lined with traffic destined
for the Midtown Tunnel, a block away. There were hundreds of people wandering along Third Avenue. I could
have been under surveillance at that moment and not
known it. I went back to Cora's apartment.

The calls continued for a week, most coming in the
evening around eight o'clock, recounting how Cora and
I had spent our day, getting raunchier with each call.
While the caller had begun by berating Cora, now she
was on my case. The woman spent the first few minutes
of every call describing in detail what she would like to
do to me sexually if given the opportunity. I offered to
meet with her. She laughed.

"Do you think I'm stupid, Jimmy?" I heard another
woman giggling in the background. "Go back to fucking
your girlfriend."

After a few more days of this kind of stuff I called the
telephone company's Annoyance Bureau.

The investigator I dealt with was very good, but all he
was able to ascertain were the first three digits of the
phone number from where the calls emanated. Our
stalker didn't stay on the line long enough to get more.

The prefix indicated that the call was coming from an
area in midtown Manhattan encompassing fifteen square
blocks. Not many cops could afford to live in that area
of Midtown, but there were still some rent-stabilized
apartments that were affordable.

I did some deductive thinking. Our dating affected no one's lives outside of the Police Academy. Whoever was making the calls had to be assigned to the Academy, and for some reason had a thing for me or Cora or both of us. I was sure of it. Unfortunately, there were three thousand recruits currently in the program, plus over a hundred civilians and tenured cops acting in support jobs.

"Can I get back in the building after hours?" I asked Cora. After hours was after midnight, because the Academy was running classes in two shifts.

"Sure, you can get in through the Thirteenth Precinct," she said. The Thirteenth Precinct station house shared the same building with the Academy, with an adjoining door in the lobby, but there was no admittance from the precinct side. "Why?"

"I want to look at the Ten Cards," I said. Ten Cards are NYPD forms that list personal information, including phone numbers, for members assigned to a particular command.

Cora said, "I'll unlock the door from the Academy side when I leave the building."

Mission Impossible was in effect.

It was one o'clock in the morning. I ambled past the desk lieutenant in the Thirteenth Precinct with a "Hiya, Loo," like I belonged there. I even felt like a real cop when he grunted back.

I went straight for the linking door and sailed through without so much as a glance. I locked it behind me.

I think I was committing a burglary. The New York State penal law defines burglary as "entering a premises with the intent of committing a crime therein." I was about to rifle the files in the Police Academy's administration office. If that wasn't committing a crime, I didn't know what was.

The building was deserted except for the janitorial staff and the lab troops in the Forensics Unit on the top (seventh) floor. I took the stairs to six, peeked into the darkened hallway, saw no one, and stuck close to the wall until I got to the administration office. The door was wide open. So much for security. These were the days before the term *urban terrorism* was invented.

I flipped on the light and made for the Ten File in the rear of the office. I figured if I was seen, I'd rather it be in a well-lit area than huddled over a flashlight.

Two hours later I had gone through over two thousand cards with no hits. A janitor rolled a bucket by at four A.M.

"You working?" he asked.

"Yeah, I'm being punished for being an asshole. Gotta refile all this shit." Punishment these guys understood; they saw recruits being subjected to all sorts of weird penalties all day and night for infractions of department rules.

He mumbled something and went on his way.

By four-thirty I had gone through all the civilians and was just about to the end of the police supervisors when I struck gold.

I found the prefix. It belonged to a female lieutenant in charge of the building's clerical staff. I ran through the rest of the cards. She was the only match.

Now it was beginning to make sense. This lieutenant was unusually attentive to me when I picked up my check every two weeks. I thought nothing of it, other than that she was friendly. This was a superior officer in her mid-forties, old enough to be my mother, and on the fast track in the department.

It was rare for female cops during the sixties to attain any rank, let alone that of lieutenant. She retired a few years ago as one of the highest-ranking women in the NYPD, and I hesitate to mention her name because she'd undoubtedly deny everything. But I was sure at the time that it was her. But who was her accomplice?

For the next few days, I managed to find an excuse to go to the administration office as often as I could, or failing that, to pass by and steal glances inside. I also asked questions of some of the old-timers who worked in the building.

I noticed that the lieutenant and a frumpy blond secretary were always talking. Rumor had it that they were more than just office buddies. These two had some serious problems. As a rookie cop still on probation and eligible to be fired for any reason, I didn't want to get into a pissing contest with someone who outranked me.

But the calls continued, except that now the stalker would speak only to Cora. I thought perhaps my frequent visits to the administration office had raised suspicions that I might be wise to my stalkers. Even though they might have suspected that I was on to them, the calls didn't stop. Two sick puppies.

With a pounding heart and sweaty palms I waited for the lieutenant to leave the building after a four-to-twelve tour. I blocked her path. There was fear in her eyes.

"Lieutenant," I said calmly, "if you and your friend keep calling me, I'm going to IAD." She began to protest, no indignation, just a lame response. I knew then that I was right. I held up a hand. "I had the calls traced," I lied, and rattled off her phone number. "Don't do it anymore. Have a nice day." I smiled, turned, and walked away.

Good news and bad news. Good: the calls stopped. Bad: my relationship with Cora didn't survive. After twenty or so harassing calls the magic was disconnected, and maybe it was a good thing. If we couldn't get past a minor, albeit unnerving, experience like the calls, how would our relationship fare if we ever got serious and had to face the realities of police work and how it could decimate even the strongest of bonds?

It was a difficult lesson because I really liked Cora, but it was just the first in a series of learning experiences handed me by the unforgiving school that is the NYPD.

3

Learning the (Frayed) Ropes

In March of 1969 I was assigned to the Fourth Precinct upon graduation from the Police Academy. Graduating rookies had filled out "dream sheets," a department form that allowed us to choose three precincts in the city. We would supposedly be granted one of our choices.

Of course we believed The Job would take care of us; hell, we were real cops now, blue uniforms and all. I realized the dream sheets were exactly that—a dream— when I caught Lieutenant Kurtz tossing them into the garbage when we filed out of our classroom. I had chosen three high-crime commands in Manhattan because I wanted to be a real cop.

I didn't even know there was a Fourth Precinct. When I found out I was going there, I nonchalantly engaged an instructor in conversation in an attempt to find out more about my new command.

"Hey, Sarge," I said, "the Fourth, that's in Brooklyn, right?"

"It's downtown Manhattan, asshole."

So much of being cool.

The Fourth, I was to find out, was a dumping ground. Every misfit, knuckle-dragging, has-been malcontent that precinct COs wanted to get rid of was dumped to the Fourth. Nothing much was expected of them, and the few unlucky rookies assigned there were sent for one reason: Someone had to do the work.

I hadn't even shown up for work yet and I approached my dad to see if he could do something to get me assigned where I'd be surrounded by real cops. My dad was only a police officer, or patrolman, as they were called in those days, and while he didn't have rank and really shouldn't have been able to exert influence over assignments, he was well respected by high-ranking bosses in the Staten Island command who would extend a reasonable favor. If getting me out of the Fourth Precinct wasn't a reasonable request, I didn't know what was. I wanted to be Supercop, and the Fourth wasn't the place to get my cape.

"Don't you think you should give it a shot?" my dad said. We were sitting at the dinner table, the rest of the family having retired to the living room to watch television. Dad twirled a highball while I polished off a wedge of apple pie.

"Hell, no, I wanna go to the Ninth." The Ninth Precinct was ground zero, the toughest high-crime command in the city. Located in Manhattan's East Village and encompassing Alphabet City (so called because the avenues are designated by letters of the alphabet), it was a small command, but what it lacked in size it more than made up for in action.

My dad looked at me long and hard. By that time he had over twenty years on The Job and had seen a lot. I could see waves of memories clouding his eyes as he recounted his first days in blue. He snorted. "Give it a while. In the meantime I'll see what I can do."

I wasn't happy doing one day in the Fourth, but later I realized why Dad let me stew there for a while. The Job, I was to find out, was full of disappointments; if I was to be granted every wish I desired, what would I learn? How would I get tough? And tough you had to be, as I was soon to find out.

I can only describe what it feels like to walk into a new command just after coming out of the Academy as the same fear you have when you drive your new car home from the showroom after picking it up. The feeling happens with every command, and every car, no matter how long you're a cop or how many cars you buy.

The Fourth Precinct was a small command located in the western tip of lower Manhattan. There was nothing much there except warehouses, piers, the Holland Tunnel, and a few hookers who laid claim to the western edge of Delancey Street. During the eighties the area would become "in" with the club crowd, and many good restaurants that couldn't afford uptown rents would lay claim to the area. But this was 1968 when the only good restaurant was a mobbed-up place called Teddy's, and the only clubs were after-hours. A good place to be put out to pasture for a soon-to-be retiree, or to hide a cop who couldn't find a bleeding elephant in a snowstorm.

I showed up on my first day for an eight-to-four tour at least two hours early. The desk officer was Lt. Arthur "Curly" Howard. Howard was one of the Three Stooges—get it? (Now you know why more cops don't become writers.) He had more time on The Job than any cop in the precinct, and ran the desk like a dictator.

A desk officer is God. He oversees the precinct on any given tour, and the commanding officer goes to him when he wants to know what's going on in his precinct.

The desk itself is set high on a platform, so the desk officer looks down both physically and socially at every cop in the command.

Howard was a curmudgeon who hated everyone. I stood before the desk with an armload of uniforms for a good five minutes before he deigned to look up from his *Daily News*. "Yeah," he growled, looking over the top of reading glasses.

"Officer Wagner," I screeched. I tried to be relaxed and confident, but my voice sounded like my balls were being crushed in a vice. "Just got assigned . . . or sent here, I mean."

"Yeah, yeah, go upstairs, grab a locker." He went back to his newspaper.

The trip to the third-floor locker room was like running a gauntlet. There had to be twelve cops filtering downstairs, hanging out, or doing paperwork, and no one so much as said hello. I wondered who was watching the streets.

Most were over forty and out of shape. A few looked

like they'd been drinking all night. Everyone, to a man, just stared at me. New cop on the block. Could I be an IAD plant sent there to spy on them? Would I turn out to be one of the boys and not a rat? My mouth was cotton dry as I made my way to the locker room, where I grabbed the first available locker.

The station house was over a hundred years old and looked like it hadn't been painted since the end of the Spanish-American War, and only then because Teddy Roosevelt was the police commissioner.

The paint was a sickening green, thick, peeling, and stained. The floor was covered in some spots by linoleum and in the rest by a layer of ground-in dirt. The locker I chose appeared to have been used as a battering ram during the Civil War draft riots in 1863. Scratched into the inside door was *Fuck the Bosses.* I could hardly wait to start my first tour.

Three hours later, after a cursory tour of the building by a hungover roll call cop, I was assigned to a squad and told to report to the lieutenant on the desk.

Lieutenant Howard's tour had ended and he had been replaced by Lieutenant Burnhardt, who was referred to as Lieutenant Blowhard (behind his back, of course). Lieutenant Burnhardt suffered from an ailment common to NYPD bosses—noballsitis, a malady one can acquire only when one is promoted to the rank of sergeant or above. It's a common affliction affecting a goodly portion of the supervisors in the NYPD, and manifests itself by the victim's inability to make a decision. There is no cure, and Lieutenant Burnhardt was terminal.

The good lieutenant would have been a great poster boy for the Save the Ostrich campaign, because he conducted his life with his head in the sand. In the short time I was in the Fourth Precinct I'd see cops torture Burnhardt unmercifully, and all Burnhardt would do was run and hide. For example, one day two cops stripped naked and paraded in front of the desk when Burnhardt was on duty. As soon as he spotted them he hastily signed out to meal and disappeared downstairs.

Another time a cop left a message on his desk for the lieutenant to return a phone call to a convent. When a nun picked up the phone Burnhardt said, "Heywood Ublome, please." Think about it.

On this day he had no idea what to do with me, so he assigned me to a foot post on Chambers Street and told me to stay out of trouble.

I was happy to get out of the station house, and gladly made my way down to my post, a nondescript street lined with office buildings. I hoped that the day would soon end so I could get home and harass my dad into moving on my request for a transfer.

I walked my post like a good little soldier, smiling at total strangers who gave me blank looks (I was to find that most cops in the Fourth avoided contact with citizens, lest they become involved in some form of police work), and swinging my baton (nightstick) like a seasoned trooper. I stopped the nightstick flourishes after the tenth time I hit myself in the balls and/or nose, backed up against a building, and looked at my watch. Only six hours to go. Piece of cake.

A Chinese guy with an apron around his waist ran up to me out of breath, yelling something in Chinese. I calmed him down and got a story.

"Someone hold me up!" His finger was bleeding, the result of a knife slash.

"Which way'd he go?"

The victim pointed eastbound on Chambers. I got a description, took off in pursuit, and broadcast a description on my radio. When I reached the corner I glanced down Broadway and spotted my archcriminal leaning against a wall, smoking a joint.

I drew my gun, approached carefully, and ordered the startled (and stoned) perpetrator to face the wall.

"Huh?" he asked. The guy was wasted and docile.

The Chinese complainant showed up right behind me and started screaming, "That the guy! That the guy!"

I cuffed the stickup man, tossed him into a responding radio car, and triumphantly marched him into the precinct.

Lieutenant Burnhardt began to shake and sweat. I was causing the good lieutenant to have to work. Shame on me.

"I thought I told you to stay out of trouble?" he said. "No one makes collars around here on a day tour."

"Yeah, Loo, but this guy stabbed—"

He held up a trembling hand, booked the prisoner, and told me to bring him upstairs to the detectives for fingerprinting. My ego quickly deflated. I went from hero to pain in the ass in a matter of minutes.

The lone detective on duty was watching the news on a tiny portable television with aluminum foil for an antenna. He was pissed that I'd interrupted his downtime.

Welcome to the Fourth Precinct.

I was branded a cowboy. While other cops were civil to me, no one wanted to work with me because I actually intended to do police work.

My squad consisted of a former Mounted Unit cop who cooped up with his horse one night in an empty train boxcar on the West Side tracks, fell asleep, and woke up in Schenectady; a cop who was assigned to a Queens precinct who was caught getting a blow job in the Bronx when he was supposed to be on duty at Shea Stadium; and another cop who had a penchant for shooting out streetlights when he was drunk, which was almost every night. These characters had been dumped to the Fourth. The remaining few cops assigned to the squad, while not as colorful, had been dumped to the Fourth because of mal- or nonfeasance (I never understood the difference between the two).

I was assigned a steady foot post at the mouth of the Holland Tunnel. This was as desolate an area as you could find this side of downtown Cleveland. My sergeant, "Shaky Bob" Carapoli, figured there was no way I could get into trouble breathing fumes and freezing my ass off on the downwind side of the Hudson River. Unfortunately, he was right.

I was stiff as a Popsicle on a particular four-to-twelve tour, the sun having set hours before. I was also in desperate need of a place to pee. Rather than walking six blocks to the closest coffee shop, I elected to whip it out in an alley and relieve myself.

There's nothing (well, almost nothing) that's more satisfying than peeing outdoors in the middle of winter. It's a guy thing. Total freedom—must go back to prehistoric days when cavemen marked their territory.

Anyway, I really had no fear of being caught. I hadn't seen a human being who wasn't driving by me in hours. My sergeant, the aforementioned "Shaky Bob," was supposed to come around every so often to check up on me, sign my memo book, and make sure I hadn't been assassinated. This is part of a supervisor's job, making unannounced visits to a cop's post to keep him on his toes.

But not Bob. Bob figured that the more time he spent on the street, the more problems he might encounter. It was a known fact that Bob and his driver headed straight for the piers soon after turnout, with enough beer to float a battleship. I assume he did a lot of peeing outdoors, too.

So there I was, marking my territory, when I heard the *whoop whoop* of a radio-car siren. I looked over my shoulder to see Sergeant Carapoli leaning out his passenger-side window. *Now* he decided to drop around. I was mortified.

"Put that thing away and climb in." The sergeant leaned over his seat and opened the back door. I complied.

The overwhelming odor of beer and whiskey hit me hard. My boss and his driver were loaded and feeling benevolent.

"You're coming with us," he said, and his driver, an old-timer named Morton, laughed and burped. I didn't dare ask where to.

After five minutes of driving down desolate, deserted streets, Morton pulled into an alley one block from the West Side Highway. There were five other marked Fourth Precinct radio cars in the alley. Those five cars were what the precinct turned out on a four-to-twelve tour. Who was answering radio runs?

They brought me into a private after-hours club. The place was packed with cops, some in uniform, some in civilian clothes, some in no clothes.

Two naked women were on opposite sides of the room, one dancing by herself to whistles and shouts, the other getting doused by bottles of beer. Both appeared to be enjoying themselves. Music blared. Morton said, "Charlie Upton's bachelor party." Upton was in my squad, and in my two weeks in the precinct, he hadn't said a word to me.

Two cops in full uniform sat watching the festivities. One held a division radio to his ear. Sergeant Carapoli drifted to the bar and Morton nudged me. "Go over there with those two cops and grab the radio. Any call comes over, you let one of them know, okay?" Before I had a chance to answer, he joined the sergeant.

I did as I was told. It was my job to get a radio-car crew on the road when a job came over. Cops took turns answering radio runs while the rest drank and had a good time. I was sure that any minute a squad of Internal Affairs cops would come swooping down and arrest us all. I was to find out later that this was business as usual. If it wasn't Upton getting married, they'd find another excuse.

After an hour or so, things got really raunchy. Those so inclined lined up for blow jobs. Surprisingly, most of the cops elected to sit that one out and just drink. Others vanished outside for brief periods, only to return happier than when they left.

I wasn't asked to participate, but apparently I was being accepted as "one of the guys." Someone tossed me a beer. I drank it, but couldn't wait to get the hell out of there.

4
The Island

I spent a year in the Fourth, the whole time angling for a transfer to the Ninth Precinct. My father had pull in Staten Island, but Manhattan, known as "the city," might as well have been on another planet.

Finally I'd had enough. My tours in the Fourth consisted of covering for cops who'd rather goof off than do real police work, what little there was of it in that command, or walking deserted foot posts. I told my father to get me anywhere, as long as I didn't have to look at the Holland Tunnel anymore. He got me transferred to the 120th Precinct, the One-Two-Oh, in Staten Island, where he worked.

This had to be something for the *Guinness Book of Records*. I'd never heard of a father and son being assigned to the same command, but then again I had never heard of the Fourth Precinct, either. I just didn't think they did that, you know, like the Fighting Sullivans, the five brothers who bought it on the same ship in World War II.

The Fighting Wagners wound up working in the same sector opposite each other. When my dad worked days with his partner, I relieved him in the same radio car on the four-to-twelve shift. Talk about strange.

I settled in nicely. The One-Two-Oh covered a large area, and as a result most of the cops rode in radio cars. I was beginning to feel like a real cop, answering radio runs, making arrests, and occasionally even helping people. Truthfully, the average cop helps very few people in the altruistic sense of the word. Mostly we keep order by subtle intimidation, with the infrequent rescue of the proverbial cat in a tree to qualify us as benevolent.

My relationship with my father was, shall I say, different. At home he was Dad, but I couldn't imagine calling him that at work. I wasn't comfortable calling him Joe either, and the hugs I got from him stopped at our front door. So I didn't call him anything. At work, to him I was Jimmy; to me he was "Uhhhm."

We saw each other briefly during the change of tours. He'd pull up in the radio car with Dave, toss me the keys, wink, and say, "Be careful out there," before he'd vanish inside the station house to sign out.

Since we worked in opposing squads, I saw him for extended periods only when our days off coincided. Still, when I had a question or problem, I'd get up early to catch him in the morning before he went to work.

As a new man in the command I took the usual good-natured kidding, which I expected. When a bunch of new recruits arrived I'd be let off the hook. I also got stuck with the occasional foot post or securing a burned-out storefront, because I didn't yet have a steady partner. When assigned to a radio car, I'd fill in for a vacationing or sick person in my squad.

One afternoon I had just arrived at work for a four-to-twelve when the desk officer told me to get dressed and relieve my dad at the scene of a quadruple homicide. All crime scenes had to be secured to maintain the integrity of the location and to await the arrival of the Forensic Unit.

This homicide was particularly grisly. A love-struck teenager was infatuated with an older woman who lived down the hall from him with her husband and two kids. For some twisted reason, the teen decided to take out the entire family of his unrequited love with a twelve-inch butcher knife.

He massacred all four of them before calmly returning home and flipping on the TV. Dad and Dave were the first officers on the scene and made an arrest in a matter of minutes. It didn't take Sherlock Holmes; all my dad and Dave had to do was follow bloody footprints to the killer's apartment. After a short (but illegal) search, my dad found the murder weapon hidden in a closet. He later backtracked, returned the knife to where he had found it, got a search warrant, then went back and "discovered" it. At the time his concern was more heavily focused on not getting stabbed in the back than on the suspect's constitutional rights.

The few dead bodies (or DOAs) I'd seen in the Fourth were relatively clean. The heart-attack victim, the drug overdose, the occasional car accident with the victim DOA from a bump on the head. A rookie's mandatory trip to the morgue to view an autopsy was a fairly mild and bloodless affair. I'd also missed the ground war in Vietnam by being in the navy. Nothing had prepared me for what I saw in the victims' Staten Island apartment that day.

My dad met me at the door. He was drawn and visibly shaken. He put his arm around me and backed me up against a wall.

"It's a mess in there, Jimmy. Gonna take a strong stomach."

I appreciated his concern, but I didn't want to be babied. I was a cop; I could handle it.

"Yeah, sure, not a problem," I said, but my stomach was beginning to knot.

I saw the woman first. She was on her back, dressed in jeans and a T-shirt saturated with blood. Couldn't accurately determine her age. Thirty-five, maybe. Her throat had been slashed with such force that her head hung by muscle, lopsided, her spinal column exposed. There were defensive slash cuts on both hands. Her eyes were wide open. Throat wounds are a bitch. She had bled out.

Two kids, a boy about five, a girl maybe nine, were butchered in the kitchen. They, too, had gaping neck wounds and had been stabbed in the back, probably as they tried to run. Both bodies had spilled their last ounce of blood.

The husband had taken the worst. His corpse was

jammed into a hall closet, pants pulled down, testicles chopped from his body, throat slashed, eyes gouged. His tongue protruded from his mouth and had taken a ripping cut that ended under the cheekbone.

None of them looked real. I willed them to move. The rage of animated violence that took their lives didn't seem as if it had been fully expended amid the gore. I looked hard for movement where there was none.

"Jimmy."

I turned at the sound of my name. Dave Ballantine was sitting on a slipcovered sofa in the living room, munching on a rare hamburger. Blood dripped from the soaked bun onto a spread of newspaper. Preserve the crime scene.

"You're not gonna get sick, are you?" he asked. Dave was a tough character and my dad's best friend. He was my prime antagonizer, the king of practical jokes, who ribbed every rookie, especially me. It was part of the game. The gushing burger was supposed to turn my stomach.

I went into the living room, stepping carefully, looking for evidence I didn't want to destroy. I reached for Dave's burger. "Skipped lunch," I said. "Mind?" Out of the corner of my eye I saw Dad come back into the apartment. He stepped over the dead woman and stopped, watching.

Dave shook his head and handed over the sopping bun with its bleeding contents. I grabbed it with both hands and finished it off in three massive bites. "Coulda been a little more rare," I said, wiping juice from my chin with the back of my hand.

Dave never ribbed me again.

"I never wanted this for you, Jimmy," my father said early the next evening. It was the first really warm day of spring. We were in the yard, both of us clutching sweating beer bottles, watching the sun go down.

"Want what, The Job?"

"It changes you, you know? I see what it's done to me, to Dave. That fucking hamburger, pure Dave."

"It's okay, Dad. I mean, I was upset, I'd be lying if I said I wasn't, but it's not every day you run across four DOAs."

"It's at least twice a week in the Ninth, Jimmy. They're killing people over there for the hell of it." He uncapped a second beer. "You always want better for your kids, is all I'm saying. You'll see when you get married. The Job's changing. Mark my words: Things are gonna happen in this city even Jack Webb couldn't handle."

My old man could have been a seer.

About a month later I was pulling into work, running a little late. As I bounded up the steps, my dad's radio car came screeching around the corner, coming to a skidding stop right in front of me.

Dave was driving, and my dad was in the backseat with a prisoner. The door flew open and the cuffed prisoner was jettisoned out, face-first. He landed with a howl as Dad lumbered out of the backseat. Dad was livid, madder than I'd ever seen him.

Dave came flying around the car, fumbling for a handcuff key. Cops began to gather, forming a protective shield around the prisoner. I knew what was coming.

Dave, cursing a steady stream of four-letter words, lifted the prisoner up by his arms. He was a white guy, maybe twenty-five, husky, with a pile of unruly hair. The prisoner screeched with pain. Dave removed the cuffs, shoved him into my father, and the battle began.

"Motherfucker! Cocksucker." My father began to pummel the guy with a barrage of punches and kicks. Cops began screaming to get the mope inside. One cop said, "Joe, witnesses!" A couple of taxpayers had stopped, staring across the street at probably more cops than they'd ever seen on Staten Island in one place.

I didn't say boo. Right then my dad was someone I didn't know. He'd always been tough with us kids, but fair, reasonable. He never hit us, never let loose with more than a "goddamn" or a "hell."

Now he was an unleashed animal. Whatever the prisoner had done, he'd done it for the last time.

The prisoner was fighting back, a wild look in his eyes. I found out later that he was high on the newest street drug: PCP.

He swung once, a powerful roundhouse. Dad stepped aside, watched the mutt go down, then kicked him in the head.

The cops were in a frenzy, ranting, screaming, hoping my dad would take out the frustration of their tough day, week, year, on the battling junkie. Dave was screaming at Dad to get the motherfucker in the house.

Dad yanked the prisoner by the wrist and dragged him to his feet. I heard a sickening snap as the man's arm broke. He yelled so loudly I was certain Mayor Lindsay heard him in Gracie Mansion.

Inside, the beating continued. My father, spent, turned the now chewed-up prisoner over to Dave, who removed him to a cell in the back of the house and proceeded to pummel him some more.

Finally it ended. Charges: burglary, attempted murder of a police officer (knife, recovered at the scene), and, of course, resisting arrest. The prisoner was in the hospital for three weeks. Eventually he pled guilty to reduced charges and got five years.

My dad didn't talk to me for two days. I didn't know why then, but I know now (since I've become a parent): He was embarrassed at losing it in front of me. The rock, the provider, the person the family could look to for stability and reason had lost it, if only for a brief time.

Would I have done what Dad did? Dave told me later that the bad guy came at my father with a steak knife, narrowly missing him. Under the best of conditions, I'd have liked to have said that I'd have been cool and professional. But cops work in a pressure cooker, told to keep everything under control, treat people with respect. Eventually you've got to blow; everyone does.

If this incident had happened in the nineties instead of the sixties, Dad would have been indicted and possibly sent to jail. The era saved him. Back then cops didn't go to jail for beating prisoners. They got medals.

The boxing up of emotions, the standing order to stifle

your feelings, leads to violence. Back then the rage was turned outward. These days cops turn it inward because of severe sanctions for losing it. The suicide rate on The Job inches up every year. I would be touched by the specter of suicide a few years later, but at that point it was an aberration. This was the sixties; we were immune.

5

Walking the EVil

Cops call it walking the grid: a systematic stroll through a crime scene, dividing the area into navigable, ordered squares, observing the minutiae that make up the setting of someone's misconduct. Catalog it mentally for future recall, photograph it for trial, store it for your nightmares. Get to know the territory that will play a significant part in your life.

That day I walked the grid through the confines of the Ninth Precinct. If I was going to work there, I wanted to get a feel for the streets. Knowledge is power; knowledge is survival. Know the streets before the streets know you.

July 1970. Finally I was transferred to the Ninth. On a Friday night, two days before I was supposed to report, I stood across the street from the station house on East Fifth Street, wearing civilian clothes and watching the comings and goings of cops as they worked toward the safe completion of their tour.

I identified myself to no one. Blending in was the plan. Walk the streets like a ghost and observe the inhabitants. The cops I would get to know; the civilians were the ones who could kill me. Know the enemy.

The first NYPD cop to be killed in the line of duty was shot in the Ninth, blown off a fire escape while investigating a burglary in 1863, as the Civil War raged. He was followed by seven more, including two doubleheaders. The Ninth's running out of wall space for plaques.

I started walking east toward Alphabet City. No white faces east of Avenue A. I was dressed down, but still made for The Man. My elbow brushed my side and found my off-duty .38 Smith. Comforting to know it was there and I knew how to use it.

Squalor City. Broken-down tenements, some dating back to the mid-1800s. I found out later that headquarters supervisors who went uptown to spy on the ground troops rarely ventured east of A. If the natives didn't blitz them with debris from rooftops, the cops they were looking to catch doing wrong would elude them in the jungle of darkened alleys and bombed-out buildings.

Kids out of school for the summer, if in fact they ever went, were running through the water spray from illegally turned-on hydrants. Some smiled as I passed. Most gave me hard looks.

Avenue D, the Lillian Wald/Jacob Riis housing project that ran for fourteen blocks. Nice view of the East River through the barred living room windows.

I turned north, then west to St. Marks Place. Hippie heaven. Ground zero for the antiwar, antiestablishment, anticleanliness movement. A one-block stretch of glitzy clubs, drug dealers, shoeless fourteen-year-old prostitutes fresh from Iowa willing to suck a dick to foster greater love among human beings. They weren't opposed to a few bucks, either.

St. Marks Place attracted runaways from all over the world. It was pumped twenty-four hours a day. Kids literally living in the street, parents from west of the Hudson River handing out eight-by-ten glossies. "Have you seen my daughter? Her name's Marcia; she's thirteen. Tell her, if you see her, that we love her and want her to come home." Oh, yeah? If you love her so much, how come the most recent picture you have of her is at least five years old?

A squad of Tactical Patrol Force cops helps keep the peace. Sixteen foot cops on one block and still there was trouble. Uptown predators scooped up the trusting and unwary as soon as their tender soles hit the concrete. Those not willing to spread free love wound up raped, sometimes murdered, often dumped in the river, gobbled up by toxic waste or tangled in rusted cables. Parents of those kids carried around pictures until they faded.

Rock clubs and showcases. CBGB (Madonna waited tables there before she donned her bullet bra), the Electric Circus, walk through the doors into another world. On Fourteenth Street, the Academy of Music, later to be called the Palladium. Bruce and Elton started out there. Let's not forget the Fillmore East on Second Avenue, a ring of Hell's Angels securing the perimeter against the mob who were there to see the show. I forgot who was there that night. Janis, Jimmy, Alice? Too long ago to remember.

South toward Houston Street (pronounced House-ton. The test of a true New Yorker: If you don't say it our way, you were born in Kansas). The southern border and a different kind of plight: the Bowery, life's last stop before the relative calm of hell. New York's dregs: queers, transvestites, the lowest-rung prostitute. Home of the two-dollar blow job.

I swung west toward Tompkins Square Park, an oasis of garbage-littered grass, with dealers hawking nickel bags, and the only block in the precinct that had trees. There were two radio cars, nose-to-nose so the partners could warn each other of approaching assassins. They sat inside drinking something out of unmarked cups. I'd be doing that in two days.

A hundred thousand people crammed into a precinct fourteen blocks long by ten wide. West of Avenue A: Polish, Italian, Russian, Jewish, hippie. East of A: Black, Hispanic. Pandemic: junkies, muggers, prostitutes, other assorted lowlifes. A cauldron waiting to boil over.

Back to the station house, where I began walking the grid. In the East Village.

The EVil.

6
The Squad, Part I

"**W**hat do they call you?"

"Wags." I was in the third-floor locker room of the Ninth Precinct station house. My reception had already been considerably warmer than in the Fourth or the One-Two-Oh. The desk officer actually smiled at me.

"Wags, cool. I'm Kenny Kenrick." He shook my hand. "You're in the Sixth Squad; we'll be working together." He was tall, thin, about my age, maybe a little older, with a shock of early gray at the temples. His grin was warm and genuine.

"What do they call you?" I asked.

"Kenny Kenrick." We laughed. The locker room was packed with the eight-to-four tour suiting up. Kenny was already in uniform, neat and pressed out, military creases ironed into his shirt. He was ex-military, served with the First Cavalry Division in Vietnam. One day I asked him why he shook out his shoes before putting them on. He told me it was a habit he acquired in the jungle. "Scorpions."

Kenny called out, "Hey, Sixth Squad, come meet Wags."

A few cops in various stages of undress ambled over. The guys in their underwear carried their gun belts. Everyone introduced themselves, hands jutting out for the shake, but the names didn't stick. I was too nervous. New kid on the block.

Kenny said, "Hey, Wags, you wanna take a few steps back."

I looked at him. "Huh?"

"Back, Wags, you gotta step away from your locker."

I still didn't know what he was talking about and gave him a blank stare. One of the cops grabbed my arm and yanked. "Over here."

I bumped against the locker behind me. They lined up, me behind them.

Kenny: "Ready!"

Everyone drew their service revolvers.

Kenny: "Aim!"

Arms extended toward my locker. What the fu—?

"Fire!"

A deafening volley of shots exploded in the cramped locker room. My ears rang and my eyes crossed. My locker had been ventilated with bullet holes.

Cops from other squads who were changing erupted into applause. Everyone laughed.

"Welcome to the Ninth," Kenny said. "If we'd heard you were a shithead we would have thrown your locker out the window. Consider yourself one of the guys."

When a new cop transfers in, a call is made to that cop's previous command for the skinny. Nice to know what kind of person you're working with. Kenny clapped me on the back, and my new squad wandered off. My ears rang for the rest of the day.

I passed a container to Kenny. "Five sugars for you, lemon for me. Your pancreas is gonna stop working."

"Good," Kenny said. "If I die it's less money for my ex-wives."

Kenny was twenty-six and on wife number three. He'd gotten hitched for the first time when he was eighteen. That lasted three years, the next one four. He was currently a newlywed.

Kenny and I were sitting in a radio car under a tree adjacent to Tompkins Square Park, sipping iced tea out of Styrofoam cups. We had partnered up, his last steady partner having retired. The platoon had just turned out, and the entire day tour was parked under the only trees in the precinct, those that ring the park. It was only a little after eight, and the humidity festival that is New York in July was attacking with a vengeance. It had to be ninety degrees.

Every tour began like this. Pick up coffee or whatever, maybe an egg sandwich, and off to the park. The only slow part of the day tour was the first hour, maybe the first two in the dead of winter, when the junkies were still in their hovels, their "workday" having just ended. The daytime burglars would be hitting the pavement soon to begin ripping off the apartments of the gainfully employed. By noon, every other person we'd see would be a junkie, dealer, prostitute, or runaway.

After about a week I'd settled in, gotten to know everyone's name, and begun to learn the layout of the command. Sure, I'd made my unofficial walking tour, and I'd been answering jobs for a while, but it takes some time to really get to know a precinct, even one as small as the Ninth.

Where to eat was the most important consideration. We weren't exactly in the gourmet capital of the world. If you didn't like greasy Spanish food or Chinese dead cat foo young, your choices were limited. Cops, however, like truck drivers, always find decent restaurants; our guts depended on it.

To pay or not to pay was also a consideration. This was the sixties; free food for cops was the norm. While I wasn't opposed to getting a free meal every now and then, I didn't want to make a fixture of myself in a restaurant where after a while the owner would think that Wags was his personal police force.

Fortunately Kenny was of the same mind, and we bounced to different restaurants every day, sometimes paying, sometimes not.

The radio was quiet. Kenny was filling me in on the other squad members.

"Pat Randazzo, supercop, or at least he thinks he is. Likes to be called Clubber. Never brings in a prisoner in the vertical position."

"Reddy doesn't mind?" Our boss, Sgt. Fred Reddy,

had over twenty-five years in and appeared to be a strict but fair boss. He was well liked.

"Pat's bringing in mutts; Reddy don't really care. He brings in Nancy Sinatra with a bloody lip, he's got a problem."

The park was surrounded by tenements. Across from us a guy was swinging from a makeshift hammock suspended from opposite ends of a fifth-floor fire escape. He was in his underwear, talking on a corded phone that extended inside the apartment through an open window. He was laughing and slugging down a beer from a long-neck bottle.

"Anybody I should watch out for?" I asked.

Kenny shrugged. "They're all good guys; no one's fucking around or gonna jam you up, if that's what you mean." He shrugged again.

I saw something in the double shrug. "Okay, who?"

"Frankie Moran's hitting the juice a little too much lately, but he's got a right. His brother was killed over Easter."

"On The Job?"

"Fireman." Kenny went on to explain that Frank's brother responded to a three-alarmer on Delancey Street on a day tour, or whatever firemen call it. He was dragging a hose up a smoke-filled flight of stairs toward the roof when he thought he saw a hot spot on the next landing. "He chased the fire, fell off a parapet, six stories. He was on the roof and didn't realize it. That hot spot? It was the sun. He was trying to put it out."

"Jesus."

"Wouldn't see me fighting fires. Too friggin' dangerous."

"What do you call what we do, bean counting?"

"Guy's got a gun, a knife, makes us even; I'm used to that," Kenny said. "That fire shit scares me." Kenny liked to speak about his service in Vietnam. He told me he was a machine gunner and he came home with a helluva tan.

The guy swinging in the hammock was giving himself

a shove against the building wall every few minutes to get some nice motion going. Then he'd ride out the momentum, sip his brew, and jabber into the phone. Looked like a nice way to spend a morning.

"So Frankie gets shit-faced every now and then," Kenny said. "No big deal."

"When he's working?" Frank was the senior man in the squad, about thirty-two, with ten years in.

"He can handle it."

I got the rundown on the rest of the Sixth Squad. The two black guys, Andy Glover and Greg Foster, were good cops, in their mid-twenties. "Glover generally drives Reddy," Kenny said. "Foster works with Laurie." Rocco Laurie was twenty-five, newly married, and lived not far from me on Staten Island.

Aside from Moran, the rest of us had about the same amount of time on The Job. Seniority meant nothing in the EVil except for vacation picks. Time in the Ninth was the barometer of how much you knew.

The radio started to crackle. Nothing for us.

Hammock Man shouted for another beer, and a slender arm passed him one through a window. He pushed himself off the wall again, this time a little harder, and his arch took him over the outer railing and over the street. He took a pull on the beer and gave himself another push. A poor man's thrill ride.

Kenny slipped the car into gear. "Whaddaya say we ride the sector?"

"Sounds go—" I was still looking at Hammock Man when the back tie on his hammock snapped. It broke loose just when he cleared the outer railing; that one split second suspended him precariously five stories above the simmering asphalt of Tenth Street.

He tumbled out of the hammock, screaming.

"Motherfucker!" I yelled.

Hammock Man kept on screaming. I watched what appeared to be a slow-motion descent. The phone cord had torn loose from its connection inside the apartment and trailed the falling man like a flying snake. A nanosecond before he impaled himself on three sharpened spires of the wrought-iron fence in front of his building, he turned and looked at me. The eyes of a dead man, fear and resignation. Then the whoosh and thud of a body in motion, air knocked out of it, suddenly stopped by an inanimate object.

Kenny blanched, silent for a moment, then regained his cool. "Don't think he'll be doing that again. Ah, shit, more friggin' paperwork." The combat vet, seen it all, holding his feelings inside.

A crowd began to gather. The rest of the squad got out of their cars and trotted over to the victim, who was still squirming. He still had the phone in his hand, the cord dangling to the sidewalk.

Pat Randazzo and his partner Frank Moran pushed the gawkers back while Kenny radioed for an ambulance on the portable. Foster and Laurie stepped out into the street to keep traffic moving. A few more guys went upstairs to Hammock Man's apartment.

In less than a minute, a pretty Hispanic woman, no more than twenty-one, flew down the stairs and became hysterical when she saw her man. She clawed at his feet and fell to the ground. No one on the street came forward to comfort her. Two cops picked her up and took her away from the dripping blood.

There was a sudden exhalation of air from Hammock Man and he was dead. I heard a siren in the distance, an ambulance on the way. Too late for this one.

Sergeant Reddy responded, called an Emergency Service Unit, and Hammock Man was cut down with acetylene torches while kids played in his shadow.

A squat Hispanic woman wearing a halter top three sizes too small came out of Hammock Man's building. "Hey, Officer, who's gonna pay for my busted fence?"

Violent death is common in the Ninth.

The following day was my last day tour, and I was looking forward to a long swing. My father was on vacation and we planned to go fishing.

The locker room was unusually quiet. Kenny grunted a greeting from down the aisle; Pat and Frank were off in a corner with their backs to me. I didn't see the rest of the crew.

I spun the dial on my combination lock and swung the door open.

A figure dressed all in black, wearing a ski mask and carrying a handgun, leaped out at me. I saw the gun in his hand too late to go for mine. His shot echoed as I grabbed my chest. I heard scurrying behind me. Then laughter.

The black-clad figure whipped off his mask. Rocco Laurie.

"Son of a bitch!" I yelled, now backed up against a locker, a hand still over my rapidly beating heart.

Kenny was howling. "I think he missed. Hey, Rocco, shoot him again!"

Laurie was laughing so hard that tears were streaming down his face. He opened the cylinder of his gun and waved it in my face. "Blanks. Go change your underwear."

Okay, so in addition to getting my locker assassinated, this Rocco-in-the-Box was also part of the initiation. My ticker slipped from its fight-or-flight mode and began to slow down. I started to laugh. I couldn't believe I found this funny. Maybe I was just as sick as the wackos I worked with.

"Kenny, you rat fuck, you did this," I said, my voice cracking.

Partners exchange locker-combination numbers for a variety of reasons, not the least of which is to remove any incriminating items in the event of an IAD raid. Until the early eighties it was common practice for a cop to carry around loose decks of heroin to give to junkies in exchange for information. Very embarrassing to have dope discovered in your locker.

"We usually wait a week or so, till your guard's down," Kenny said. "At least you didn't have to wear the Arrest Helmet."

The Arrest Helmet was a kid's red plastic fireman's hat with a blinking dome light that some cop spray-painted black. When a rookie assigned to the Ninth straight out of the Academy made his first arrest, he was told he had to wear the helmet to Central Booking to identify him if he was in civilian clothes. Kenny told me that only one dumb kid fell for it. It was more common for the rookie to be told he needed to carry it with him to Central Booking, and if he needed help with forms or procedures he was to put it on, switch on the light, and someone would rush over to help him. This gag worked many times, but I was spared because I wasn't a rookie when I got to the Ninth.

For the next few months I opened my locker standing off to one side. I never told anyone when I was going to use the bathroom, where I'd be at my most vulnerable. I wouldn't put anything past my squad.

Police humor. Keeps you sane in an insane world.

7

Nun Too Soon

My social life was less than good. In fact, it sucked. Since I was working around the clock I rarely got weekends off, plus I was making arrests and got stuck in court on my days off more often than I would have liked. The time-and-a-half was good for the wallet, but I had nowhere to spend it. Quite frankly, I had more laughs when I was in the navy on a ship in the middle of the Pacific. This had to change.

I was invited to a party on Central Park West by a friend attending Columbia University. It was a typical Friday-night get-together, about two hundred sweaty, stoned undergrads jammed into a three-bedroom apartment belonging to a student's parents who were cruising the Mediterranean. They probably told Junior he could have a few friends over, and the party animal invited the immediate world.

I was definitely in enemy territory. The police had been called to the Columbia campus on numerous occasions to quell antiwar demonstrations that had gotten out of control. Cops were not on the student body's list of favorite people.

A friend in the Tactical Patrol Force told me that they had used experimental methods of crowd control on the rioters, including something sinister called Foo Gas, which, when inhaled, opened every orifice in the human body. It rendered the rioters incapable of doing much else except taking a shower. A slippery liquid substance called Banana Peel was also used, and made it impossible to stand, let alone walk. End of riot.

When Columbia students barricaded the entrance to the campus in April of '68, the TPF lowered a bunch of their troops into sewers and infiltrated the campus through a labyrinth of interconnecting drainage pipes. It was a tough battle, with one cop killed by a brick and many students injured. A TPF cop once told me that there's nothing more violent than a student peace demonstration. Go figure.

Anyway, I wasn't about to tell anyone that I was on The Job, and most guests were too stoned to realize that I was the only guy there with short hair. If anyone gave me a suspicious look I'd raise a clenched fist and say, "Off the Pig."

I was all set to vacate the place after fifteen minutes anyway because I felt like a pair of brown shoes in the tuxedo section of Bloomingdale's. I imagined I could have a better time walking a foot post on St. Marks Place fielding insults from runaways.

I begged off from my friend and had almost made it to the door when a gorgeous brunette hooked my arm.

"Where're you going?" She was a few inches shorter than me with chin-length hair, huge brown eyes, and a killer smile. The tight jeans and tube top didn't hurt her appearance, either.

"Out of here. I don't think I fit in."

"Stick around; I like men with short hair." She laughed; I melted. Her name was Maureen O'Brien. We left for a bar called the Sacred Cow on Seventy-second Street.

Maureen was a student nurse at St. Clare's Hospital on the West Side, attending nursing school in the hospital during the day and working the wards two nights a week. She had weekends off. She resided in the dorms on the top floor of the hospital.

I told her I was a cop before we got out of the elevator. I figured if she was turned off by men in blue I didn't want to waste my time. Turned out her father and two uncles were cops in a small-town PD in Maryland, where she was raised.

We hit it off. I'm not much of a drinker, but she could put them away. We listened to live music, told bad jokes, sipped cocktails, and touched each other until eleven o'clock. Then she looked at her watch and turned into Cinderella.

"Shit, I gotta go. I didn't realize it was getting so late."

"Late? I thought you said you had weekends off. It's Friday night."

She stood up. After my third drink I'd noticed her tube top had gotten tighter. Must have been the humidity. "Jimmy, St. Clare's is run by nuns. Student nurses have curfews, eleven-thirty on weekends, ten on weekdays. C'mon, take me home."

We had thirty minutes and she wanted to walk the fifteen blocks to the dorm. We got into a clinch on the corner of Fifty-fifth and Ninth and backed into an alley.

There wasn't much we could do fully clothed, standing ankle-deep in debris, but we came as close to duplicating the elevator scene in *Fatal Attraction* as you can get without some director yelling, "Cut!"

She wouldn't let me walk her to the entrance of St. Clare's. "Nun on security at the front door," she explained. It was just as well, because as excited as I was, I figured some sharp-eyed cop would stop me for carrying a concealed weapon.

I gave her my phone number (she said personal phone calls to the dorm were frowned upon and went through a switchboard manned by a nun). She called the next day. That night I met her at an Italian restaurant in the West Village on the civilized fringe of the Ninth.

We saw each other at least three times a week. This would have been Cora revisited except that Maureen shared her accommodations with fourteen other student nurses and I was still living at home. I had been apartment hunting on Staten Island for about a month, but now I was so desperate for my own place that a cardboard condominium under the Manhattan Bridge with the homeless people was looking more and more attractive.

There were various hotels in Manhattan that comped a cop. While I didn't want to take advantage of the system, I was going broke springing for motels in the outer boroughs. So after a month or so of playing musical motels, we pretty much settled into a particular hotel in the Gramercy Park area.

Maureen was as effervescent as a person could get without bubbling over. Never in a bad mood, liked every kind of restaurant I took her to, enjoyed the same kind of movies I liked—in short, too good to be true.

Me, being the sharp cop I was, after a few months of seeing her to the corner of St. Clare's and no farther at the end of the evening, I began to get suspicious. Also, I had met only one of her friends, a live wire named Susan, and that was an accidental meeting in a bar lightyears away from the hospital. We never went out with other couples either, something I hadn't minded until recently. I suspected that she was seeing someone else, possibly a doctor, and couldn't afford to have me seen too close to where someone could spot us together and report back to Dr. Kildare.

I realized that I had no claim on her or her time, and while I would have liked her to be with me exclusively, I couldn't very well object to her seeing other men. I had made no commitment other than lining up the next date. "I love you" hadn't been uttered by either of us.

Still, my curiosity started to take over and I found myself slipping into cop mode. I could also say that I was thinking with my big head for once, not my little one.

"A good friend of mine just broke up with his girlfriend," I said as we attacked a plate of fried calamari at our favorite Italian restaurant. "Think maybe we could set him up with a nurse friend of yours?" Susan was out. I was told she favored women.

"Gee, I really don't know anyone available. Everyone I'm in school with is sort of . . . involved."

"Everyone?"

"Yes, everyone."

Okay, so that didn't work. How about, "The precinct's having a reunion racket in two weeks; want to go with me?"

"What date would that be?" I told her. "Um, I've got finals the next day; gotta study."

I looked at my appointment book. "Oh, made a mistake; it's the following week."

"Going back home to Maryland for a few days; you know, see the parents." She giggled, but it was forced.

So I had to decide if I was going to press the issue or let it go. I was having a good time, I liked Maureen, and the jealousy thing wasn't me. So I let it drop.

October 5, 1971. A day that shall live in infamy. I was working a day tour and Kenny had called in sick. This left me the odd man out, and I was available for any shit assignment the desk officer had dangling.

"Wags," Lieutenant Hulsman said, "grab a hat and bat and report to the CO Manhattan North, southeast corner of Forty-second and Broadway. NYU peace demonstration."

Great. I'd rather go up against a platoon of Black Panthers than police a bunch of spoiled college kids, but that's why they paid me the big money. The big money, in 1971, was sixteen grand a year. Twenty years later, when I became a PI, I wouldn't even put on my shoes for anything less than that for one case. Dedicated, that was me.

So I stood with a bunch of other frustrated cops under the extinguished lights of Broadway and ignored taunts, curses, and the occasional rock or bag of human feces flung at us. After seven hours of this I was ready for a cocktail, maybe two.

I had brought my car and a civilian jacket with me, so after we were cut loose I called the Ninth and had a cop sign me out. I headed for the nearest gin mill with two cops from Midtown South.

So there I am, crossing Eighth Avenue at Forty-third Street, when I spot two nuns in full regalia crossing the street walking toward me.

Now cops and nuns have always been more than cordial to each other (just how cordial I was about to find out). I think it has something to do with us relying on the same employer: a nun for spiritual sustenance, a cop to save his or her ass when the shit hits the fan.

So it's normal for a cop to greet a nun with, "How ya doing, Sister?" and to get a nod and a smile in return, the cop hoping that he'll get points to be used when God judges him after he takes a bullet between the eyes.

Even though I was out of uniform, I intended to offer my salutation, nuns generally being able to spot a cop anywhere, in uniform or out.

As we passed in the middle of the street, I smiled and waved. Both nuns did likewise.

One of the nuns was Maureen.

Did you ever see the movie *The Longest Day*? There's a scene where a squad of American GIs on patrol pass a squad of German soldiers walking in the opposite direction, separated by a low stone wall. Each group is aware of the other's presence, but they choose to keep walking, avoiding confrontation.

That scene is exactly what sprang to mind as Maureen and her companion walked past me and the other cops. Only she and I knew what was passing between us.

Our eyes met, disbelief in mine, terror in hers. Street sounds became muffled, and it seemed as if we were walking in slow motion. The nun with Maureen continued to jabber, as did the cops with me. I didn't look back.

When we got to the bar, I downed three quick scotches. Needless to say, I wasn't very good company, and I bowed out early.

I went home to a darkened house and waited for the phone to ring. I waited in the living room until sunrise. No call.

I never heard from Maureen again. For a long time I gave every nun on the street more than a passing glance, wondering if I was about to meet an old friend. I did the same every time I passed a hooker. You never know.

*   *   *

It took me weeks before I was able to function with a clear head. Clarity is important in police work. Wandering minds tend to catch bullets. Kenny knew I was in a funk, so one day I told him what went down as we sat sipping coffee in our usual spot by the park.

"Hey, broads are a dime a dozen," he said. That Kenny, a real philosopher.

"That's because you don't date them; you marry them."

"Well, this one's gonna work out, buddy. I'm going broke on engagement rings."

Kenny never spoke much about his ex-wives, but his current wife, a knockout named Kathy, had his heart. He had pictures of her in his locker, wallet, memo book, and of course in his hat, where every cop who ever lived carries *the* picture of the person or persons who mean the most to them.

I was happy for Kenny, but was still in a foul mood a few weeks later when I stopped by my local hangout on Staten Island, the Colonial Inn.

I'd been going to the Inn since I'd gotten my first phony ID at seventeen. It was a large bar/restaurant with a fair-sized dance floor. It was a typical Friday night, crowded shoulder-to-shoulder. All I wanted to do was have a few beers, shoot the breeze with the regulars, and go home.

After my third brew, I realized that Archie Bunker was right when he said, "You don't buy beer; you merely rent it." The trip to the john was akin to running a gauntlet. I collided with numerous bodies boogying on the dance floor as I made my way to the men's room. There was no way anyone could have made it through that crowd without bumping into someone, so I was a bit taken aback when a guy in a cream-colored suit told me to "Watch where the fuck you're goin', shithead."

Normally I'd let something like that roll off my back. One thing you learn on The Job is to ignore taunts and challenges, because if you didn't, you'd be in fights several times during a single tour. But on this fateful evening I was in no mood to take shit from anyone. So the dick-measuring contest began.

Me: "Go fuck yourself."

Suit: "You talkin' to me?"

Me: "Yeah, you. Go fuck yourself."

Suit: "Fuck me? Fuck you!"

Two brain surgeons. The Suit was about my size, and I was itching for a fight. The crowd parted as much as possible, but we were still within arm's length of the circle of people surrounding us.

I wasted no time in throwing a right haymaker. My punch missed the intended target and caught the cheek of a petite brunette who was standing perilously close to the action.

She flew back through the crowd, bounced off a wall, and slid into unconsciousness. I forgot about The Suit momentarily, but was reminded of his presence when his punch coldcocked me square on the chin. The battle was on, but was soon broken up by three bouncers.

I rushed over to the woman I'd just knocked out. She wasn't moving. I was scared shitless; I thought I'd killed her. Another woman was cradling her in her arms. Someone passed her a cold towel, which she applied to the injured woman's head. She stirred, but didn't open her eyes. At least she was alive. For now.

"Listen," I said, "I think we should get her to a hospital."

The woman with the towel said, "What, you're gonna take her? Haven't you done enough already?"

I felt like shit. The prostrate woman couldn't have been more than twenty-five, and looked exactly like Liza Minnelli (the old Liza, not the new Liza, who could have taken the punch and probably knocked *me* out). She could have been Liza's twin, right down to the haircut, body, everything. "Holy shit," I said, "did I just deck Liza Minnelli?"

"No, asshole, her name's Pat Russell," her friend said. Liza—uh, Pat—wasn't moving.

"I'm getting my car," I said. "I'm taking her to the

hospital." Pat's friend gave me a suspicious look. "You, too," I added. All I needed was to be accused of rape on top of everything else. As it was, I saw my job circling the drain. The Job lives by one credo: Get involved in an altercation in a bar, look for another job. This would certainly be the case if the comatose Pat Russell lodged a complaint against me, if and when she woke up.

Pat's friend (whom I'll always remember as Angela Asshole, because that's the way she introduced herself to me in the car: "My name's Angela, asshole!") held her in the backseat while I broke the land-speed record to Doctor's Hospital.

Pat came to on the gurney as she was being wheeled into the emergency room. She was given a battery of tests and admitted for a severe concussion.

Pat was in the hospital for three days. Every day after work I visited her, always bearing gifts. The first trip I brought flowers, the second candy, the third a pile of magazines.

Initially I was trying to put on the charm, hoping she wouldn't charge me with assault, but that fear quickly faded when we began to talk.

"I can't tell you how sorry I am," I said for the tenth time in as many minutes.

She laughed a sweet infectious giggle and smiled at me with gleaming white teeth. "For what? Last thing I remember was watching two Neanderthals square off. For all I know, I slipped. Forget it."

I was sitting on the edge of her bed. "Anyone ever tell you you look like Liza Minnelli?"

"Can't tell you how many times I'm asked for her autograph. After a while I got tired of denying it, so I just sign." She flashed those radiant teeth again.

"You're kidding."

"Would I lie to you after all we've meant to each other? Want to go to Studio 54? I get in all the time, just make like I'm Liza."

We talked for an hour; the next day a nurse had to ask me to leave. I took Pat home when she was discharged; she lived about three miles from me on the Island.

I was definitely interested in her but felt a little gun-shy about asking for a date, not so much because I met her over a right cross, but because of my experience with Maureen. We were parked in front of her house. Ah, what the hell.

"Hey, you aren't a nun, are you?"

Pat looked at me like I had three heads. "Huh?"

"Or perhaps entertaining the idea of a life devoted to God?"

She began to laugh.

"How about the Jehovah's Witnesses? You have the urge to knock on strangers' doors on Saturday mornings?"

"You're a hoot. I work for Met Life, for God's sake."

I dismissed the God reference and asked her out. These days we're approaching our twenty-fifth anniversary and have four great kids. After our initial meeting, it was all uphill.

8

Bosses

The Ninth Precinct station house is a fortresslike structure located in the middle of East Fifth Street, between First and Second avenues on Manhattan's Lower East Side. The command has been there for over a hundred years, and the building's facade has been blasted smooth by years of extreme weather.

The Ninth and the Lower East Side are steeped in legend and lore and are as much a part of the city's history as is Trinity Church, only not as well remembered. The Ninth has certainly had its share of "colorful" police bosses.

Alexander S. Williams was one such person. Assigned to the Houston Street area in the 1860s, Officer Al coined the phrase, "There is more law on the end of a nightstick than in a decision of the Supreme Court." Very profound, our Officer Al. He was famous for throwing members of the Gas House Gang, a notorious bunch of street toughs, through glass windows to make the point that he was the law in those parts. Late in his career he perfected the clubbing of prisoners into a science. He could beat someone senseless with a cocobolo nightstick and not leave a mark. He retired with the rank of Inspector and the sobriquet "Clubber." More than a hundred years later, Pat Randazzo, a cop in my squad, purloined the nickname as his own (more about Pat later).

Another colorful boss was Capt. (later Chief Inspector) Max Schmittenberger. Captain Max never met a dollar he didn't like, and ruled the Ninth at the turn of the century like it was his own personal fiefdom. He collected over $30,000 a year from brothels and shook down six hundred bookies a month for $15 each. That was big money in those days—hell, it's big money *these* days. Max died in 1910 a multimillionaire.

Another entrepreneur was Lt. Thomas Byrnes (later chief of detectives) who ran the precinct in the 1880s like a business. He wouldn't investigate a robbery unless the victim offered a reward, which he would collect upon apprehending the bad guy. In addition to being a thief, Tommy was an innovator who invented the rogues' gallery, the forerunner of mug-shot books, and established the Dead Line, an imaginary line encircling Fulton and Greenwich Streets, the Battery, and the East River. A criminal (by Tommy's definition) found within these boundaries was subject to a severe beating and arrest just for being there.

The award for holder of the Most Tarnished Tin, however, goes to Lt. Charles H. Becker of the Gambling Squad, who has the unique distinction of being the only active police officer to have been executed in the electric chair. He fried in 1915 for murdering a gambler named Beansy. Celebrated author Stephen Crane was harassed for years by Becker for calling the lieutenant "the crookedest cop who ever stood behind a shield."

Another cop who parlayed his graft money into a financial empire was Big Bill Devery. In 1903, he and gambler Frank Farrell bought an American League baseball franchise. They called their team the New York Highlanders. The team was renamed the New York Yankees in 1913 and sold in 1915.

The Job has its share of hero bosses, too, the most notable being Lt. Joseph Petrosino, who went after the Black Hand (later known as the American Mafia) and was lured to Italy and assassinated in 1909.

Well, times change, as did the types of people The Job attracted who later became bosses. These days a Lieutenant Becker, Clubber Williams, Chief Tom Byrnes, and the like couldn't exist in the heavily internally policed

New York City Police Department. Of course, this is a good thing, because if cops today were given the freedom they had at the turn of the century, we'd see a lot more criminal activity within our ranks. It would be human nature for cops, as well as anyone else, to push society's envelope without the fear of extreme sanctions.

Precinct-level bosses run the NYPD, headquarters brass notwithstanding. While the chief sitting on his ever-expanding duff in the ivory tower of 1 Police Plaza thinks he's got a grip on the troops, it's the sergeants, lieutenants, and captains in the precincts who implement the policy created by the chiefs. Or not.

You would think, and fervently pray, that a precinct supervisor would be a superqualified manager who was given rank because of his ability to lead men (and women). Without their expert leadership, street cops would sink into morale morass and decay, and the city would crumble into a pile of ashes. Think of the tragic results if a combat platoon leader in Vietnam was a bumbling idiot, and in charge of thirty-three armed soldiers let loose to do whatever the hell they wanted because they lacked proper guidance. Eventually the trickle-down effect would have the Viet Cong landing on the beaches of Coney Island. The same could be said for similar circumstances in the NYPD, on a precinct level.

With the aforementioned in mind, I now introduce you to the frontline supervisors assigned to the Ninth during my years in that command. Those of you who might consider moving to Montana after reading the following, take heart: Most of those described are now retired.

A precinct commanding officer holds the rank of captain; sometimes, in a larger command, he's also deputy inspector. We had a captain, Baker by name, ballbuster by design.

Captain Baker came to the Ninth from a desk job somewhere downtown. His goal was to straighten out the "cowboys" of the Ninth and make it into a precinct a visiting diplomat from Yemen wouldn't be afraid to walk into.

Ninth Precinct cops had a reputation for being wild men. More often than not, any high-crime command was a world unto itself. Rules generally didn't apply in precincts where walking to your radio car at the start of a tour could turn into a near-death experience. We made up our own rules as we went along.

Wild parties, drinking on duty, brutality, and a sloppy appearance were generally accepted in a ghetto command, as long as you got the job done. Parties were a safety valve to let off steam. Drinking on duty prepared us for the after-work parties. (Why waste valuable minutes getting a buzz on your own time?)

In the seventies it was commonplace—indeed, accepted—to slap around prisoners and other miscreants who gave us a hard time. The cops were greatly outnumbered, and if for one moment the street people thought you were soft, you'd pay the price with a garbage can thrown from a roof or a direct confrontation on the street. The tougher you were, the more respected you were in your sector. Show weakness and you were screwed.

Captain Baker was determined to change our image by implementing rules that would have met with resistance even from the Royal Guard at Windsor Castle.

"Men," he said at his first roll call, "from here on in every officer in this command will wear a hat when outside the radio car." I hadn't seen my hat in weeks. "Two, no smoking in uniform, no drinking in uniform, and above all, I want a greater amount of respect shown to the citizens of this command."

Citizens? I thought. I had recently locked up a fifteen-year-old kid for setting his parents on fire—this shortly after someone tried to blow up my radio car with a homemade bomb. No, Captain Baker had to go, but first we had to find where he was most vulnerable.

While we did our research, Captain Baker issued a blizzard of memos, putting his verbal orders on paper. Baker, by the way, wrote everything in calligraphy, and I mean everything, from precinct directives to lunch orders. The cops couldn't read a thing he drafted.

"What the fuck is this?" Kenny asked me one morning as he waved around the Baker memo of the day. The writing was elaborate and unreadable.

I examined it. "I dunno; looks like maybe King Arthur's orders to invade Scotland."

While every cop in the command continued his research, Captain Baker went on a rampage. I received my first of only two command disciplines in my entire career from him for not wearing a hat at the scene of a three-alarm fire when Kenny and I had dragged a half-dozen people from a burning building. A command discipline is a reprimand that carries mild sanctions (loss of vacation, accrued time, etc.) and is kept in-house. No big deal, but the pettiness rankled me, considering the circumstances.

Baker was a beefy guy with a pile of red hair and appeared to be in the best of health. One day, however, I got a call from a source in the Health Services Division advising me that our fearless leader had a pacemaker. Anyone else would have retired on three-quarters pay for life with a tax-free disability pension under the Heart Bill, which makes heart disease among cops a line-of-duty injury. Not our Captain Baker. He chose to drive us to *our* first coronaries instead.

I quickly spread the word about the pacemaker and, within a day, Pat Randazzo came up with a plan.

"Let's give the son of a bitch a heart attack." Pat's idea of a good time was shooting rats on the Hudson River piers, so his proposal wasn't out of character. Besides, Captain Baker had found out about Cal's, and drastic action needed to be taken.

Cal's was a gin mill located next door to the station house. Calling it a bar or a restaurant would be elevating its stature. To enter Cal's, you descended three steps from street level, both physically and socially.

It was also our home away from home. It was so much a part of our daily lives that the roll calls were posted on the bar for the upcoming tour. Instead of reporting to the station house to find out what you were doing that day, you'd go to Cal's. Before the day tours, Annie, the ancient cook who bragged about pouring drinks for

Al Capone *before* he went to Chicago, would prepare breakfast for the troops and eye-openers for those who needed them. Sometimes there were some die-hard drinkers who would still be there from the previous day.

On bad-weather days when things were slow, the entire platoon would turn out of the station house after roll call and go directly to Cal's, answering calls when required but otherwise drinking, playing cards, or watching TV.

Even as we conspired, Captain Baker was preparing another illegible memo making Cal's off-limits at all times.

We didn't think so.

"How're we gonna give him a heart attack?" I asked.

Pat whipped out an automatic garage-door opener. "With this."

"What're we gonna do, catch his head in a closing garage door?" Frank Moran offered. Frank was particularly upset about the idea of losing Cal's. He sometimes spent entire weeks there, leaving only to shower in the station house.

"No, dickhead," Pat said. "I read somewhere that these things can stop a pacemaker."

"So we're going to kill the precinct CO. Smart," I said. "Maybe we can shoot the mayor when he shows up for the funeral."

"Nah," Pat said. "It'll stop the thing, maybe have his heart go into fibrillation. Probably won't kill him."

Probably? What the hell, it was worth a try.

So Pat hit up a local hardware-supply warehouse for fifty garage-door openers.

For the next couple of weeks every working cop started clicking away every time he got within three feet of the captain. Nothing. A bunch of us even got together and stood outside his office (he always retreated behind closed doors, afraid some disgruntled cop would lob in a grenade) and held a massive click-in. Still nothing.

Pat came into Cal's one day and we threw twenty garage-door openers at him. "What do I look like," he said, "Mr. Fucking Wizard? I gave it a shot."

*   *   *

Lt. Bob Hulsman solved our problem. Hulsman was a desk officer and loved being a cop. He was one of the few supervisors on The Job who never forgot what it was like to be in the trenches, and he treated cops with respect and admiration.

Whatever a cop wanted, he got. Need a day off because you were too hungover to come to work? Call Hulsman; he'd give it to you. Cops used to call him from Cal's five minutes before the start of a tour and ask for the day off. Hulsman would give it to them, even if the precinct was understaffed.

He also acted as the buffer between us and irate citizens making complaints against us. "Don't you worry, sir," he'd say to Joe Citizen, "you fill out this Civilian Complaint Form and I'll personally see to it that the officer you caught sleeping with your wife will be punished to the fullest extent of the law." As soon as the complainant left the station house, Hulsman would tear up the form.

While you might think that he was a pushover and easily taken advantage of by conniving cops because of his attitude, you'd be wrong. When Hulsman worked, the cops backed him, worked their asses off for him, and would do anything for him. Too few bosses really appreciated us, so when we found one who did, we cherished him.

One day Lieutenant Hulsman was turning out the four-to-twelve tour, reading department orders, calling the roll, and inspecting the troops, when Captain Baker strode out of his office to watch the show.

When Hulsman was finished he saluted us, gave a "Left-face," and marched us toward the door to commence protecting the taxpayers.

"Hold it there, Lieutenant," Captain Baker barked. Hulsman gave us a "Platoon, halt!"

Captain Baker, hands behind his back, sneered at the lieutenant and said, "You neglected to read the platoon my memo on unauthorized meal locations." Baker had listed the only four good restaurants in the command as off-limits because they occasionally didn't charge cops for meals. "You're not doing your job, Lieutenant. I specifically gave you that memo to be read at five consecutive outgoing roll calls."

It's not good managerial protocol to dress down a supervisor in front of subordinates. This applies to all arenas, not just the police department, and is a basic tenet of effective management theory. It is particularly bad manners to do this in an organization where everyone is armed, specifically the supervisor who is being chewed out.

Hulsman had no love for Captain Baker and telegraphed those feelings whenever possible. Unlike our other bosses, Hulsman didn't give a rat's ass what Baker thought of him. He got steamed every time Baker came out with another silly rule. Now he'd had enough.

Hulsman flung his pen and clipboard to the floor and physically attacked the CO.

He and Baker were both pushing fifty, about the same size, and not in the best shape, but the lieutenant had surprise on his side.

He grabbed the captain in a headlock, and they both waltzed around the sitting room floor in a not-so-fond embrace. There were no punches thrown, only a lot of bumping bellies and cursing.

Initially we stood stock-still. When the shock at what we were seeing wore off, we started whooping and hollering. "Kill the motherfucker, Loo!" and "Stomp his fucking pinhead," were not uncommon.

Sergeant Reddy ran from behind the desk and separated them in a matter of seconds, but not before the captain had had his shield ripped from his shirt. There was no real winner, and perhaps Sergeant Reddy's quick response prevented two coronaries.

What Hulsman did was a firable offense, if not an arrestable assault, but I don't think he gave a damn. After months of petty bullshit, he had had enough.

Captain Baker, sporting a bruised ego and a torn shirt, didn't say a word, but simply turned and went into his office. He slammed the door behind him.

Lieutenant Hulsman, red in the face and out of breath, straightened his tie. "If there are no questions, gentlemen, take your posts, and have a safe tour." He walked back to the desk like nothing happened.

Everybody dropped their gear and gave him a two-minute ovation.

Captain Baker never filed charges and was transferred to a headquarters job within a month. During his last weeks in the Ninth he never mentioned the incident, but made certain that he never worked the same tour as the good lieutenant.

Lieutenant Sugarfoot, another desk officer, was so named because my squad derived great pleasure from pouring maple syrup in his shoes. The lieutenant might have been a great boss at IBM, where bean counting was important, but in the often unpredictable world of the Ninth, where split-second decisions were the norm, Lieutenant Sugarfoot couldn't decide what to have for lunch, let alone how to charge a prisoner.

I'd never pass up on an opportunity to break his balls. I pulled one gag on him constantly, and he fell for it every time.

Desk officers are constantly bombarded with phone calls. At any given time there's a pile of messages waiting to be answered. When Sugarfoot left the desk, which was often, I'd slip a message into his waiting stack that would say something like, *Call Ed, very important,* and leave a phone number. I'd vary the message and handwriting, but always left the same phone number, which belonged to Fur Kew, a Japanese restaurant on Third Avenue and Fifty-second Street.

The Japanese person who answered the phone would say, "Fur Kew," when he picked up on his end, but it sounded like "Fuck you." Sugarfoot must have been suckered into the Fuck You gag at least fifty times, each time getting more and more steamed. Making his life miserable was a crusade with me. No one deserved it more.

When the proverbial shit hit the fan, the lieutenant

would excuse himself and go to the bathroom, out, of harm's way. He was petty to the point of being ridiculous and would chastise cops for minor infractions. While Captain Baker's nit-picking came out of meanness, Sugarfoot's emanated from a desire to adhere to the rules to the letter, no matter how ludicrous they were.

He used to conduct sideburn inspections. During the seventies, sideburns were in vogue, and most cops had them. Department rules stated that sideburns could extend no more than halfway down the ear in length. Anything longer got a cop a command discipline that cost a vacation day. Sugarfoot actually had a cardboard ear that he would place up against a cop's head. If the cop's sideburn extended below Sugarfoot's ear, you lost a day.

We tried to show him the error of his ways by throwing his locker out a fifth-floor window, but he didn't get the subtle message.

"You think he has a pacemaker?" Pat Randazzo asked. Pat was researching a magnet theory that he was dying to try out.

No such luck. Sugarfoot appeared healthy as a horse.

As good fortune would have it, one day a homeless psycho wandered into the station house, stood in front of the desk, and began waving a twelve-inch butcher knife.

Sugarfoot panicked. He tried to talk to the nut, but everything that came out of his mouth made him sound like Ralph Kramden trying to explain to Alice why his no-cal pizza idea cost them three months' rent. "Hamna, hamna, hamna . . ."

Sugarfoot was armed, of course, but he didn't draw his gun even though he was the only heeled person in the room. Two civilian clerical workers screamed.

Pat Randazzo, who was on a foot post that day and in the house for lunch, heard the commotion and ran to the desk, a gun in one hand, slice of pizza in the other. He could see only the psycho's back as he entered the room. The knife wasn't visible.

"What the fuck's going on?"

Sugarfoot, by this time a lovely shade of red, pointed to the knife wielder. "Knife," he managed to squeak.

The women were still screaming.

"What?" Pat yelled.

One of the women blasted out, "Knife!"

The nut turned on Pat.

Pat raised his pizza. "Hey, drop the fucking knife!"

The psycho hollered something unintelligible and took a step toward Pat.

Pat dropped his pizza. This pissed him off. He emptied his gun into the guy with the knife, all six chest shots, killing him instantly. Pat mumbled something about ruining his meal, turned, and went back to the lunchroom.

One of the two typists fainted, and Lieutenant Sugarfoot had a heart attack. He survived, but never came back to work and retired on the Heart Bill.

I hate to say it, but cops can be the cheapest people in the world. For the most part, cops are generous to a fault, often contributing their own money to a destitute crime victim or paying snitches out of their own pockets. But when you get a cheap cop, you get a world-class miser.

The propensity toward frugality is often exacerbated in the police department because if a cop really pushes, everything is free. It's even easier for a boss to live for nothing because he makes policy. He can put a cop on foot post in front of a "friendly" place of business at the stroke of a pen.

In twenty-two years on The Job I've never worked with a cheaper boss than the sergeant we called the Hitchhiker.

The Hitchhiker had twenty years on The Job, nine as a boss in the Ninth. He never spent a dime on anything. This was a guy who used other people's pens because he didn't want to waste his own ink.

For the Hitchhiker, food was free, clothes were free. Since this was the early seventies, he had to wear a lot of iridescent shirts and bell-bottomed jeans, because that was all that was sold on St. Marks Place. We also called him the world's oldest hippie, but the name Hitchhiker stuck because he thumbed a ride to and from work (still in uniform) to save the cost of commuting.

He'd stand on First Avenue after a tour in full uniform, thumb extended, and catch a ride within minutes. Having a uniformed cop in your car while riding through the neighborhood seemed like a pretty appealing idea to some suburbanite on his way to the Midtown Tunnel.

The Hitchhiker lived so far out on Long Island that he had Indians for neighbors, and it took him at least three hours to get home. Coming into work, he'd snag Suffolk and Nassau County police radio cars to deliver him to the Queens border.

The logistics of these daily trips were mind boggling. It took less planning to land 150,000 troops during D-Day than it took for the Hitchhiker to line up his relay of police cars to get to work. How he worked out the problem of a radio car being on a job or stuck with an arrest, no one ever found out. All I know is that in all his years in the Ninth, he was never late once.

My goal on The Job was to be a boss. Most cops wanted the coveted gold shield of a detective, but I wanted to lead men the way they should be led.

Most of our supervisors were top-shelf bosses who took The Job and their responsibilities toward their cops very seriously. Men like Sergeant Reddy were dedicated professionals and took up the slack for some of the incompetents I've written about in this chapter.

If I ever made boss, I vowed, I'd never forget what it was like to be a cop.

9

The Squad, Part II:
Pat Randazzo

Pat Randazzo's goal on The Job was to win the Medal of Honor. And he didn't want to do it by saving lives; he wanted to win it by taking them. A blazing shoot-out was a lot more glamorous than jumping into the East River to save a drowning child.

The New York City Police Department Medal of Honor is presented to very few individuals. Most of the recipients are awarded the coveted medal posthumously. Pat hoped to be one of the breathing winners, but as strange as he was, the alternative would probably have been acceptable.

Pat was born and raised in Howard Beach, Queens, home to many made mob guys and wanna-be gangsters. To his credit, Pat took the high road, and stayed out of trouble as a kid when most of his buddies were boosting cars, beating up homosexuals, and shooting dope. A swarthy, dark, muscular guy, Pat spent most of his off-duty time in a local gym pumping iron.

His father was the legendary first-grade detective Roger Randazzo, whose career Pat wanted to emulate. Roger, however, served the citizens of New York in the fifties, when outlaw cops were the norm rather than the exception. Roger had a deserved reputation of being the most brutal cop of his time, but also one of The Job's best detectives.

To be fair, during those days cops needed to be heavy-handed to survive. There was no such thing as the Civilian Complaint review board to monitor violence-prone cops, but Roger took his brutality to extremes and killed more bad guys than Dirty Harry dispatched in the movies.

Pat, however, craved his father's approval, and was going to show his dad that he could be just as good a cop, if not better. His dad, it seems, won every medal The Job had to offer *except* the Medal of Honor. Pat would win it for his dad, or die trying.

What Pat failed to realize, or take into account, was that what passed for good police work in the 1950s got you locked up in the 1970s.

Looking back on Pat's tragic life I wonder if his father didn't bring some of his violent tendencies home from the office. We're all products of our environment.

Pat was a member of the infamous Class of '68, and went on to prove the hypothesis that most rookies from that year were destined for trouble.

I had just come off my last four-to-twelve and was looking forward to a nice long swing with my wife, Pat, and our newborn, James Junior. I was one of the few cops who actually liked being with his family (maybe that's why I'm one of the scant number of cops who has never been divorced) and forgot about police work as soon as I left the station house.

The commute was a lot shorter after midnight and I was in the house a little before one. I wound down in front of the TV until it was time for Jimmy's two A.M. feeding, then crawled into bed.

The phone rang at three-thirty. It was on Pat's side of the bed, so she answered it. I propped myself up on an elbow, mostly awake; my REM sleep hadn't kicked in yet. Cops are notoriously light sleepers anyway, the effect of catching a few z's in our radio cars on slow midnight tours. Go heavy into dreamland while working and you could wake up dead, or worse, with an Internal Affairs boss taking your picture.

"Who wants him?" Pat said softly, painfully aware of little Jimmy's habit of waking up at a sound as subtle as rustling leaves. Pause. "I'll see if he's here." Pat was not typical of police wives in that she didn't socialize with other cops' wives or have much interest in police social activities (for which I was grateful). She fell into the mold, however, when it came to protecting me from work calls.

Many times cops are called at home if there's an emergency and ordered in to work, even if they're on vacation or their swing between tours. The basic rule is that if the cop doesn't personally speak to the boss who's ordering him in, then he doesn't have to show up for work. Pat screened all the calls. I never answered the phone at home.

She put her hand over the mouthpiece. "It's Sergeant Reddy. Are you here?"

"Yeah, gimme the phone." I swung my legs out of bed, a knot developing in my stomach. I expected bad news, dead cop kind of bad news. Reddy had left for home the same time I did.

"Don't give me bad news, Sarge."

"Wags, you've gotta come back to work. I'm here now."

My heart was pounding. "What happened?"

"Remember Pat's collar?"

I thought for a moment. "Yeah, you mean the drunk?" The squad had been dispatched to the Bowery to sweep the street for homeless drunks. Back then public intoxication was still on the books, and the Ninth made periodic arrests on the block in response to complaints from the last of the few taxpayers who lived there.

The entire squad made collars, some more than one, and filtered in and out of the house all night with the prisoners. Pat, I recalled, made three arrests, the last one right before the end of the tour. I had gotten on the books with my one pitiful wretch and had called it a night. Not my idea of quality police work.

"Well, when the Broom went back to the cells to check on the prisoners, Pat's was dead." The Broom was an inside man in charge of cleaning up the station house and monitoring prisoners in the cells, usually assigned to that job because he was useless on the street.

"Whaddaya mean, dead? What was it, a suicide?"

"Beaten to death, Wags," Reddy said. "Looks like a skull fracture. An ME's back there with him now. The cells are a goddamn crime scene. IAD is here; the entire squad and the desk officer are being ordered back. You've been officially notified."

"I'm on my way."

We were interrogated separately. I told the sergeant from Internal Affairs all I knew, which was nothing. Sure, I had seen Pat bring in his last prisoner when I was on my way upstairs to change for the trip home, but other than having to be dragged in (the most common mode of transportation for the comatose homeless), the drunk looked and smelled like every other prisoner booked that night, disheveled and stinking.

The desk lieutenant was new; he'd been assigned from a detective command after he was promoted. Not only was he pissed at being bounced back to the bag (uniform) because of his promotion, but after a week in his new rank he was now under investigation. All newly elevated supervisors have a one-year probationary period, and I was sure our new lieutenant was sweating being reduced back to the rank of sergeant.

We were forced to stay until eleven in the morning, after which we adjourned to Cal's to discuss the incident. Pat wisely passed and went home, certain he was being followed by IAD.

Reddy gave us the story.

"Pat booked a dead guy."

There was a collective "Huh?"

"He crushed the poor schmuck's skull with his nightstick, maybe because he was giving Pat some lip," Reddy said, "realized he'd offed the guy, decided to bluff the new lieutenant, brought him in, and booked him dead. Told the Loo he was unconscious like the rest of the mutts last night. The Loo was a second whip in some hotshot detective squad, probably hadn't been that close to an unconscious homeless mutt in ten years."

"Jesus," Greg Foster said, "the Loo back him up?"

Reddy snorted. "What choice did he have?"

The lieutenant was caught between the proverbial rock and a hard place. A desk officer is responsible for making certain that all prisoners are in decent shape prior to being lodged in the precinct cells. This meant that if he admitted that he didn't personally check the prisoner while Pat had him propped up in front of the desk, he was derelict in his duties. Translated: demotion back to sergeant and probably transferred to the auto pound in the swamps of Queens.

He should've checked Pat's collar, if only because Pat had a precinct-wide reputation for beating up prisoners. Pat would make regular stops at Shinbone Alley, a short patch of garbage-strewn land between two buildings on Sixth Street, so named by the members of the Ninth because that's where you went with prisoners who needed a lesson in humility. A short couple of raps on a shinbone fostered instant compliance.

So the lieutenant had no choice but to say that the prisoner was in tip-top shape at the time of booking.

Pat, of course, swore his collar was ready to run a marathon and never looked better. Skull fracture? "Probably had it awhile and checked out in the cell," Pat said. "Hey, when it's your time, it's your time."

Nothing came of the incident, and no charges were ever brought against Pat. If I'd been him I would have counted my blessings, reformed my violent ways, and straightened out. That wasn't about to happen.

Two years later Pat's girlfriend committed suicide. A tragic occurrence to be sure, but even more tragic because she'd shot herself with Pat's off-duty revolver. In the front seat of Pat's father's car. With Pat in it.

His story was that she was despondent because Pat gave her the bad news that he didn't want to see her anymore. Of course, he told her after he had sex with her in the backseat of his father's Cadillac, hopeless romantic that he was.

Prior to the act, he had placed his gun on the dashboard of the car, as most cops would do in a similar situation. After they climbed back into the front seat,

Pat hit her with the Dear Joan. The poor thing was crushed, Pat said, and she reached for the pistol and blew her brains out.

Questionable, to be sure, but Pat had an answer for everything.

IAD interrogator: "You've got powder residue on your hands, Officer Randazzo. How do you explain that?"

Pat: "Gee, Sarge, I went to the range yesterday. How long does that shit last?" Powder residue can last up to four days; every cop knows that.

IAD: "Witnesses heard screams."

Pat: "She's a screamer; you know what I'm saying?" He winked.

IAD: "You know your girlfriend was three months pregnant?"

Pat: "Really?"

Pat beat the charges once again. Now I'm not saying that it wasn't a case of straight-up suicide, but it stank. The general consensus was that Pat, a confirmed bachelor, found out about the pregnancy and, after getting a resounding "No way!" to his suggestion of abortion, decided to abort the baby *and* his girlfriend utilizing the Randazzo Method. After that, the squad tended to stay away from Pat unless police work dictated otherwise.

Pat's undoing came about a year later. He was walking a foot post by himself on a four-to-twelve tour when he got involved in a chase that began on Avenue A and Tenth Street and culminated on the roof of a tenement on Eighth Street and Avenue B.

Pat had called in a 10-13 (Officer Needs Assistance) during the chase, and every available cop from our precinct and bordering commands came to his aid. A "thirteen" is the most serious of calls and indicates a life-and-death situation. In this case, Pat screamed that he was pursuing a man with a gun. Cops responded from everywhere, on foot and via siren-screaming radio car.

Kenny and I were the first on the scene. Pat was on the roof, a dead Hispanic male, about thirty-five, at his feet. A .25-caliber automatic lay at the corpse's side. Pat still had his gun out and was breathing heavily.

"Fucking Spic took a shot at me."

"Put that thing away," I said. Pat holstered the gun. More cops were spilling onto the roof. I looked over my shoulder at the oncoming herd. "Crime scene!" I hollered. Everyone froze.

As the recorder in the sector (Kenny was driving that night—the recorder rides shotgun and does all the paperwork), I was the "first officer," and as such would be testifying as to what I saw and what I did.

What I saw was a very dead, slightly built Hispanic male, maybe a hundred and forty pounds, arms like pipe stems, covered with the track marks of a veteran junkie. His chest was sunken, his face pinched and lined beyond his years. A hard life lived in the EVil.

At center mass was a neat bullet hole, and very little blood, indicating a heart shot.

The lighting was poor. We were many feet above the tallest street lamp. The sky was moonless and cloudy.

"Good shot," I said to Pat.

"Fair to middling," Pat said. "Scumbag whipped out the piece when I asked him to empty his pockets. Chased him here; then he threw a shot at me on the first-floor landing." Forensics would find a .25-caliber bullet lodged in a wall downstairs.

Bosses were spilling onto the roof. I knew I'd be out of the picture soon, but I had to ask Pat a question before we'd clear the crime scene and Pat was brought into the house for interrogation.

"You outsized this guy by a hundred pounds. You couldn't talk to him?"

Pat shrugged. "Some guys you can talk to; others you gotta shoot." I saw the look in his eyes; he was already composing his request for a department medal. Not Medal of Honor stuff, for sure, but if shots are fired at a cop during a sustained period and the cop fires back, that's Combat Cross material, especially if the perp is killed.

* * *

Three days passed. It looked as if Pat's shooting was justifiable. No one cared about the dead guy. Just another junkie. Then the report on the .25 auto came back.

It had been reported stolen in Queens six months ago. The owner of the gun? Pat Randazzo.

Now, what are the odds that a gun stolen from Pat in Queens would not only surface months later, but be the same gun that was used against him in a gun battle on a rooftop within the confines of the Ninth Precinct?

IAD smelled blood. They wanted Police Officer Pat Randazzo in the worst way, not only for his current indiscretion, but for the crimes he had allegedly gotten away with over the years.

The Manhattan DA didn't see it IAD's way. While the evidence was certainly suspicious, it was circumstantial at best. Even though the aforementioned odds were pretty high against such a thing happening, it wasn't inconceivable. Besides, an ADA said, "He didn't shoot the pope; it was a junkie, for chrissakes."

While he beat the criminal charges, Pat was brought up on department charges of failure to safeguard his firearm (the .25-caliber automatic). He was found guilty. Normally that was a five-day rip (loss of five vacation days), but the police commissioner is the final arbiter in all departmental trials. He fired Pat Randazzo.

Pat, bitter and resentful, cleared out his locker and vanished.

In March 1991, one year after I had retired, I read in the *Daily News* that the body of a male was found stuffed in the trunk of a Cadillac parked in the long-term parking lot at Kennedy Airport. The victim had been shot in the head and had been in the trunk an estimated two weeks before the odor of the decomposing corpse had led to its discovery. Homicide detectives suspected a mob hit. Great piece of detection.

The body was identified as that of Patrick Randazzo, a known mob associate and former police officer reported missing by his father over a week prior to the find.

I made a call. A veteran mob watcher from the *Daily*

News told me that after Pat left The Job, he gravitated
to the only thing he knew: hurting people. He hooked
up with the Gambinos, who utilized him as a debt collec-
tor and enforcer. My source suspected some contract hits
along the way, although Pat had never been locked up.
The Randazzo luck had held.

What hell must his dad be going through, I thought,
old, looking back on a checkered career, but reveling in
a reputation that had become golden over the years, as
most do when the facts are clouded by lore, then having
to bury a son who died because he yearned so desper-
ately for his approval?

I speculated that Pat's attitude had gotten him
whacked. Trying to be the big shot. While that posture
will get you fired from the NYPD, it'll get you dead in
the circles Pat traveled in.

I remembered that night on the rooftop on Avenue B,
Pat standing over the man he'd just killed, a familiar
sneer etched across his face.

"Some people you can talk to; others you gotta shoot."

Patrick Randazzo, cop philosopher, predicting his
own future.

10
The Shrine

St. Marks Place, in the late sixties and early seventies, was a mini Las Vegas without the money. Party central, existing under the guise of a political safe haven for the left-leaning, make-love-not-war generation, fueled by drugs and the dislike of anyone in authority.

This revolutionary paradigm stretched for only three blocks, between Seventh and Ninth streets, from Avenue A to Cooper Square, but what a block it was. Fellini could have left his makeup man at home had he decided to shoot a movie on St. Marks Place.

The block consisted mostly of neon-drenched head shops, drug dealers hawking homemade pharmaceuticals, and runaways from all over the world, average age fifteen.

There were two clubs on the street, the Electric Circus and the Dome, both hard-rock emporiums catering to any age group regardless of sexual orientation. On any given four-to-twelve Kenny and I would have at least three radio runs in the clubs, mostly for drug overdoses. Not many fights or violent crimes; this was the Age of Aquarius: make love, not war.

The St. Marks Bath House was on the corner of Cooper Square and catered to gays. These were the days prior to the AIDS epidemic, and anything went. Parties raged; orgies abounded.

The police were rarely called to the Bath House. Disputes were settled on the spot by bouncers. Cops were called when the inevitable partying and drug use resulted in an accountant from Scarsdale, away from his wife and kids, suffering a heart attack while taking one too many hits of amyl nitrite.

But St. Marks Place exuded an aura not to be confined to its physical boundaries, its reputation sucking in businesses not actually located on the legendary street. The renowned rock club Fillmore East was located two blocks away on Second Avenue off Sixth Street, but was often mistakenly referred to as being situated on St. Marks Place.

The Fillmore had a reputation approaching the mythical. Every major rock group played there in the sixties, most remembering it as their first paying gig.

I was single then, and a big rock fan. I remember seeing Janis Joplin, the Allman Brothers, Albert King, Joe Cocker, Jethro Tull, Led Zeppelin, the Doors, the Who, the Animals, Ray Charles, and many other famous and infamous rockers of the time on the celebrated Fillmore stage.

The lines often stretched two blocks to the tip of St. Marks Place, and even though I could have "tinned" my way in for free, I elected to wait and pay rather than be made as the enemy and have to sweat twenty-six hundred hostile cop haters in a darkened room for two hours.

The place reeked of pot, and bottles of cheap wine and beer were passed around indiscriminately. I always managed to get to the first row in the balcony, the best vantage point in the house. The local Hell's Angels chapter provided security.

The bands rocked with a steady blast of earsplitting music that pounded through your head with aural pyrotechnics resembling exploding mortar rounds. I'd leave the Fillmore unable to hear for hours. Man, what music.

In June 1971 the Fillmore East went out of business. Its last hurrah was a series of shows featuring Alice Cooper. I tried getting tickets the legitimate way, but when the box office sold out, I began making calls to contacts I had met on the street. No luck.

The best I was able to do was get assigned a foot post

in front of the Fillmore the day of the last show. I remember it as a bright, sunny, typical June morning in the city, humid, with a beaten copper sky threatening a sneak attack of thunderstorms.

When the rain did come, it came in torrents. I got soaked crossing the street from a coffee shop where I'd taken a break, and sought refuge under the Fillmore awning.

Music blared from inside, rehearsals in full swing. Sergeant Reddy and his driver, Andy Glover, pulled up right about then, and Reddy signed my memo book as supervisors are obligated to do up to several times a tour. He winced at the music as I bobbed my head to the beat.

"You like this shit, Wags?"

I smiled. "Shit is in the eyes of the beholder, Sarge. There's good shit and bad shit. This is good shit."

Reddy looked at his watch. "Getting to be mealtime; then I've got some paperwork to catch up on. Don't think I'll be back. You need me, I'll be in the house."

The sergeant was telling me that he wouldn't be looking for me. I'd worked for Reddy, made him look good with quality arrests, never getting into any trouble. He was a fair boss who appreciated his men and never forgot what it was like to be a cop. A good cop, he said, never gets cold, hungry, or wet. Words to live by.

I saluted him as the car slid into Second Avenue traffic. As soon as it rounded a corner, I went into the Fillmore.

The room was long, cavernous, and dimly lit. On a lighted stage Alice Cooper and his band were rehearsing songs from his *Welcome to My Nightmare* album. Even from the back of the theater and without makeup, Cooper was easily recognizable. At about six-three and extremely thin, with a long face and thick black hair, he stood out like a Klansman at an NAACP rally.

I inched silently into a seat about midtheater so as not to disturb the work in progress, although the music reverberations could have masked a charge up Hamburger Hill.

I listened to Cooper and his band for about twenty

minutes as they did alternate takes of the same tune and riffed through various other songs, jamming, pausing, and fine-tuning as they went along.

They stopped abruptly at a hand signal from Cooper and began to unplug their instruments. The drummer tossed his sticks into the air. Rehearsal was over.

"Bring up the lights," Cooper said, and the house got bright. The band was leaving the stage when he spotted me in the orchestra. He shielded his eyes. "Hey, Officer, c'mon up.

"You got the post?" he asked as I approached the stage. He knew the lingo—probably had off-duty cops for security.

"Just got out of court," I said.

He lifted the lid on a plastic cooler and produced two bottles of Rheingold beer. "Join me?" Cooper was a notorious beer drinker in those days and had a legendary capacity for the stuff.

I'm not much of a drinker. Even my days in Cal's had me downing coffee during the day tours. I'd never drink on-duty until the end of a tour, and then only one beer. To this day my friends call me a cheap date, since I'm unable to consume more than three drinks over the course of an evening.

But how many times in your life are you invited to share a brew with a rock icon like Alice Cooper? "Yeah, sure," I said, and hopped onto the stage.

We sat with legs dangling into the pit. He raised his bottle. "To the Fillmore; may it rest in peace." He took a long pull on the beer.

"I'm here every weekend," I said, "when I'm not working."

Cooper seemed surprised. "A cop with a rock jones. Cool." He extended his hand. "Alice Cooper."

No shit. "Jimmy Wagner. Call me Wags."

"Wags it is. Want another?" He had downed the beer in one gulp. In the course of the next hour he would kill two six-packs.

I expected questions about police work, my attitude toward peace demonstrators, and my position on the

Vietnam War, but all we talked about was the demise of the Fillmore. In his mellow, sandpapery voice he waxed nostalgic about his gigs in the most famous rock emporium on the East coast.

"I played a lot of rooms, mostly on the left coast, but this room is history. You can hear Jimi, Janis, the Allmans. All of them. The sound's still in here, soaked into the walls." He pointed toward the balcony. "My craziest fans are always up there, man. Halfway through my first set I always expect someone leaning over too far to drop off. The diehards, that's where they are."

"My spot, too," I said, feeling a sudden kinship and relaxing as I sucked on beer number three. "Know what they're gonna do with this place?"

"Just going under far as I know, but whatever they do with the building eventually, they'd better do it justice; it's a shrine."

For a few hours I wasn't a cop, only a fan in uniform, but on equal footing with a down-to-earth guy.

I was feeling the beer, and I knew that as soon as I got out into the sun I'd be sorry I ever had the first one. I looked at my watch. "Shit, I gotta sign out." I jumped up to leave.

"What, you're not gonna ask for free passes to the show? Last one's tonight, but I guess I don't have to tell you that."

I had debated asking him for tickets, but I felt it would be like asking him for his autograph, decidedly not classy for a cop in uniform, so I opted not to do it.

"That's okay; I've already got two," I lied.

Cooper leaned back and dragged a battered attaché case between us. He popped it open and produced four tickets. "Now you've got four more. You have any more friends can stomach two hours of me tonight?"

I still have the stubs.

It was the best show, rock or otherwise, I've ever seen. Alice Cooper played with a passion that spoke of his love for the Fillmore and the knowledge that he was part of history.

In the years that followed, I took to calling the shuttered Fillmore the Shrine. Rock bands still rehearsed there, but the building was closed to the public.

In 1981 construction began on a new facade, and word immediately spread around the neighborhood that a new club was opening where the Fillmore East once stood. I hoped the new owners would keep the spirit of the Fillmore alive and not destroy any of its history.

Weeks went by. I'd walk past the building every day and watch construction crews tearing up the exterior of the building. Apparently major changes were going to be made. I hoped these changes would be restricted to the outside of the building, and that the developers would allow the ghosts of rock to jam in the halls of the old interior.

It physically pained me to see the layers of history being ripped away to be replaced by a new modern marquee that proclaimed the new club, The Saint, would be opening in two months.

The owners of the club were hiring off-duty cops as security, and I was first in line to apply. I bypassed The Job's requirement to get permission to moonlight. I figured the regime at 1 Police Plaza would have an off-duty cop working for Idi Amin before they'd allow one of their members to work in a former rock club, enlightened as they were.

Opening night was a bubble burster. The Saint was a gay club. It seemed like every gay male in the city was waiting patiently on line to gain admittance. Management wisely replaced the Hell's Angels as line security with members of the gay community. The off-duty cops worked inside.

The room had been destroyed. Every orchestra seat had been removed to make way for a dance floor. Walls had been stripped to bare brick. Strobe track lighting, coupled with blaring music, started my head pounding as soon as I got there.

Undulating, sweating, seminaked male bodies jammed the dance floor. The place was packed to capacity; I estimated over three thousand people. And four off-duty cops to keep order. If a fight broke out I had plans to shoot myself in the head and bypass the unnecessary pain I'd undoubtedly suffer trying to break up a fight while outnumbered six hundred to one.

The only reminder of the old Fillmore was the balcony. It was still standing, albeit sagging under the weight of several hundred men. From the floor I could see a crowd peering over the edge of the railing.

Three hours into my shift, I couldn't take the music anymore and asked the manager if I could be reassigned to the balcony.

"Yeah, but you'd better take someone with you," he said, and rolled his eyes. Most owners and managers of gay clubs in New York are mobbed up. This guy was no exception. He had Brooklyn wiseguy written all over him. He was trying to tell me something, but wouldn't elaborate.

I grabbed Bob Gries, a sandy-haired off-duty cop with a devilish gleam in his eye. Bob was from the Sixth Precinct in Greenwich Village. "Let's go upstairs; maybe it's quieter up there."

The balcony was dimly lit and packed almost to the point of overflowing. Cliques of totally naked men cavorted and danced (by themselves and with others). What drew my attention was a crowd of men surrounding something or someone in the far corner.

"I wanna check this out," I said.

"Lead the way."

We elbowed our way through the crowd. Everyone was either otherwise engaged or tripping on some illegal substance. No one paid any attention to us.

As we neared the group, a thunderous round of applause exploded, barely masking a ripping, bloodcurdling scream.

I wasn't about to get up close and personal with this group, many of whom were in studded leather regalia and looked meaner than junkyard dogs.

I pulled a chair to the perimeter of the mob and jumped up, and what I saw I don't think I'll ever forget. A naked man—a naked older man; he was at least sixty—was down on all fours. A young guy wearing jeans and a leather vest had his arm shoved up the man's ass, almost to the elbow. I would imagine the insertion produced the scream. The arm's owner proceeded to pump his fist into the guy's ass repeatedly, as the pumpee screamed in agony.

Now, I've been around and seen some pretty nasty things in my police career and in the navy, but I never even imagined something like what I was witnessing.

The crowd was wild, yelling, whooping, clapping. I grabbed Gries by the collar and pulled him onto the chair.

"Can you believe this shit?" I said, half expecting him to fall off the chair at the sight.

Gries was almost nonchalant. "Yeah, so?"

"Yeah, so!" I hollered above the din. "Yeah, so! Doesn't this shock you?"

Gries snorted. "I'm in the Sixth Precinct, remember? Most of these guys live there. You expect this shit to shock me? Lemme tell you something: When I caught a tractor-trailer load of priests going down on each other under the West Side Highway, *that* shocked me. When I saw two grown men fucking a sheep in a warehouse on Twelfth Avenue, *that* shocked me. When a guy walked into the station house complaining that he had a lightbulb stuck up his ass, *that* shocked me. But this? We see this shit every day in the Sixth. Apparently you've never heard of the Fist Fuckers of America."

The crowd had grown, now attracting gays from the far corners of the balcony as well as a new bunch who had just filtered upstairs from the dance floor. I had to scream to be heard.

"You gotta be fucking kidding me!"

Gries raised his right hand. "It's a real club; they meet in the Anvil." The Anvil was a notorious leather bar with a view of the Hudson River. "The guy with the tears in his eyes is actually enjoying this."

Now, at this time the term *politically correct* had not yet entered the American lexicon. I had always, however, considered myself a fairly liberal thinker, at least compared to the average New York City cop.

My attitude was that as long as you weren't hurting me, my family, or my friends, and if you weren't committing a crime, you were pretty much free to do whatever the hell it was you wanted to do. If you wanted to be gay and insert your fist up someone's ass, more power to you, but I'd appreciate it if you'd wash your hands if you work in McDonald's.

The victim—or, more properly put, the "recipient"—in this case seemed more than eager to be the fist fuckee, and I wasn't about to object to his idea of a good time.

However, these perverts were desecrating the Fillmore! My blood began to boil as I envisioned the spirits of Janis Joplin and Jimi Hendrix having to witness this depravity in a place where they had made history. I flashed back to my afternoon with Alice Cooper and the whimsical look he'd gotten on his face when he talked about "the Shrine." Tears actually came to my eyes and Gries noticed it.

"Come over here with me," he said, the aforementioned devilish gleam becoming more pronounced.

We jumped off the chair and repaired to a vacant corner. Gries looked around, then pulled a foot-long metal rod with two prongs sticking out of the front from inside his jacket pocket.

"You want to take back the balcony?"

"You're goddamn right," I said. "What the hell is that thing?"

"Cattle prod. Fifteen thousand volts. It'll move a herd of cattle; whaddaya think it'll do to three hundred crazed perverts? Great for crowd control or waking up homeless drunks in the winter before they freeze to death on the street."

"You're a real humanitarian."

I should pause here because you're probably wondering if Officer Gries was part of the infamous class of '68. Well, he was, but it should also be noted that Gries was a damn good cop, and given the times, he wasn't the only cop to use extraordinary means to survive the street. After this initial ignominious meeting, Gries and I became fast friends. He was a bright guy who, after getting his B.A. from John Jay College of Criminal Justice, went on to St. John's Law School and today is a successful New York attorney with offices in several other states. Of course none of this precluded his being dubbed "Electric Man" until he retired.

Gries showed me how the thing worked and said, "Go get 'em. I'll back you up."

And I did.

I waded silently into the crowd and began zapping everyone within reach. Howls, not unlike that which emanated from the gentleman on all fours, pierced the balcony. Some of the more stoned celebrants fainted.

I cleared a path through the mob in seconds, driving everyone downstairs. Anyone who gave me a problem, or those I couldn't reach with the prod, were dispatched by Gries, who came up behind me with the metal folding chair we had been standing on.

I was in a frenzy of hate and sweat as I jabbed any and all available moving bodies. "This is for Janis, you perverted prick! This is for Jimi!" And on it went until I was exhausted and soaked in perspiration. Gries, too, was spent. He opened the chair he'd wielded as a weapon and sat down. Field expediency.

After only a few minutes, we had reclaimed the balcony amidst a bunch of prostrate bodies and the smell of burning flesh.

We had little time to congratulate each other before the manager came charging up the stairs.

"What the fuck are you doing?" He had his fists balled, but thought the better of using them when he saw the weird look in my eyes.

Gries said to the manager, "I wouldn't fool with him; he's pissed."

So he stuttered and stammered for a few seconds, then blurted, "You guys are fired!"

I pushed past him, Gries right behind me. "Take this job and shove it up your ass!"

"Pardon the pun," Gries said, and tucked the cattle prod back under his jacket.

I burst into the street, gulping what passes for fresh air in New York, leaned against a car, and lit a cigarette.

"You okay?" Gries asked.

Now I began to realize that we'd just assaulted half the gay population in Manhattan. I visualized a jail door being slammed on a hapless prisoner: me.

"You think we have a problem here?"

"Doubt it," Gries said. "Would you want to be the guy who reports that while you were cheering a guy getting his asshole reamed, someone jabbed you with a cattle prod? Who wants that kind of publicity?"

Well, he was right. Nothing came of my rampage, and I felt a little remorseful for losing my temper the way I did. I was more and more physical lately with prisoners, and my thoughts went back to Pat Randazzo and the way he conducted himself. I hoped I wasn't falling into that mold, although the frustrations of police work often led the average cop to vent his angst at the very people he was sworn to serve. As time went on I'd find myself becoming the brutal cop I abhorred, and it would lead to problems toward the end of my career.

This time, however, I assuaged my guilt knowing that I was defending the honor of the heroes of rock 'n' roll.

11
Celebrities

A New York City cop will meet and mingle with celebrites throughout his or her entire career. So meeting Alice Cooper, while a thrill and an honor, wasn't an aberration.

Take an average cop, any cop, and no matter where they work, be it in the glitter of midtown Manhattan or the shrubs of Staten Island, they'll be guaranteed to meet the famous and infamous. Some under less-than-flattering circumstances.

Ninth Precinct cops weren't in the habit of making arrests for driving while intoxicated (DWI). There were real criminals on the street, and the time spent dragging a drunk through court was time wasted when we could be catching real bad guys. Also, the precinct was so small that by the time you followed a car long enough to make a determination that the driver was drunk, he was in Brooklyn.

Most important, during the seventies and early eighties, Mothers Against Drunk Driving (MADD) wasn't the powerful political force it is today. In short, no one took a drunk driver too seriously. Besides, cops have been known to have a few for the road themselves, and it would have had to be one serious drunk for a cop to take action.

Kenny and I were working a horrendously busy midnight-to-eight tour. Normally things would slow down after three A.M., but it was a hot summer night and the natives were restless.

Finally, a little after four A.M., things quieted down and we stole five minutes to go to the park for a few iced teas.

I was holding mine to my head (this was the period before air-conditioned radio cars) and Kenny was sipping his, both of us grateful for even a few minutes' respite, when a late-model Cadillac weaved down the street in front of us.

Kenny was beat. "I suppose we gotta do something about that."

"I suppose." I slipped the car into gear. We pulled the Caddy over off Avenue B, thankful for the late hour and the deserted street.

Car stops can be dangerous—you never know who's inside—and we approached the car with appropriate caution.

Kenny took his position at the right rear of the Caddy while I shone my flashlight in the driver's face, less to see with whom I was dealing than to blind his aim should he have a gun.

"Hi, Officer," the dark-skinned driver slurred, his head stuck out the window at an odd angle.

He looked familiar, but at that hour I probably wouldn't have known my wife. "License, registration, and insurance, please," I said. I watched his hands carefully as he dug out a wallet and gave me the necessary paper.

As I focused on the ID he said, "Hey, Officer, I'm Tonto," after which he opened the car door, leaned out, and projectile vomited all over the street, narrowly missing my shoes.

I blinked and read the license: Jay Silverheels and a Brooklyn address. I lowered the light and scrutinized the driver's face.

Son of a bitch. Tonto.

"Hey, Kenny, Tonto's driving this car!" Kenny loved the Lone Ranger, and had a repertoire of Tonto and Lone Ranger jokes.

"Yeah, sure," he said, but he saw I was serious and came around the car.

"Holy shit!" Kenny was starstruck.

Now, not much impresses a street cop, and even if there is something that would require this response, a cop would keep it to himself, once again maintaining the upper hand in a situation. Be cool. In control.

But Tonto? That was worth a "Holy shit!"

Well, Tonto was wrecked and coming home from a party in the West Village. But he was a happy drunk, and within fifteen minutes we had every working sector on the scene trading "Hows" with Jay Silverheels.

We parked his car and took him to Ya Ya's and pumped coffee into him until he was passably sober. He "kemo sabed" us all to hell and signed autographs, telling us stories about the series and about Clayton Moore, who played the Ranger ("Love him like a brother"). Then we drove him back to his car and sent him on his way.

As the Caddy slowly made its way toward the Brooklyn Bridge, Tonto stuck his head out the window and yelled, "Gettum up, Scout!"

Kenny said, "Say, Wags, who was that man?"

"I don't know, partner, but he left this." And I pointed to the pile of Tonto's vomitus in the street.

Only in New York.

Central: "In the Ninth Precinct, listen up. Six-boy is in pursuit of a late-model canary yellow Ferrari or Maserati heading eastbound on Fourteenth Street toward the Ninth. Units to respond?"

"Adam-Boy."

"Charlie-David-Frank, Central," Kenny said, "we're coming up Fourteenth Street now. We see the lights. We'll stop 'im."

Another nutty four-to-twelve working with less-than-minimum manning and just managing to keep up with the jobs. Now we had to help a sector from the Sixth Precinct catch a sports car.

"Pull across the lanes, Kenny," I said wearily.

"He'll ram the fucking car, for crissakes!"

"So we'll get out."

Kenny thought about this for a moment, nodded, and blocked the eastbound lanes with our radio car. "Okay, un-ass the vehicle," he said after he came to a screeching halt. He didn't have to tell me.

The car—I think it was a Maserati—braked sharply and slid to a stop. The driver remained inside.

The pursuing Sixth Precinct radio car came to within inches of rear-ending the Maserati, screeching to a halt behind it.

Cops from two precincts converged. This is when people get hurt. The cops are so angry that they've had to risk their lives pursuing a car that they sometimes lose their tempers and beat the shit out of the driver when they finally catch him. Human nature. You have to drive 80 mph to catch a car going 70 mph. The adrenaline is pumping and you're pissed.

Fortunately, Sergeant Reddy responded and kept the situation under control.

"It's the Sixth's collar; we stay back," he told responding Ninth Precinct units.

The driver was dragged out of the car by a cursing Sixth Precinct cop. The driver was Miles Davis, legendary jazz trumpeter. He was sober, but not very friendly, and was swearing right back at the officer. I guess this could be expected from a guy who played entire concerts with his back to the audience.

His car was loaded with alligator shoes; there had to be thirty pairs of them still in boxes. No crime there. But he also had a blackjack, and carrying a concealed weapon is a misdemeanor. Bye-bye, Miles.

The Ninth Precinct station house has been used by the Hollywood community for years, mostly for exterior scenes. The outside shots of the station house in *Kojak* and *NYPD Blue* are of the Ninth Precinct.

Telly Savalas would stop by every so often to shoot street scenes and liked to mingle with the cops. He had a gnarled knuckle on his right hand, which made shaking hands awkward, but that didn't stop him. A nice guy who loved a cop, he was always friendly and would talk to us for hours. "Who loves ya, baby?" he'd say.

The *NYPD Blue* cast arrived after I retired, but I understand they were also friendly. Not too many prima donnas when they needed us as a buffer between the actors and the street people, or sometimes needed that extra-special favor that even the most powerful people in the movie industry couldn't provide.

Charles Bronson was filming scenes from *Death Wish* within the confines of the Ninth. One particular scene had Bronson chasing some bad guys over a rooftop.

These locations are not chosen haphazardly. When a location is selected it can't be changed on a whim. It takes literally all day to set up lighting, coordinate airplane flyovers, wait for the right weather, etc.

So when the day of the shooting arrived and a dead junkie was found OD'd on the roof where the chase scene was going to be filmed, all hell broke loose.

Time is money. Hours spent sitting around cost thousands of dollars. The director was going crazy. I had the foot post, assigned to provide security, and called an ambulance to remove the corpse.

The good news: The ambulance arrived in minutes. The bad news: The EMT people couldn't remove the stiff because it was on private property.

I told the director we'd have to wait for the morgue wagon.

"How long's that gonna take?"

"There's only one for the entire borough. Busy day, lots of dead people, could take all day."

The director flipped.

When shooting stops, the star of the picture usually repairs to his trailer to have a few cocktails, get a massage, whatever. But Charles Bronson walked over to me and asked what was going on. I told him.

"Can't we get the morgue people here any sooner?" he asked.

"Depends on the backlog of bodies."

"Okay, thanks, Officer." He smiled and left.

I've dealt with a lot of shitheads in my time, and I'd heard stories about temperamental movie stars ordering cops to get them coffee on sets (you can imagine what the response to *that* request would be) and generally throwing their weight around. But Bronson was a genuinely nice guy, so I decided to lend a hand.

Kenny was off (one of the reasons I got stuck on a foot post), so I strolled over to Ya Ya's, got on the radio, and reached out for Frank Moran.

"Nine foot post," he responded. At least he was monitoring the radio.

"Call me on landline," I said, and gave him the number of the pay phone in Ya Ya's. He called within five minutes.

"You okay?" I asked him.

"Yeah, yeah, fine," he said. You never knew with Frank. He could be drunk by eight in the morning or not touch the stuff for a week. Today he was sober.

"I'm stuck on the movie detail. Do me a favor and go to the house and borrow a radio car. Meet me on the corner of the shoot."

"Not a problem."

I knew no one would be looking for Moran. He walked the entire precinct, basically wherever he wanted, and no one bothered him.

Frank showed up with the radio car and I told him to wait around the corner. While everyone was bitching and complaining I went to the roof, tossed the dead junkie over my shoulder, and carried him down four flights of stairs and out through the rear basement door to the radio car.

Moran was leaning against the car smoking a cigarette. I was winded. "Pop the trunk, will ya?"

"Yeah, sure. Whatcha got there?"

"Dead junkie."

Moran didn't even blink. "Oh, okay."

I dumped the body in the trunk, slammed it shut, and told Moran to drive to Bellevue.

We dropped the body in the morgue, where it would

have wound up anyway, and told the startled attendant, "Part of our new service. We deliver our own bodies on slow days," and drove back to the shoot.

"Thanks, Frank."

He looked at me, said, "For what?" and drove away.

I grabbed an assistant to an assistant producer. "Body's gone."

"Huh?"

"Morgue helicopter. Just plucked the guy off the roof."

"Hey, you guys are great."

"Tell that to the mayor."

Many scenes from *The Godfather, Part II* were shot within the confines of the Ninth Precinct.

Sixth Street, between Avenues A and B, was transformed into Little Italy, circa 1910, and remained that way for weeks during the extended filming.

One mom-and-pop grocery store was redesigned to be Abbandando's Market, where Don Corleone worked as a boy and was fired when the local Black Hand boss wanted his nephew to have the job.

That little grocery store remains the same today, the "Abbandando" sign and facade architecture still in place. The owners liked the "new old" look and decided to keep it that way.

Most New York neighborhoods have block associations that are vocal in local politics. During the filming, local block leaders shook down the producers for a lot of money, claiming that without their muscle, neighborhood troublemakers would disrupt the shooting.

A fact of life when filming a movie in New York.

In the late seventies I filled in for a cop friend who moonlighted as a bodyguard. He worked in Midtown North, made many contacts in the entertainment industry, and picked up a lot of security assignments.

The Job requires that you get permission prior to taking a second job, even if it's only for one day. Bodyguard work is particularly scrutinized, because at one time a group of cops were caught hiring themselves out as body-guards to organized-crime figures. Very embarrassing at 1 Police Plaza when Officer Smith gets his picture taken with a local don and it winds up on the front page of the *Post*.

The problem with the system, however, was that by the time the necessary paperwork was approved by various commanders up and down the line, eventually winding up on the police commissioner's desk, the bodyguard assignment had come and gone. So cops rarely sought permission to work bodyguard jobs, and prayed that their charge wouldn't be the target of a terrorist attack while they were working.

My friend from Midtown North is still on The Job, so therefore he shall appear here under a pseudonym. Let's call him Officer Knapp. By the way, these days Officer Knapp makes more money doing private bodyguard work than he ever thought of making as a police officer.

"What do I have to do?" I asked. We were in a bar on the West Side.

"Meet my buddy Danny—he owns a limo—on Fifty-third and Lex; then you go pick up the couple at the Plaza Hotel," Knapp said. "Young Hollywood hotshots, husband and wife. After that you go wherever they go."

"What's the itinerary?"

"Party time. Usually some clubs, maybe some shopping first, nice restaurants, like that."

"That's it?"

"Yep, that's it." He reached into his pocket. "Here's two hundred dollars; have a good time."

Two hundred bucks in the late seventies went a helluva lot further than it does now, and was about what I was taking home each week from The Job after taxes. I pocketed the cash. We made small talk, had another drink (which I happily bought), and I went off to meet my clients.

Danny, the limo driver, had a beautiful stretch Lincoln that was illegal as hell. No Taxi Limousine Commission plates, which were required by law, and no insurance.

"How do you keep from getting summonses?" I asked.

He shrugged. He was a boxy Irishman, about forty. "Get 'em all the time. Don't pay them, though."

"What happens if they hook your car?"

"Fuck them; I ain't made a payment in six months anyway. I'll get another."

Great.

At the hotel we picked up the couple, who introduced themselves as Jose and Kitty. They spoke unaccented English, but had a Hispanic last name, which I immediately forgot. Very informal, pleasant people.

These nice people had plenty of money. She was a little on the heavy side, blond, dripping jewelry, and wearing a short, revealing dress. He wore a conservative suit accessorized by a gold Rolex and a diamond pinky ring.

They had dinner at the Four Seasons (Danny and I stayed with the car), followed by a little partying at Studio 54, supplemented with plenty of champagne in the car.

I discovered the reason Jose and his wife used Danny's illegal limo rather than a legitimate service when they came to New York—because Danny had the best blow in town. Coke and Dom Pérignon flowed. This was going to be a long night. I didn't sign on to bust my clients, so I kept my mouth shut and enjoyed the ride.

We wound up at Club A under the Queensborough Bridge on the Manhattan side a little after two A.M. By this time my charges were so juiced that they invited Danny and me inside the club with them.

It was wiseguy central in the crowded disco. At that time I hadn't had the exposure to gangsters I would acquire after I retired and went into the PI business, but I knew enough to realize that these guys pick fights for any reason. I was hoping I wouldn't have to shoot my way out of the place.

Fortunately, Jose and Kitty were satisfied to sit at a table and guzzle champagne, stopping periodically to make frequent trips to the bathroom to powder their noses.

Jose showed me pictures of his sons, two handsome

little boys. I showed him pictures of my son. He told me a little about his movie production business. I told him funny stories about police work. Danny sampled his own product. Time flew.

The evening ended a little after four A.M. with us dropping off the soused-but-under-control couple back at the Plaza. Jose palmed me two hundred-dollar bills.

I wasn't to take another bodyguard job until after my retirement, for no other reason than that police work and my growing family kept me pretty busy and I wasn't all that money hungry. That would come later, after I left The Job and got a taste of what *real* money was like. And, of course, I remembered the incident because of the double-ace tip.

Fast forward to August 1989. I was on vacation, sitting on my porch reading the *Daily News*. A story on page three detailed a grisly murder in Los Angeles. Jose Menendez, an executive with Carolco Productions, and his wife Kitty had been shotgunned to death in their home, the bodies discovered by their sons, Erik and Lyle.

The boys were arrested shortly thereafter, were subsequently convicted at trial, and are now serving life terms.

I remembered how proud Jose had been of the two smiling boys in the picture that night in Club A. He beamed with parental joy, as I had when showing him pictures of my son.

I looked at my son Jimmy, who was twelve, playing in the yard with his friends. My daughter, Jennifer, ten, was shopping with her mother. Patricia, seven, was watching television.

I hugged my son; he was closest.

"You're weird, Dad," he said, embarrassed by the display of affection in front of his buddies.

But he hugged me back.

12

Murder in the White House

Lest you think that I'm confessing to being the ghost-writer for the Margaret Truman mystery series, this chapter will deal with a homicide that occurred in the infamous Ninth Precinct hotel, the White House.

The White House was an SRO—single-room occupancy—hotel located on the inglorious Bowery, the last stop for the lowest common denominator of drunk or junkie.

SROs were subsidized by welfare money, and many of these hotels dotted the bleak landscape that was the Bowery. For over a century, men down on their luck and in the hopeless throes of alcohol addiction gravitated to the slum of the Bowery and remained there for the rest of their limited lives.

Until the sixties, the Bowery had a mystique. It was said that many Wall Street tycoons who had lost their money in the Crash of '29 lived on the Bowery, anonymously, until their livers exploded from one too many bottles of Hombre (the Wine for Men!).

Then came the tidal wave of drugs, specifically heroin, and what had once been a haven for male alcoholics became a pangender hole-in-the-wall hideout for depraved junkies. A class structure emerged, as it will in all segments of society, with the alkies on top of the heap. As with jewel thieves in prisons, the alky dominated the sub-echelon of their world.

Sammy's Bowery Follies, a throwback to the golden days of vaudeville, often featured habitués of the neighborhood in starring stage roles. The locals also had their own newspaper. The newspaper went belly-up in the fifties, followed by the demise of Sammy's in the late sixties. In their place came the influx of the SROs.

Single-room occupancy hotels were a necessary evil when drugs took over the Bowery. As if heroin weren't bad enough, cocaine, inhalants, and later the crack epidemic had the battered neighborhood bursting at the seams. In the seventies, runaways with drug joneses ruptured the dyke, and the city decided to hide its unsightly netherworld by giving them living space.

The Bowery denizens received vouchers for $1.75, good for a single night's stay in one of these hotels. These one-night flops stretched into weeks, months, and sometimes years for their tenants. Often tenancy was terminated by a hot shot of bad (or, most times, good) horse, and as a dead body was carted out, a walking corpse dragged itself in to take over the digs.

The most notorious hotels in the Ninth were the Kenton, the Palace, and the White House, located within a block of each other. Living arrangements consisted of cubicles just big enough for a cot and a washbasin, facilities down the hall. Each cubicle had a stretch of chicken wire across the top that served as a roof and kept uninvited guests out. There were no locks on the doors because there was nothing to steal, unless you counted the shoes of the sleeping, which only turned into salable commodities during the winter.

Generally the drunks kept to themselves; trouble came in the form of junkies. The Kenton and the Palace were notorious havens for hard-core drug addicts, and we'd get many radio runs to both hotels. Most were for ripe dead bodies who wound up that way from natural causes (we considered an overdose a natural way to go for these people), but there were a surprising number of suicides, occurring mostly, I would imagine, during a rare moment of lucidity when the drug money ran out and the victim was clearheaded enough to realize what he had degenerated to.

Hanging was the most popular way to do oneself in.

The cubicles hadn't any windows to leap from, and egress to the roof was impossible without a key to the padlock that secured every roof door in Manhattan south of Houston Street. A week never went by when Kenny and I wouldn't find some poor wretch on his knees hanging from a doorknob by his last pair of shoelaces, his tongue swollen to the size of a cow's and his eyes bulging like Rodney Dangerfield's.

These were equal-opportunity hellholes, and strictly male enclaves. All you needed was a voucher and you had a flop for the night. Black, white, dwarf, or Martian, all were welcome. The absentee owners didn't care about your appearance; they cared about the subsidy reimbursement they got from the city. Landscaping in Scarsdale doesn't run cheap.

The White House, however, catered only to male drunks, although the occasional junkie slipped in if he didn't have visible track marks. Transvestites were okay because they still had their original equipment.

The White House was aptly named, because only whites were permitted to stay there. Everyone in the area knew the house policy and no one cared. This was the Bowery; the federal law barring discrimination was scoffed at.

For the most part, the White House was one of the more staid SROs in the precinct. Accommodations were a step above the norm, because steady tenants were permitted to break through the cubicle walls to form larger living areas. Most of the time radio runs dealt with petty disputes involving the ownership of a jug of Swiss Up or the occasional heated debate over the vintage of a bottle of muscatel. ("My bottle says 'Drink before Tuesday,' so it's gotta be better than your shit.")

But not all was glum. The Bowery was in our sector, and to keep from going nuts from our dealings with the citizens, Kenny and I devised Quiz Show Sundays.

Liquor stores were closed on Sundays. You would think that people whose lives revolved around cheap wine would take that into consideration and squirrel an extra bottle or two away to tide them over until Monday. This never happened. An extra bottle had a way of disappearing during that end-of-week, thank-God-it's-Saturday party. So by Sunday morning every drunk on the Bowery was hungering for a little eye-opener.

There were a few enterprising drunks, outsiders to be sure, who would go down to the Bowery on Sunday mornings with duffel bags full of fifty-cent bottles of Hombre, which they would sell for a dollar. These guys couldn't be Bowery regulars because they'd get their throats slit for preying on their brethren the first time they closed their eyes in their flop. No, these entrepreneurs often journeyed from as far away as Tompkins Square Park (only a few blocks north, but a world removed from the ghetto that was the Bowery).

Kenny and I would confiscate the duffel bags and give the wine to the regulars we had come to know. The wine wasn't free, however. The drunk would have to answer a question, usually dealing with current events, before we'd hand over a bottle. They wouldn't have to answer it correctly, mind you, just come up with any answer that would make it seem like they weren't getting a free handout. It was on such a Quiz Show Sunday that we came across a possible homicide in the White House.

"Okay," I said, "who's the president of the United States?"

The drunk reeling by the radio car was white, about thirty-five, dressed warmly for this Sunday morning in December, in greasy tan pants, a ripped turtleneck sweater, mismatching sneakers, and a torn navy pea coat. His oily hair hadn't seen soap in at least a week, but he was clean-shaven. Go figure.

I didn't know this one. I knew most of the drunks by name; he was probably new to the area. A lot of these guys had outstanding warrants, and whenever we needed a collar we'd stop the first alky we saw and usually score. Today, however, was Quiz Show Sunday. He could have been Martin Bormann; we didn't care.

"Oh, man." The drunk pressed his lips together, brow

knit in heavy concentration. "Oh, man, I know it, I know it! I got it! That Dick guy!"

Richard Nixon had been called a lot worse. "Absolutely correct!" I said. The drunk beamed. "Kenny, what has the gentleman won?"

Kenny, who was behind the wheel, leaned over the backseat and dug into a duffel bag. "In addition to a year's supply of Rice-A-Roni, the San Francisco treat, he's won a bottle of vintage port!" He retrieved a bottle of Hombre and handed it to me. I passed it along to the winner.

He clutched it to his chest, tears in his eyes. "Oh, thank you, Officers, thank you." He twisted open the cap right there and guzzled half the bottle in one gulp.

I felt a sudden urge to cry. I felt extreme pity for the poor soul standing in front of me and couldn't understand why. Was it because I could see myself in this guy's place? Couldn't be, I reasoned; I wasn't a drinker. After a while I began to realize that the feeling came of empathy. The alky was one of society's outcasts, and as a cop, so was I. I didn't feel I could share the moment with Kenny, so I kept it to myself.

We still had over thirty bottles of wine to give away when we pulled in front of the White House. Carl, a neighborhood fixture, who some said was a doctor who'd lost his license and served time after he'd killed someone on an operating table, performing surgery stone drunk, shuffled over to the car.

We had to be a little tougher with Carl, because he was sharper than most and he'd be insulted if we asked him too easy a question.

Kenny's turn. "Hey, Carl. How're ya doing, buddy?"

Carl was of indeterminate age. When he was sober he looked somewhere on the plus side of fifty. Today he was strung out, hungover, and looked to be in his seventies.

"Hey, Wags, Kenny. Listen, I got a problem."

"No shit," Kenny said, and went back to the game. "When was the Tet Offensive, Carl?" Kenny tended to go with Vietnam lore, most answers to which I didn't even know. Once he'd told me that all the marines

marching with Jim Nabors in the opening credits of the
TV show *Gomer Pyle, U.S.M.C.* were real marines, and
that all had been subsequently killed in Vietnam.

"No, man, forget that for now," Carl said, waving off
the jug. "Bermuda's missing."

Bermuda Schwartz—we didn't know his real first
name—was a disabled World War II veteran on a pension and was given the nickname Bermuda because of
his affection for the like-named shorts. He wore brightly
colored shorts even in the dead of winter. Between his
monthly military stipend and his Social Security check,
he was one of the few Bowery regulars who could have
afforded to move to more palatial digs. But he had spent
the better part of twenty years in the White House, had
his friends and sources of cheap booze, and decided to
stay.

"What do you mean, 'missing'?" I asked.

"I seen him in the building on Thursday, then no more
Bermuda. He vanished." Bermuda was Carl's best friend;
all they had in the world was each other. Carl was visibly shaken.

"Maybe he's on a bender somewhere," Kenny offered.

Carl shook his head adamantly. "Oh, no, no way. He'd
just got his army check. Bermuda gets his check, me 'n'
him got to Paddy Rose's downtown, get some real good
Italian food. Bermuda woulda said somethin' he was
goin' somewhere."

We got out of the car. I hooked Carl by the arm and
ushered him into the lobby of the White House. Being
seen talking to cops for any extended period of time on
the Bowery could label you a snitch and be hazardous
to your health.

Kenny flipped open a writing tablet. "Okay, Carl, we'll
make a note of it. If he doesn't show up in a few days
we'll file a missing persons report." He gave me a sly
wink.

No one cared about the drunks and junkies who lived
on the Bowery. Most of its inhabitants had families who
had deserted them. Certainly the system didn't much
care either. Kenny and I knew that Missing Persons

would shit-can any report involving a resident of the White House.

But Carl was clinging to hope. "Would you? Oh, thank you. You guys are the best. But could you do me a favor? Could you ask around the building right now? I mean, he had a coupla four hundred bucks, you know?"

Yeah, I knew. People died for a lot less down here.

Kenny snapped the tablet closed. "We haven't got the time, now, Carl, but—"

"Yeah, Carl, we'll check around," I said. Kenny shot me a look. "What's the harm? We're here."

Carl had last seen Bermuda on the fourth floor, where most of the regulars lived. First we spoke to the desk clerk in the cage, an old man with a face like a crumpled paper bag. He was in the middle of handicapping the day's race card at Hialeah.

"Fucking skells all look alike to me. Don't know 'im, ain't seen 'im."

We went upstairs.

The hallways were narrow, built to accommodate smaller Americans who lived here over a hundred years ago when residents weren't ashamed to call it home. Grime crunched beneath our feet as we made our way down a darkened passage knocking on doors. We got the same response from all the broken-down men who knew Bermuda: "Ain't seen him." From those who didn't: "Don't give a fuck."

"C'mon," Kenny said, "let's go." Carl was hanging on our every movement, pleading in his eyes.

"No, we've only got one more room up here." I banged on the door of the last "suite." No one answered, but a foul, unidentifiable odor wafted through the rotting wood. It was strong enough to make my eyes tear.

I ordered Carl to move to the side. Kenny and I framed the door, standard operating procedure before entering a room, the unpleasant arrival of a bullet between the eyes always foremost in our minds. Carl just stood there with a blank look on his face until I dragged him toward me by his coatsleeve.

I turned the knob, pushed the door open, and Kenny

went in first, his service pistol extended. I did a Groucho Marx and came in right behind him, my gun sweeping the room.

Two sleeping bodies lay naked in a sagging bed at the far end of the hovel, which had been made double-wide with the removal of a partition. A beat-up, threadbare convertible-type couch with greasy upholstery that must have been dragged upstairs from someone's junk pile was in one corner. A hot plate was on a shelf, and on a battered Formica folding table was a rotting tuna sandwich, encrusted in maggots. There were no windows, and the room was freezing, in contrast to the rest of the building, which had radiators hissing steam. Cockroaches scattered along the walls. Four empty wine bottles were strewn about the floor.

"Jesus!" Kenny said. "What a fucking stink."

"Be it ever so crumbled, there's no place like home." I pointed to the tuna. "Today's special. Hey, Carl, wake up the sleeping beauties." Carl shook the two men. They woke up gradually, last night's drunk still with them.

Both were white, in their thirties. The older of the two was a heavily made-up transvestite with thick rouge, running eyeliner, smeared purple lipstick the color of an overripe eggplant, and a two-day growth of beard. He had a butch haircut, but pulled a blond wig from beneath his pillow and placed it askew on his head.

"Hey, motherfucker, what're you doing in here?"

The second man was thinner and shorter, with bad teeth and bloodshot eyes. He rubbed his face. "Sally, what are—"

"You hush, Robert," Sally said, and swung his hairy legs to the floor. He grabbed a terry-cloth robe and climbed into it. Robert slipped on shorts and dove into a soiled sweatshirt.

I wanted out of there. The place stank and I could see my breath. The interview was going to be short.

"Have you seen Bermuda?" I asked. Kenny was already out the door, Carl right behind him.

"No, we ain't seen him," Sally said. His husky voice boomed like a carnival barker's.

"What's with the tuna sandwich?"

"Last night's dinner."

"Sorry I missed it," I said. "Bermuda was last seen on this floor. Sure you didn't see him?"

From out in the hallway Kenny said, "Jesus, Wags, let's go."

Robert was using a wall for support. "We ain't seen him. No, maybe I seen him about a week ago." His stomach was heaving, and I didn't want to stick around for the inevitable.

As I turned to leave, I kicked an empty wine bottle. A cork shot across the room. "We'll leave now, give you a chance to tidy up for the pope's visit, maybe turn on the goddamn heat—"

"We like it nippy," Sally interjected.

"You hear anything about Bermuda," I continued, "you call the house; ask for Wags, okay?"

Sally sneered. "Yeah, sure. Now get the fuck out."

We stood in the street gulping fresh air. Carl was wringing his hands. "What do I do now, Wags? Where's Bermuda?" He looked like he was going to burst into tears.

"We'll get back to you, Carl," I said. Kenny was already in the car, turning the heat up to nuclear. We left the dejected Carl standing in the middle of the street looking like he'd lost his best friend. He had.

Kenny blew a string of lights getting to FDR Drive, the only highway in the precinct where you could get a car up to seventy, especially on a Sunday morning. Kenny floored the pedal.

"Gotta get the smell out of my clothes." He opened the window, and frigid air blew through the car. I felt like I was sitting in a meat freezer. The few cars on the road moved over to the right when Kenny hit the siren. Within minutes we were passing the U.N. building.

"You satisfied now that we just have another drunk who probably went belly-up in some alley somewhere?" Kenny said.

"I'm satisfied Bermuda's dead, all right, but I'm pretty sure that transvestite and his buddy killed him."

Kenny pulled the car over under a shady spot on the Drive. "Who're you," he said, "Sherlock fucking Holmes?" I smirked. "Okay, what makes you think the two gay caballeros did it?" he asked.

"You were already halfway down the hall. I gave a wine bottle a kick on my way out. I saw a cork."

Kenny's eyes brightened. We both knew there wasn't a wino on the Bowery who drank anything other than cheap shit with twist-off caps. A corked bottle meant those two mopes had come into some money—Bermuda's army money—enough to buy four bottles of vintage wine.

Uniformed cops don't solve crimes. When you see uniformed TV cops like T.J. Hooker or Reed and Molloy on television track a criminal and solve a crime, that's fantasy at its best (or worst, depending on if you like cop shows or not).

Uniformed cops are there for the immediate. We see a crime being committed, we made an arrest, grab a bad guy on the word of a recent victim, or collar someone based on a description circulated soon after a crime has occurred. There are no uniformed Columbos.

We reported what we had to the detectives. After four days they reported back.

"You got nothing," a second grader told me. He had a stomach bigger than my wife's (and she was pregnant with our second child).

"What about all that good guinea red lying around?"

"The transtesticle"—he chuckled at his own joke—"said him and his boyfriend hit the number. They bought the good shit to celebrate. Who are we to say they didn't?"

"You toss the place?"

"You kidding? I couldn't wait to get the fuck out of there. What a stink, and they're fresh-air fiends. I froze my frigging ass off. Besides, the place is as big as an envelope. What's to hide? Maybe come up with a spike or two, maybe some smack residue, but I ain't putting my hands on either of those two to make an arrest."

Something didn't sound right. "Still stinks? The same tuna sandwich?"

"I didn't stick around to examine it, but it didn't look like tuna to me. Some kind of green mystery meat, covered with bugs." He shuddered.

I had an idea.

"Aw, Christ," Kenny said as we once more approached the fourth floor in the White House, "there's that fucking smell again." He put a handkerchief to his face.

The hallway reeked, all right, but the odor, while vile, was different from the previous eye-tearer we had encountered.

Carl was with us, although we had asked him twice to wait in the lobby. "He's my friend," he countered. "I'm comin'."

This time we didn't knock. Kenny drew his pistol, extended his gun arm, and nodded.

I kicked the door off the hinges with one try, a testament to the rusting hardware, not the force of the blow.

Sally and his boyfriend were fully clothed this time, sitting side by side on the unmade bed. They sank into it like they were reposing in quicksand. Robert was cooking a spoonful of dope while Sally (in a pleated wool frock, I might add) tied off his left arm with a shoelace.

Both looked like the proverbial deer caught in the glare of headlights. Robert stuck the spoon in his mouth and swallowed the evidence, while Sally made a grab for the residue-laden plastic bag the dope had come in. I was quicker and snatched it from his hand.

The tuna had been replaced on the table by a wedge of rotting chopped meat. The smell was overpowering, and I wondered how Sally and his friend could stand being in close quarters with a pound of ptomaine, even if it was the middle of winter, and the room was as cold as a Bowery hooker's heart.

"So okay," Sally said, "you got us for the smack."

"Give up easy, don't you, shithead?" I said, and grabbed Robert's arm. "Sit over on the couch."

Robert struggled off the bed and eased himself down on the couch like he was sitting on feathers. Kenny noticed it.

"Just take it up the ass, Robert?" Kenny had a way with words.

The junkie looked scared, too scared for a simple drug bust. Besides, we had no warrant. This was a toss-out in court for sure. So why the consternation?

"My partner asked you a question," I said. I turned to Carl. "Hey, Carl, you hear Kenny ask Robert here a question?"

Carl was standing in the doorway. He looked menacing. "Yeah, a question."

Robert was shaking visibly. He looked toward Sally pleadingly.

Sally: "You don't say nothing, honey." To me: "You got us; you take us." He started to get up. I grabbed a bony shoulder and pushed him back on the bed; then I drew my gun and inched backward toward the door.

The wheels were turning. "Now I gotta ask you this; Sally, I'll ask you, because you seem to be the brains of the outfit. Why would you be sitting on this swaybacked bed balancing two decks of dope when you could be on the couch cooking your shit on the table?"

Sally's eyes darted around the room. "The hamburger, it spoiled, I didn't wanna—"

"So you throw the meat out," I said. "Like you did with the tuna. Remember the tuna?"

Sally forced a smile; Robert blanched. "Yeah, the tuna," Sally said.

"Get up, Robert," I said.

He didn't move.

"Carl, get him up." Carl grabbed Robert's ear and twisted, forcing Robert to his feet. "Kenny, give me a hand."

We threw two sagging cushions from the couch to the floor, then pulled on the opposite ends of the mattress bar. The bed unfolded.

Of course, crumpled inside was the body of Bermuda Schwartz.

"It was the meat, huh?" Carl said later in the station house. We had just booked Vincent (Sally) Nalo and Robert Hirschbaum for the murder of Myron (Bermuda) Schwartz.

"Not so much the meat as the fact they replaced one form of rotting food with another. Soon as they did that I figured they were doing it for a reason. Ever smell a ripe DOA? That's why they turned off the heat, so the corpse would preserve better. And what better way to hide the odor than with a stronger smell? They either were afraid they'd get bagged carrying out the body or were too fucked up to care."

Kenny came into the squad room. "We're signed out, Wags. I'm going home to take a three-hour shower. Unless, of course, you wanna stop in Cal's to brag."

I snorted. "I'd like to see my family and sleep on clean sheets. Besides, got court tomorrow. C'mon, Carl, I'll give you a lift back to the hotel."

"Yeah, okay." Carl had been pretty quiet during the arrest procedure, and I was afraid that he'd jump the two prisoners right there in the room. He'd insisted on going to the station house with us.

Carl kept to himself during the ride to the White House. He got out of the car without a word, but knelt by my window.

"Hey, Wags, you know no one gives a shit about us down here. I wanna thank you for doin' what you did." There were tears in his eyes.

"I'll tell Kenny."

"No, it was more you. Kenny, he's a good cop, but you got it here." He touched his chest. He wiped wetness from his face.

"You gonna be okay?"

"Yeah, yeah, I'll be okay. Don't know what I'm gonna do without Bermuda, though. He was good people, had an education, you know, was easy to talk to. Had an opinion."

"Like you?"

Carl's eyes darkened. I was getting to close to his past. "He was my friend." He struggled to his feet with the aid of the car door. I realized then that Bermuda had probably shared his wealth with Carl, and that Carl might now be broke.

I felt uneasy about asking the question, but felt I had to. "You need anything?"

Carl blinked. "Nah, got a few bucks behind a loose brick." He winked. "Thanks anyway."

As I pulled away, Carl called my name. I braked and stuck my head out the window. "Yeah?"

"Tell Kenny, January twenty-first, 1968," he said, smiling.

"Huh?"

"That Tet thing. I looked it up."

Bermuda's $10,000 military life-insurance policy went to Carl. I'd like to report that he straightened out his life, took his unexpected gift, moved out of the White House, and got himself a decent place to live, maybe even a job. But it didn't happen.

Carl drank up the money and bought booze, good booze, for those tenants of the White House he liked, until all the money was gone.

Years after, I'd see him on the corner of Bowery and Delancey wiping car windshields with a filthy rag. We always waved to each other.

The last DOA case I responded to as sergeant before I retired was that of a body found beaten to death in a garbage-strewn lot off Canal Street.

It was Carl. There was no family to notify, so he was buried in Potter's Field, somewhere, I'm sure, within viewing distance of the place Bermuda was buried years earlier.

13
Psycho

On September 23, 1974, police officers and partners Donny Muldoon and Tommy Cimler were working an eight-to-four tour in Ninth Precinct Sector George.

It was a quiet autumn morning, and they had parked their car on Avenue A and were enjoying an early lunch when a signal 10-30 was broadcast over the division radio.

A signal 10-30 is a robbery in progress, a potentially hazardous radio run to be sure. Both cops hurriedly packed away their sandwiches and raced to the scene, 102 St. Marks Place, with lights flashing, siren wailing.

The dispatcher had told them to see the complainant in apartment Three-Boy, adding, "No other information available."

As they entered the building, Muldoon remembers seeing a water truck, the kind that delivers bottled water to office buildings. He thought this odd because the closest office was blocks away. He quickly forgot about the truck as he and his partner entered the four-story tenement.

The door to apartment 3-B was ajar. While Cimler, a seven-year veteran, positioned himself beside the door, his partner, Muldoon, on The Job ten years, leveled a gun at the door from the stairway, his forearm resting on the top banister for support.

Cimler yelled, "Police, open up!"

A large Irishman, later identified as William Talmadge

Connell, a former minister and marine, opened the door. He was wearing a T-shirt and jeans and had a wild look in his eye.

"I have a bottle of nitroglycerin behind this door! Go away!" What he didn't tell the cops was that he also had a fully loaded .357 Magnum in his waistband in the small of his back. Without waiting for the cops to respond, he stepped into the hallway and began shooting. Muldoon and his partner returned fire.

A fusillade of shots followed, the cops and their adversary just a few feet apart. Muldoon was struck in the leg. He and Cimler emptied their revolvers into the man, killing him instantly.

Inside the apartment, responding officers found an arsenal of firearms. They also found the driver of the water truck handcuffed to a steam pipe, but otherwise unhurt. He'd been lured there with the promise of a big sale. A second hostage, the super, had also been cuffed, but broke loose with the aid of a screwdriver he was carrying. It was he who had called 911.

The dead man had planned to use the hostages to help carry his arsenal to a waiting truck parked down the block. He then planned to hijack the boat that ferried tourists back and forth from the Statue of Liberty. What he planned to do with a boatload of hostages was unclear; the mad Irishman was no longer around to answer questions.

Connell's cache was considerable. In his apartment he had over 40,000 rounds of ammunition, plus numerous rifles and shotguns. So extensive was the stockpile that the street was roped off and inventory was taken on the sidewalk in front of the building. The officer taking the inventory piled up a hundred hours overtime cataloging the weapons. The cop chosen to do this was Stanley Swiatoka, the only cop on the NYPD who was drawing welfare in addition to his salary. He had thirteen kids. The hundred hours OT certainly helped his family.

I wasn't working the day Donny Muldoon got shot, but when I heard the news on the radio I rushed to

Bellevue Hospital. Donny, while in another squad, was a good friend, and we spent time together whenever our divergent schedules allowed.

Donny was lucky. He was hit with shrapnel from a fragmented bullet that had ricocheted off his metal flashlight. He and Tommy would receive the Combat Cross for their heroic actions in the gunfight.

I sat on Donny's bed. He was pretty groggy, just out of surgery, but he wanted to talk.

"What happened?" I asked.

He licked his lips. "Psycho," he said, as if no further explanation were required.

Psycho. These days The Job uses the more politically acceptable term Emotionally Disturbed Person, or EDP. When not talking to the press or a boss, however, a street cop will refer to the city's mentally unbalanced contingent as psychos.

Understandably, psychos account for the largest number of officer injuries in the NYPD, followed by participants in family disputes. What sets psychos apart is that a cop usually can't reason with them; a battling husband and wife may listen to reason if diplomacy is employed. The State Department has nothing on a seasoned ghetto street cop when it comes to defusing a dispute among sane or marginally sane adversaries.

The average cop handles hundreds of radio runs involving psychos, and God knows I handled more than my share. The stories I'm going to relate were among the most bizarre, and heretofore never repeated outside the police fraternity. Most are hard to believe, but I was there. Believe them.

Psycho with a Blackjack

The radio run came over around noon on a rainy-day tour. "Report of a man throwing furniture out a fifth-story window, corner Avenue B and Seventh Street. Units to respond?"

Kenny was the recorder for the second half of the tour. He grabbed the radio. "Sector Frank on the way."

Frank Moran picked up the call from a foot post a block away. "Nine foot man, Central, I'll back up."

"You think he'll remember to load his gun?" I asked as I threw the car into gear.

Kenny rolled his eyes and hit the siren. Frank Moran was still in a pit of depression following his brother's death. His drinking had gotten out of control, and he was ordered to see the department shrink, who advised him to get a hobby to get his mind off his dead brother and booze.

So Frank took up boxing. He fought in the middle-weight division for The Job against other PDs, lost most fights, and kept right on drinking. Now he was losing brain cells to both alcohol *and* right crosses.

Six months back he had gone to his semiannual pistol qualification at the outdoor range in Rodman's Neck and had forgotten to load his gun when he left. The error wasn't caught until five months later, when he went back to the range for his next qualification. He had worked the street for five months in uniform with an empty gun.

Kenny said, "He can forget his gun. All he needs to do is breathe on the bad guy." It was midday and Frank was probably shit-faced. We were to find out later that Frank had been walking the wrong foot post for over a year. No one ever bothered to look for him.

A crowd had gathered in front of a tenement. Moran, already there, was pushing pedestrians into the street. A pile of furniture, broken glass, utensils, and clothes lay scattered in front of the building.

As we got out of the car a sofa hit the ground with a thud, narrowly missing Moran. The crowd cheered. A shirtless black man with a shaved head hung out a fifth-floor window shouting vulgarities. He was huge and easily filled the window frame.

The guy ducked back inside the apartment. Within seconds a console television came crashing to the street.

"Jesus," I said, "helluva way to rearrange the furniture." I kept my eyes glued to the window, afraid I'd have my hair parted by a refrigerator.

I heard sirens in the distance. Within minutes an Emergency Service Unit (ESU) truck pulled up. Emergency Service cops possessed the necessary equipment, including stun guns and full-body shields, to control psychos. They also had automatic weapons and shotguns in case the job went bad.

A burly sergeant wearing body armor and a helmet bounced out of the back of the truck and jogged over to us. He looked like he had more time on The Job than my entire squad combined.

"Okay," he said, "here's the plan. We're gonna sit tight until my other unit arrives." He glanced at his watch. "They're on another job, should be here in ten minutes or so."

The psycho made another appearance, this time throwing a recliner out the window. He yelled, "I'm gonna burn the fucking building down!" and went back inside.

"Okay," the sergeant said, "change one. We can't wait for the rest of my guys; we're going up. You're coming with us."

"Who, us?" Kenny said.

"Yeah, you. He could light up the whole friggin' neighborhood by the time my other guys get here. There's only three of us; we need you guys. We'll go in first; you follow. Normally we can handle these guys, but this is a big motherfucker; we may need you." He had one of his men give us handheld ballistic shields. "Keep these in front of your faces. Psychos like to throw shit at cops, too."

"Like what kind of shit?" Kenny asked.

"Like human feces, urine, battery acid if he thought far enough ahead to stockpile some."

Great, I thought, I wasn't ugly enough; now I was gonna get an acid, shit, and piss facial.

The sergeant sighed. "Let's do it."

We didn't have to evacuate the floor. Everyone had already abandoned their apartments. As we walked down the hallway, I heard the muffled sounds of breaking glass and muttered curses coming from the nut's apartment.

One of the ESU cops wielded a metal battering ram.

We stood aside as he hit the door once. It flew off the hinges. The ESU cops piled in, followed—albeit reluctantly—by Kenny and me.

The apartment looked like ground zero in the eye of Hurricane Hugo. Every piece of furniture was gone; holes were punched in walls; light fixtures were ripped from the ceiling.

The psycho confronting us made George Foreman look like Tattoo from *Fantasy Island*. He stood in the middle of the living room floor, about twenty feet from us. He had to be at least six-five, about four hundred pounds. He was wearing only boxer shorts and was covered in more blood than I'd ever seen on a living person. And, oh, yeah, he was carrying an enormous blackjack.

His eyes lit up when he saw us. He smiled, his mouth dripping blood. He was gonna kill him some cops; I saw it in his eyes.

The ESU guys stopped the forward charge when they saw him. Kenny and I ran into their backs. The sergeant, probably for the first time in his career, was speechless. Five cops gawking at a seminaked, bleeding black guy. It was a stare-down. We blinked.

The sergeant said, "Put down the blackjack. How'd you get hurt?" The blood flow was prodigious. I assumed he'd slashed his wrists, as is common with psychos.

We had our hands on our guns, but no one had drawn. While we were within our rights to shoot a guy with a blackjack (a deadly weapon as defined by the New York State penal law), the average cop is hesitant to take a human life unless there's no other way to quell a potentially dangerous situation. There were five of us and only one of him, although the one of him weighed as much as two of us.

He let out a bellow that could have been heard by a rutting moose in Saskatoon, and charged. Within a nanosecond he was on us.

The force of his body weight knocked all five of us to the ground. Now we were five cops rolling around on the floor with a psycho who had an enormous amount of strength.

The shields were useless. Instead of being used to pin him or block objects or blows, they were now being used to pin *us* to the ground.

"Use the fucking Mace!" a cop screamed.

ESU cops carried federal Streamers, an early type of pepper spray, originally issued department-wide but withdrawn from all but specialized units when patrol cops began spraying each other, toilet seats (try sitting on one of those after its been saturated with the chemical), and passersby who just pissed us off.

I was on the bottom of the pile when two ESU cops managed to unload two containers of Streamers into the nut's face. Most of it splashed back and blinded us, the burning so searing I thought I'd lose my eyesight.

It just pissed off the psycho, who began pummeling us with the blackjack. I was hit numerous times, but felt little pain, maybe due to the diversion created by the Streamer effects.

Kenny screamed into his radio, "Ten-thirteen, Ten-thirteen!"

Cops came from everywhere. Within five minutes the nut was wrapped in a blood-soaked sheet and finally subdued. Two ambulances rushed the nut and seven cops to St. Vincent's Hospital.

A local roving television news crew was on the scene as we left the building. I was saturated with blood, fortunately not my own. My eyes were tearing and I had trouble breathing. A young woman reporter grabbed my arm and shoved a microphone in my face.

"What happened up there, Officer? Are you okay?" Through a blur I saw a look of astonishment on her face. She seemed to be amazed that someone covered with so much blood could be standing.

"Got a direct hit with a mortar round," I said as I pushed past her.

I had my eyes flushed with what seemed like the spill-over from the Grand Coulee Dam. The rest of the cops were treated for a variety of cuts and bruises. No one was seriously injured. This amazed me, because a black-jack can create some nasty damage.

A young doctor breezed into the ER.

"You okay?"

"Eyes hurt like hell."

"Well, don't rub them. You'll be okay in a few hours."

"Thanks." I jumped off the gurney.

"Hey, don't go anywhere. You have to go back to the apartment; that's where we think it is."

"Huh?" I asked. "Where what is?"

He told me.

Kenny was in the radio car, a bandage on his forehead, his eyes a nice shade of fire engine red. "Let's get back to the house. I gotta take a shower."

"Can't," I responded. "We have to go back to the apartment."

He looked at me like I was crazy. "What're you, out of your mind? This is a line-of-duty injury, my man. I'm taking a few weeks off." He slipped the car into gear and eased into traffic. "What's back at the apartment?"

"The guy's dick."

Kenny slammed on the brakes. "What?"

"The blackjack? It was his dick. He cut it off. That's where all the blood came from."

I thought Kenny was going to throw up. He looked like he wanted to crawl out of his skin. "You mean to tell me that nut beat up five—"

"Seven," I corrected.

"—guys with his severed dick?"

"That's what I'm telling you. Now they want us to go back and see if we can find it so it can be reattached."

"Fuck 'em; let them find their own dick. I shoulda known anyway."

"Whaddya mean?"

"The forehead. He had a forehead like glass, just the type to do what he did. Shoulda known."

Kenny had a theory that the crazier the psycho, the smoother his forehead. A grizzled head-case could be slicing up folks on the Staten Island Ferry with a machete (it actually happened), he could have a face like Bette Davis in *Whatever Happened to Baby Jane,* and still he'd have a forehead as smooth as a baby's ass. I hated to admit it, but there was something to the theory.

Well, we had initially picked up the job, so we had no choice. We went back, found the offending phallus, scooped it up, placed it in an ice-filled shoe box (it barely fit), and raced back to St. Vincent's, lights and siren all the way.

Four days later I was in a sector with Rocco Laurie (Kenny milked the dick whipping for two weeks off) when we were called to St. Vincent's on an aided case. As we were leaving, the young intern who asked me to go back to the apartment spotted me.

"You'll be happy to know we successfully reattached the gentleman's penis."

Yeah, I was thrilled.

How's It Hanging?

There were very few trees within the confines of the Ninth. One August night at the end of a four-to-twelve tour, an apparently depressed man decided he was going to hang himself from the tallest tree in the precinct.

Kenny and I arrived on the scene on East Fourteenth Street to find a white male about thirty-five, dressed neatly in slacks, a button-down white shirt, and polished black shoes near the top of the tree. He had a rope with a precisely tied hangman's noose around his neck. The other end was securely fastened to a limb.

We moved the crowd back as other patrol units and Sergeant Reddy responded. Within minutes we had the street cordoned off.

I estimated that the guy was at least thirty feet off the ground. He had his hands clasped in prayer and appeared to be mumbling.

"You," I said, "c'mon down!"

The man shook his head. "I'm gonna kill myself!"

I'm thinking, No, you're not; I've only got fifteen minutes to the end of my tour and I'm supposed to meet my wife at a neighbor's party. "Can't we talk about this?" I shouted.

"No! I'm gonna kill myself!"

"Yeah," I muttered, "you said that."

"Ask him why," Sergeant Reddy said. "Keep him talking. I'll call ESU." He went back to his car to retrieve his portable radio.

"Why would you wanna do something like that?" I hollered.

"My girlfriend left me for my best friend!"

Kenny chimed in. "You're supposed to kill her, not yourself!" Under his breath he said, "Fucking idiot." I shot him a look. "Hey," he said, "I've been there."

He told us his name was Albert and that he was an accountant. We tried to coax him down for ten minutes until the ESU arrived. They couldn't do much either, but at least they had a bullhorn. I had nearly screamed myself hoarse.

Suicides, particularly those who choose to do themselves in in public, usually want someone to talk them out of it. The ESU sergeant seemed to be making headway when the crowd, which had grown to over two hundred people, started chanting, "Do it! Do it!"

Well, this was all our lovelorn friend needed. Now he was convinced that no one loved him, and he made his move. He spread his arms like an Acapulco cliff diver and dove off the tree.

The crowd gasped in unison; Kenny and I sighed, "Oh, shit," and down he came.

In a split second the rope around his neck became taut and, fortunately for him, snapped the securing branch. Poor Albert tumbled like a Plinko chip on *The Price Is Right,* hitting every limb on the way down. The branches broke his fall (and two legs and an arm). He hit the concrete with a thud. He survived.

"Hapless son of a bitch," the ESU sergeant said, "loses his girlfriend and fucks up his own suicide."

Some people can't do anything right.

Are Those Cherry Bombs Up Your Nose, or Are You Just Happy to See Me?

Bellevue Hospital is known worldwide for its psycho ward. Cops spend a lot of time transporting psychos to the hospital for treatment. Every time we went into the wards, we'd have to empty our guns, per department rules. Psychos can sometimes possess superhuman strength (as noted with our dickless furniture mover) and can easily rip a gun out of a security holster or a cop's hand.

Kenny and I had just delivered a compliant nutcase to the mental ward on the first floor. We were on our way out of the building when a six-foot-six black guy (at least this one had his clothes on, and I assumed all his parts) strode into the lobby, not twenty feet in front of us. His face was painted white and he had a cherry bomb crammed into each nostril, fuses exposed. In his right hand he held a fired-up Bic lighter.

The lobby was jammed with the usual Friday-night mob of the sick, lame, and lazy waiting to be examined by a small army of exhausted residents and nurses. The din was murderous, but the entire room lapsed into an abrupt silence when the black man screamed, "I'm gonna blow my fucking head off!"

The short silence was followed by screams. The waiting patients started scrambling for exits. The hospital staff, who had seen just about every sort of maladjusted fruit-cake who ever walked the face of the earth, looked to Kenny and me as if to say, "Okay, do something about this nut so we can get back to work."

It took a few seconds for the scene to soak in. Kenny slowly went for his gun. Out of the side of my mouth I said, "Don't bother; it's not loaded." We hadn't as yet reloaded our weapons, a task normally accomplished when we got clear of civilians.

"Wonderful," Kenny said. "Now what do we do?"

The man was still frozen in place, but the flame was getting precariously close to the fuses. I called over my shoulder to the nurses' station, "Call the cops, will ya?"

A veteran nurse who had probably seen more blood than a Delta Force commando said, "You are the fucking cops."

"Guns aren't loaded," I said. "We just came from the back." Somehow using the term *psycho ward* didn't seem appropriate. She ducked behind her desk after snatching a phone.

"C'mon, mister," I said, "put the lighter down. Whatever your problems are, there're enough drugs in this place to make you forget them."

He advanced on us. We backed up. He grinned the twisted leer of the North American psycho, a species that only inhabits areas frequented by cops. "Put up your fucking hands," he said, and began to laugh, clearly having a good time.

If a cop *ever* loses the psychological advantage during a confrontation, it can only lead to a life-threatening situation. We weren't about to comply.

Kenny and I had worked together long enough that we could read each other's minds. We backed up a few more paces and drew our revolvers at the same time. The black guy looked dumbfounded. We figured it was better to shoot the guy in the lighter arm than risk a fistfight where the cherry bombs could explode with us in close proximity.

When we broke open the cylinders on our revolvers and went for our speed loaders, he knew he had a few seconds to light the fuses. He raised the open flame to his nose.

Ever try to light cherry bombs in your nose? I hope not, but if you ever find yourself in a similar situation, you'll find that it's not that easy to bring the flame to the fuse in one try.

The black guy burned his chin on his first try and let out a scream. Kenny and I fumbled with our speed loaders. Finding six tiny holes in a .38 cylinder isn't any easier than detonating cherry bombs in your nose. We were shaking like cheap tin signs in a howling hurricane when the Mad Cherry Bomber brought his light north for a second try. This time he wasn't going to miss.

Just then a Thirteenth Precinct foot cop, responding to the radio run of cops in trouble, barged through the lobby door. The black guy whirled and brought up the lighter.

The cop grasped the situation immediately. He went into a combat crouch and yelled, "Drop the lighter!" The black guy laughed. The cop fired once, hitting Cherry Bomb Man in the kneecap. Nice shot. We tackled him. He probably walked funny for a while, but that cop saved his life.

When we finally left the hospital Kenny said, "We gotta retire; this job is getting weirder every day."

We had seven years in, thirteen to go. It was going to get even weirder.

After a while, cops begin to have a certain affinity for psychos. They're loners, just like us, set apart and shunned by the rest of society. I think the average cop fears that by some twist of fate he or she may wind up like some of the people we admit to mental wards. A blow to the head during a family dispute, wrapping a radio car around a lamppost rushing to a Ten-thirteen, given a megadose of a hallucinogen by some twisted waiter who hates cops.

We do, however, have our favorite nutcases, the kind who can't really hurt us and who provide comic relief.

Remember Ruthie? For those of you who've forgotten, Ruthie built her life around grabbing the testicles of every New York City cop she could lay her hands on. I was christened by her in the Academy, although most cops didn't meet Ruthie until they were walking a foot post surrounded by civilians. Truly embarrassing. And painful.

Well, it turned out that Ruthie lived within the confines of the Ninth Precinct.

Ruthie hadn't aged well. In addition to the scabs and sores on her legs and the Xs and Os tattooed on her ass, her face looked like the rough-salted rim of a margarita glass.

She loved Sergeant Reddy. Every day without fail Ruthie

would show up on a day tour with her dog (still wearing a stylish red bandanna around his scruffy neck) and ask for the sergeant. Sergeant Reddy was always a gentleman. He smiled and said good morning, but always steered clear of her. Ruthie had a viselike grip. Once she got you by the balls, it took the Jaws of Life to release her hold.

Uninitiated rookies would be introduced to Ruthie as part of their rites of passage into the Ninth Precinct.

But no one ever abused Ruthie. The cops felt sorry for her and treated her with respect. She was a legend.

Of all the psychos we met, no one made more of an impression on Kenny than Oric Bovar. But just how crazy was he?

14

Oric Bovar and the Temple of Doom

Kenny and I were never what you would call good friends. We trusted each other with our lives, but our personal lives never intertwined because of our divergent lifestyles.

Kenny was a terminal partyer, currently on wife number three, and a Vietnam veteran who couldn't forget the war. I found my thrills in being home with my family, never thought once about divorce, and couldn't handle more than two drinks. The closest I ever came to fighting a war was being on patrol in the Ninth Precinct.

Partners don't last long together if their personalities clash. We got along well, but our relationship ended after work or after a few cocktails at Cal's.

Still, I knew him almost better than I knew my wife. Spend at least eight hours a day in a radio car with a guy for years and you can read his mind.

It was during the mad minute, one cool September night, before the rush of calls for service on a four-to-twelve tour. We had just turned out and were in the car by the park gulping coffee when I noticed something was wrong with Kenny. He was unusually quiet and withdrawn. Kenny's normal state was manic, particularly on a four-to-twelve, when our adrenaline was pumping and we could expect anything in the way of assignments.

Despite the workload—we usually handled anywhere from thirty to forty jobs a tour, as compared to three to five for a quiet precinct—Kenny would always manage to squeeze in at least a few bad jokes. He had a remarkable memory when it came to jokes. I never recall hearing the same one twice.

He would come up with something like, "The Lone Ranger and Tonto are sitting in a bar. A stumblebum cowpoke comes in and tells the Ranger his horse, Silver, collapsed in the street. The Ranger says, 'Shit, I forgot to water him before we came in here. Tonto, would you give him something to drink and run him around in circles for a while? It'll cool him off.' Tonto says, 'Sure, kemosabe.' Twenty minutes later, another cowboy comes in the bar, asks the Ranger if that's his horse out there running around in circles. The Ranger says, 'Yep.' The cowboy says, 'Well, you left your *Injun* running!' "

I would say, "Kenny, you're a riot," and usually yawn. It was either listen to lame jokes or watch him tell the performing mimes in Tompkins Square Park that they had the right to remain silent.

Today, however, no jokes.

"What's the matter, run dry?" I asked.

Kenny was lost in thought. He snapped out of it. "Huh? What?"

"No jokes today? I need something to put me to sleep."

"Uh, not today. Say, Wags, let me ask you a question: You still love your wife?"

I looked at him. "What kind of question is that? Of course I love my wife."

"Yeah, okay, I'll accept that—"

"Gee, thanks."

"But are you still . . . you know, attracted to her?"

"Are you serious?" He was staring at me intently. He *was* serious. I thought about it for a while.

"I'll tell you a story. A couple of weeks ago I'm almost home after a day tour and realize I'm out of smokes. So I'm passing the neighborhood Pathmark Supermarket, decide to get a carton. I go in and as soon as I get inside, I see this woman way across the other side by the produce. She has her back to me. Short skirt, great legs, phenomenal ass. I go out of my way to get a look at her. Turns out it's my wife. That answer your question?"

He snorted. "Yeah."

There was a moment of awkward silence. We had about three minutes before the dispatcher would start spitting out jobs. Our division dispatcher was good; he empathized with us street scum, probably did his time in some hellhole, and would hold back jobs for the first ten minutes of a tour so the troops could have their coffee.

"Okay," I said, "talk to me."

Kenny ran his fingers through his hair. "My wife caught me in bed with another woman."

"Oh, shit, Kenny. Man, I'm sorry."

"Sorry for what? That I got caught or that I was fucking around?"

"Sorry you may be chalking up another bride. What happened?"

"She was supposed to be out of town visiting her sister. I picked up some young broad in a bar after work, brought her home. We fell asleep. Eight o'clock Tuesday morning, Kathy walks in. She came home a day early. She missed me." He was looking out the window at three Hispanic kids climbing a tree in the park.

"I probably know why I did it. Me and Kathy, we've been sorta drifting apart, you know what I mean?"

"Couldn't you have drifted over to the girl's house? What were you thinking?"

"I dunno; maybe I wanted to get caught. You think?"

I didn't know what to think. Pat and I had a good marriage because we worked at it. I never took advantage of her by using The Job as an excuse. I can't tell you how many overtime tours, midnight grand jury appearances, and off-duty arrest excuses are used by cops—all cops, not just NYPD cops—as excuses to cheat.

To my way of thinking, The Job provided enough stress without having to live a double life at home. My home and family were my escape, the only place where I could be myself, unwind, and relax. I didn't need the worry of some bimbo I banged showing up on my doorstep.

"So what did you do when she walked in on you?"

He shrugged. "I denied it."

I was puzzled. "I thought you said the girl was in your bed."

"She was. Kathy flipped, the girl panicked, grabbed her clothes and ran out the door. I told my wife to calm down. Told her she was seeing things."

"But she caught you red-handed. How the hell do you talk yourself out of that?"

"For the last two days I've been telling her she imagined it."

"What're you hoping for, to drive her crazy? I saw a movie like that once. Hitchcock, I think. Guy tries to convince his wife she's imagining that someone's trying to kill her. Figures she'll flip out, he'll commit her and get all her money."

"I saw the same movie."

"Apparently."

The dispatcher chimed in. "Holding forty-one jobs in the Ninth."

"Jesus," Kenny said, and we poured our remaining coffee out the window. We tossed the Styrofoam cups onto the backseat, where they joined their brethren.

I grabbed the portable radio. "Sector Frank, Central, what've you got hot?"

"Let's see, I'm holding a maternity—don't think that can wait. I've got a bleeder from a knife fight, perp fled the scene, the loser's already at the hospital. And I've got a report of a vampire at three-twelve East Thirteenth Street, apartment Four-Boy. Nothing further on this one."

A word about delivering babies: I helped bring six children into this world over the course of twenty-two years in uniform. There's nothing remotely readable about delivering a baby. Actually, other than the various odd locations where I helped deliver these kids (elevator, car, restaurant bathroom), maternity cases are all the same. Babies deliver themselves. I stood there like Johnny Bench, sans catcher's mitt, and the tykes shot into my hands. Had a breech once, but by that time the ambulance had arrived. Every now and then a roving reporter from the *Daily News* picked up the radio run and took a picture of me holding a newborn that looked like a boiled chicken. Don't even want to mention the blood and accompanying mess.

I'd like to say there's at least one Wags Gonzalez running around the Ninth, but despite what mothers tell you about how grateful they are that you helped bring their future little mugger into the world, it's rare that a cop gets a namesake.

So . . .

"We'll take the vampire, Central."

A chorus of verbal jabs from other units followed. "Bring a crucifix." "Stop off for some garlic," and a poor Bela Lugosi imitation, "I vant to sock your blood!"

"Yeah," Kenny mumbled, "sock this."

I peeled into traffic.

The complainant who made the 911 call was an elderly Hispanic male with a neck like a turkey. He was waiting in front of the building, a ratty tenement of mostly abandoned apartments known to harbor junkies who used them as shooting galleries.

Directly across the street, a squat, dark-haired man was on his knees in front of another tenement. Beside him was a bucket. He appeared to be scrubbing the sidewalk with a wire brush. We made eye contact and he smiled and waved. I waved back. Wags is my name; community relations is my game.

Our complainant frantically flapped his arms to get our attention. "There's a vampire on the top floor," he told us as we got out of the car. He made the sign of the cross.

"Oh, yeah?" Kenny said. "How do you know it's a vampire?"

The complainant's eyes went wide. "She pays the junkies five dollars to suck their blood. Up there"—he pointed—"in her apartment."

Kenny and I looked at each other and rolled our eyes. "What does she do, bite their necks?"

He nodded. "Yeah, yeah. Sometimes she'll suck their fingers or their arms after she cuts them with a knife."

"She's been doing this how long?" I asked.

"About a year."

"So why call us now?"

"I just heard someone scream for help in her apartment."

It was late afternoon, and the light was dimming fast. The top floor of the building was almost dark, the soot-smeared window at the end of the hallway blocking out what was left of the natural light.

The complainant had told us that the vampire's name was Helen; that's all he knew. As we neared Helen's apartment we heard a muffled scream.

Without exchanging a word, Kenny and I took our places on opposite sides of the door. "Your turn to knock," I said. We drew our guns.

Kenny rapped on the door. "Police, open up!" Another scream, this one louder.

"Your turn to break down the door," Kenny said. So I did.

Old tenement doors are usually very thick and sturdy, but the jambs are less than substantial. One kick and the door went flying.

The fair-size room was black—not unlighted, mind you, just black. Illumination was supplied by a bare bulb, also painted black. The walls and ceiling were painted a matte black, and a black blanket was draped across the window. I could vaguely make out two figures in front of me. Fortunately we came in from a dim hallway and my night vision kicked in almost immediately.

A skinny woman dressed all in, you guessed it, black was hovering over another, even thinner woman tied to a chair with thick rope. She was stripped to the waist, her bra and sweatshirt were on the floor, and her left arm was bleeding. The woman over her appeared to be sucking her victim's arm.

Our supposed vampire straightened up and growled at us. Her teeth were filed to points and blood dripped from her mouth. She wasn't carrying any weapons. This had to be Helen.

"Back off!" I shouted.

Kenny said, "Jesus, look at this nut."

Helen hissed. I guess she thought the growl wasn't effective. Her prisoner screamed. I holstered my gun.

"Okay," I said in a calm voice, "back up against the wall." Kenny was maneuvering behind her.

Helen said, "Fuck you!"

"Hey," Kenny said, sounding offended, "a vampire's not supposed to say that. Be nice and go up against the wall."

Helen flashed her nails, also filed to sharp points and at least two inches long. She hissed again. The prisoner flipped the chair over trying to get free from her restraints.

I had no desire to get close to those nails. I sighed. "I've had enough of this shit." I took three giant steps to Vampira and laid her out with one slap from a spring-loaded sap.

End of problem.

A weepy, undulating autumn rain was falling as we watched an ambulance take Helen's victim to St. Vincent's Hospital. "I guess she didn't need the five bucks," I said.

Helen was secured inside a straitjacket for her trip to a padded room. Her last name was Rosen, she was thirty-nine, and according to her, she had been a vampire ever since getting bitten on the neck by a rabid wolf while journeying through Transylvania in search of Dracula. The closest I thought she'd ever come to being bitten on the neck was getting a hickey from a horny fifteen-year-old boy in Canarsie High School. Helen had some identity problems. I was certain Bellevue would set her straight or hang her from her ankles so she'd feel right at home.

We had a pile of paperwork to write. "C'mon," Kenny said, "we'll pick up some Chinese before we go to the house."

No one would be looking for us for a while, so a detour to Sam Wo's in Chinatown sounded reasonable. Sam Wo's was virtually unknown to anyone other than Chinatown residents and cops until Woody Allen mentioned it in his movie *Manhattan*. After that it turned into a must-see for every tourist from Westchester who wanted to be a real New Yorker. Happily, we were still a few years away from that.

What surprised me about crazy Helen wasn't so much that we faced down an honest-to-God vampire (well, sort of—the woman drank at least a quart of blood a day), but that the whole episode didn't faze me.

At this point, I'd been on The Job only a little over three years, but even six months in the Ninth Precinct was like a lifetime anywhere else. I also had no compunctions about hitting a woman, even though I wouldn't have put Helen in the same category as June Cleaver. My life was changing a little at a time, but I failed to notice, and neither did my family. When I was home I was a different person.

"Hey, Wags," Kenny said as I slipped the car into gear, my stomach growling and bird's nest soup calling my name, "what's with this guy?"

Our squat friend was still across the street scrubbing away despite the fine mist of rain. "Wanna see?" I asked.

"Sure, why not?" Kenny said.

The man with the wire brush looked up from a kneeling position and smiled. He was wearing a bulky sweater and khaki pants, both soaked through, and GI jump boots. "Good evening, Officers."

"Yeah, good evening," I said. "May I ask what you're doing?"

"Preparing."

Kenny said, "Preparing what?"

"Preparing for the end." Despite being olive-skinned and swarthy, he had the brightest blue eyes I'd ever seen. He saw that we were puzzled. He grinned.

"Allow me to introduce myself," he said with a flourish and a half-assed bow. "My name is Oric Bovar, and I'm the pastor of the Church of Everlasting Life. This is our place of worship." He gestured toward the building behind us, which looked to me like every other tenement on the block, although with cleaner windows.

"We believe that the end is near, and we are readying ourselves for that eventuality. Cleaning our living and working area is part of our preparation." He explained that he had just thirteen "parishioners" and they all lived in the tenement. I was thinking maybe Helen was one of Bovar's followers.

The rain came down harder. I'd heard all I wanted to hear; one nut was enough for the tour. "C'mon, Kenny," I said. "Sam Wo's awaits." Bovar smiled serenely. It could have been raining pigs for all he cared.

As we neared the radio car Bovar called, "Kenny," just loud enough to be heard over the common noise of the city. He sounded like he'd known Kenny for years, rather than having heard his name for the first time just minutes ago.

We turned to find Bovar back on his knees, brush in hand, a radiant smile on his face. He had dazzling white teeth and they glistened through the falling rain.

"Yeah?" Kenny said, slipping into the front seat.

Bovar pointed toward the low-slung clouds. "Death from above."

Kenny said nothing. I rolled my eyes and we drove out of there. I hadn't gone three blocks when I had completely forgotten about Oric Bovar and his Temple of Doom or whatever the hell he called his church.

Kenny was closemouthed. I figured he was still stressing over his wife catching him in bed with the bimbo and the distinct possibility that he'd just written off marriage number three.

I was willing to talk with him, offer advice, do whatever I could to help him, but I wasn't about to volunteer my services until I was asked.

When we reached the narrow streets of Chinatown, Kenny said, "Hey, Wags, this guy Bovar, he gives me the creeps." He was staring straight out the windshield, his voice flat.

I almost said, "Bovar who?" Thoughts of one from Column A and one from Column B occupied my mind. "What about him?"

"Death from above. You know what that is?"

I double-parked in front of the restaurant. Sometimes The Job has its benefits. "Yeah, the ramblings of a nut."

"I was in the First Cav in Vietnam. We were an airmobile unit. 'Death from Above' was our motto."

15

The Runaway and the Hell's Angels

Kenny became obsessed with Oric Bovar. Whenever he was driving, he made sure to pass Bovar's building. Sometimes we'd do this five, six times a day. He couldn't get "Death from Above" out of his mind. More than once he asked Bovar what he meant by the remark. Each time, Bovar smiled that mystical smile of his and changed the subject or ignored Kenny completely. It drove my partner nuts.

"How'd he know I was in the Cav? Huh? I ask you, how'd he know?"

"What makes you think he knew you were in the First Cav or the friggin' first grade? C'mon, Kenny, that coulda meant anything, like a flowerpot was gonna come down on your head, the sky's falling, anything. The guy's a whack."

"I dunno about that."

Kenny's wife had left him. I thought he was losing it. He had no appetite, had gotten thinner, and had stopped ironing those military creases in his uniform shirts.

It was a little after eight P.M. on a November night and autumn was making a frigid exit. Still, there was Bovar under a streetlight on the sidewalk in front of his building. Only now, instead of scrubbing the sidewalk, he was painting it.

"What's he doing?" Kenny asked for the second time as we passed the little guy with his paintbrush in hand.

"Kenny," I said, a little exasperated, "who gives a damn. He's painting the sidewalk. Who cares?"

"I gotta know." We got out of the car and walked across the street.

"Good morning, Kenny, Wags." We were on a first-name basis by this time.

"I don't suppose you want to tell us why you're painting the sidewalk?" I said. He had painted a neat red circle, about the size of basketball, right in the middle of the sidewalk.

"Pre—"

I raised my nonshooting hand, "Yeah, I know, preparing. C'mon, Kenny."

Kenny stood his ground. "So when's the end coming?" He tried to make the comment light, but I read something much deeper into it. Kenny wanted an answer.

"When I decide. I'll go first, then come back and tell my flock they have nothing to fear from death."

There was a moment of silence. I thought Kenny was about to ask Bovar a question when the portable blared.

"Sector Charlie available?"

Kenny keyed the radio. "Charlie."

"We've got numerous reports of a fight at the Ritz. Hell's Angels may be involved."

The Ritz was a nightclub located on Eleventh Street, between Third and Fourth avenues, and was a popular watering hole for the Hell's Angels.

Normally the club policed itself, hiring enough bouncers to nip any fight in the bud before it got out of hand, but you can have a bouncer contingent larger than the First Panzer Division, and it's going to do you no good when the Angels get frisky.

Even if just two Angels cause a ruckus and get tossed out of a club, you can bet that those two will return, bringing forty of their biker buddies to level the place.

The cops of the Ninth Precinct and the Angels maintained a grudging respect for each other. A lot of the Angels were Vietnam vets (some went back to the Korean War), as were quite a few cops. And cops, for the most part, are very orderly, regimented people who adhere to a list of rules that would make a dominatrix proud. Angels, too, live by a strict code, and despite what the press led readers to believe, the Angels were for the most part law-abiding citizens. Except when you fucked with one of them.

They didn't bother us and we didn't bother them. When Kenny and I drove by their clubhouse (which is still there, by the way) we'd wave and they'd wave back. Very civil.

We pulled in front of the Ritz with four sector cars, sirens blaring, right behind us for backup. Since this was a fight possibly involving the Hell's Angels, we could use all the backup we could get.

There were three bodies on the street, bruised and battered, but breathing. These were the bouncers, big, muscle-bound, and unconscious. Inside the foyer, two more bouncers were nursing head wounds, and the manager, a tall, well-built guy with a neck full of gold chains, was arguing with six burly Angels, one of whom had to weigh four hundred pounds. The big guy was wearing a leather vest with no shirt, sporting full-sleeve tattoos.

When the manager, a mob-connected wanna-be with slicked-back hair that looked like it was brushed with a buttered roll, spotted me, he began screaming. "I want these motherfuckers arrested! They wiped out my security team!" He ranted for a minute about the murderous Angels whom he wanted to get locked up for life (if not longer). "They attacked my men with no fucking provocation!"

The gorilla in the vest, who introduced himself as Big Vinny, calmly explained the Angels' side of the story.

"That's not how it happened, Officer. The shithead outside with the black jacket cornered one of our brothers in the john and started pushing him around." He indicated a smaller (by comparison) Angel who was wiping blood from his forehead with a cocktail napkin.

"Yeah, that's what happened," the head bleeder said.

"So we found the mutts," Big Vinny said, "and defended our friend. Simple street justice. You gotta lock us up, do what you gotta do."

I was impressed that the Angels had stuck around. Had they gone to the clubhouse, it would have taken a frontal assault by a regiment of cops to extract them.

We were twelve people, including the backup cops, jammed into a small foyer. Since my sector had the job, we had to make some kind of a decision as to who was getting locked up, if anyone, before the fight resumed.

I grabbed the manager by the arm. "Can I talk to you alone?" I asked. I ushered him into the street without waiting for an answer.

"Listen," I said. "We lock these guys up then your guys go, too."

"I don't give a fuck!" He was hot. "I'll have my men out in a few hours. These assholes gotta learn a lesson. Bust up my men, no fucking way."

I put my arm around him and took him out of earshot of passersby. "You're not thinking. They're gonna get out, too, you know? You want these guys coming back? Maybe with their friends? Besides, who was wrong here? You know, me and my partner, we've got better things to do than break up fights. Maybe next time we'll take our time getting here. Get my drift?"

He thought about it. "Yeah, yeah, okay."

We went back into the club. Kenny gave the Angels a half-assed dressing-down—in private. They left, and we went back on patrol.

An hour later we were in Ya Ya's, a coffee shop on Fourteenth Street where you could get a decent burger without going into cardiac arrest. As I was paying the check, I heard the earsplitting and easily identifiable roar of Harley-Davidson motorcycles.

Outside at least a dozen chopped bikes were pulling up on either side of our parked radio car. The riders wore the unmistakable colors of the Hell's Angels. They cut their engines and sat on their machines, waiting.

The handful of patrons in the coffee shop stopped what they were doing and looked at us, then the Angels, then back again. Like a tennis match.

"Oh, shit," Kenny said. "I think we've got a problem." He reached for the radio. I stopped him.

"What're they gonna do, kill two cops in uniform in front of witnesses?"

"Maybe just fuck us up a little. These guys don't give a shit about anything."

"C'mon, let's see what they have to say." I unlocked my revolver from its safety holster, just in case.

We went outside and stood on the sidewalk. The bikers stared at us. The whole spectacle was surreal, like a scene from the movie *High Noon,* magnified.

One of the bikers dismounted and walked toward us. I put him at about thirty, a little under six feet tall, wavy black hair, and built like a bodybuilder. His denim jacket was opened, stretched at the shoulders.

"You guys handle the Ritz thing?" he asked calmly. He was almost nose-to-nose with Kenny.

"Yeah," Kenny and I said in unison.

The biker extended his hand. "Name's Chuck Zito." Handshakes all around. "I want to thank you for treating my brothers like gentlemen. It doesn't happen too often."

"Just doing our job," I said. John Wayne, or what?

"I think it was a little more than your job. You need a favor—anything—you call me." He handed me a card. "Anytime." With that he got back on his bike, and the outlaws screamed down Fourteenth Street.

We stood there a few seconds. Kenny broke the ice.

"See, piece of cake."

"Turned out better than I thought."

Kenny said, "You can trash that card. If we ever need those guys, we've got a problem."

It turned out we did indeed end up needing the Hell's Angels' help despite Kenny's thoughts to the contrary. Fortunately, I held on to the card.

About a month later, close to Christmas, we were turning out for a four-to-twelve, and Sergeant Reddy had just finished conducting the roll call. As was department policy, he read us a list of unsolved crimes, wanted persons, and other items of interest to conscientious, intelligent, caring cops. And us, too.

In recent months we'd been getting a lot of reports of runaways. After a while they all sounded the same: female, white, fifteen to seventeen years old, from some tiny town in the Midwest, ran away after telling friends she was headed for New York, where she would live among the flower children, protest the war, and get high. Didn't sound like too bad an idea.

Anyway, New York City is a big place. The odds of finding one of these waifs was infinitesimal. The case Sergeant Reddy was telling us about, however, was different.

It started out the same, female, white, etc., but that's where the similarities ended.

"This kid," Reddy said, referring to his report, "is Lisa Anderson." He passed around copies of Lisa's picture, a fresh-faced kid who made Doris Day in her prime look like a slut. "She called her mom in some town called Milton Freewater, Washington, two days ago saying she was being held prisoner in a building on Thirteenth Street in Manhattan. Then she was cut off. We don't know if it's East or West Thirteenth, which would put her in the Sixth Precinct, but we gotta check East Thirteenth, which is ours. Talk to your snitches; see what you can find out. Take your posts and, hey . . . Be careful out there."

During the course of the tour we talked to the street people, who seemed to know everything about everybody within their own little world. We never expected to find out anything useful; we were just doing our job.

"Yeah, I seen her," said a junkie with the street name of Charcoal, so named because of his unwashed face. "Somewheres over on Thirteenth Street."

My adrenaline began pumping. "Where exactly, Charcoal? You gotta be specific."

He stroked his stubbly chin. "I dunno . . . hold it, it was three-twelve, yeah, three-twelve, that was it."

Helen the Vampire's building.

I rewarded Charcoal with three bags of the finest confiscated China White and we raced to the tenement.

Oric Bovar was sitting on his stoop admiring his handiwork. The red circle on the pavement was now surrounded by a blue circle. It had taken him a month to paint the latest addition to his work of art. A real perfectionist. Also a goddamn polar bear. It had to be twenty degrees and he was wearing his now-familiar sweater and khakis with the same boots.

"Hey, Oric," Kenny said, "you seen this girl?" He waved the picture out the window. Bovar ambled over like he was marching up the aisle with a new bride.

"Oh, certainly, Kenny. She lives across the street. Don't know what apartment, though."

We knew the building was full of junkies. "Seen her lately?"

He shook his head. "Not for at least a few days. Kind of cold, you know? These people don't have much money for clothes."

Yeah, I thought, all their money goes for heroin. "She seem, you know, under restraint, like she's a prisoner?"

"Now that you mention it, I've never seen her alone. She's always with someone, always a man. Could be she's being held against her will."

I called for Sergeant Reddy. He met us around the block. No sense in alerting the enemy.

"Goddamn building," he said. "All the years I've been here it's nothing but trouble. Stabbings, shootings, ODs—"

"Let's not forget the vampire," Kenny said.

We formed a plan of attack. Sergeant Reddy assembled those who were available from the remaining sectors, which included Foster and Laurie and Frank Moran, who was still wandering around the wrong foot post.

"Okay," Reddy said, "it's gonna be a full-frontal assault." Foster and Laurie took the first floor; the sergeant and his driver, Glover, took the second floor; and Kenny and I took the third and fourth floors. Moran went around back to the alley to scoop up any escapees.

While this was the dawning of the era of guarding one's constitutional rights, cops from the Ninth generally ignored the first several amendments when dealing with junkies or violent felons. We hadn't the time to apply for search warrants or play nice-nice with whomever might be living—if you could call it that—in those crash pads and shooting galleries. A kid's life was at stake; screw the Constitution.

Kenny and I broke down doors like Patton invading Italy. Out of four apartments on the third floor, one was vacant and the remaining three were littered with passed-out junkies, lying amid used spikes, twisted bottle caps, spent matches, and the occasional cast-aside condom. We left the nodding junkies to their heroin-induced dream states and tossed the lucid junkies into the street, but not before showing them a picture of Lisa Anderson.

One strung-out hophead admitted seeing her on the fourth floor, but gave that information up only when I gave him a nickel bag of smack from the stash in my memo book. Who knew if he was telling the truth.

We scored in the first apartment we hit on the fourth floor. The one-bedroom pad hadn't been legitimately rented in years. The one window in the bedroom had been shattered during the Kennedy administration, and a cable ran from a nearby lamppost on the street through the window to pirate city power for light.

A lone dim bulb swinging from a rope in the center of the ceiling cast eerie shadows across the room.

The only piece of furniture was a beat-up brass bed with a sagging bare mattress at the far end of the room. On that bed, facedown, naked and unmoving, was a young woman.

She was on her stomach and tied with rope sideways across the bed. Her arms and legs were secured to opposite ends of the rusted metal bed frame, her legs spread wide enough to kick a field goal through.

Blood and dry, caked semen adhered to her buttocks and thighs. Her back was scratched; dry scabs ran down its length. The picture we had of Lisa showed her with long, flowing auburn hair, shiny and healthy. Now her hair was matted and dirty. Someone had butchered her long tresses with what might have been nail clippers. Her hair was chopped, short and uneven.

I turned her head to one side to see if she was breathing and saw the remnants of semen caked on the side of her face.

Lisa Anderson was being used as a sex receptacle for any junkie who passed through the apartment.

"She's alive," I said, as if her current state could be called living.

"Jesus fucking Christ," Kenny said.

A cop sees a lot of misery during the course of his career, and I'd seen my share, but the sight of this kid—that's all she was, a kid—sexually abused and debased in this shithole, when she should have been going to high school dances in her small town of Milton Berle, or wherever the hell she lived, incensed me.

"Check the other room," I told Kenny. I was mumbling a tirade of "motherfuckers" and worse as I cut the kid free with a pocketknife.

"No one here," Kenny reported back. He got on the portable. "Central, Nine Charlie. Send a bus to three-twelve East Thirteenth Street, top floor, ASAP. We've got an unconscious white female, about fifteen, the victim of a gang—" He stopped and chose his words carefully. ". . . sexual attack. Fast, Central, okay?"

Cops began to fill the room. I brushed by them after blurting out, "Crime scene!" and headed for the last occupied apartment we'd found. I was livid, and the junkies were going to pay. Sergeant Reddy was right behind me.

He spun me around as I reached the stairway. "Where the hell you going?"

I yanked my arm away. "I'm gonna throw a junkie out a fucking window." I got one step before the sergeant grabbed my pistol belt.

"On, no, you're not. What's that gonna solve? You kick some junkie's ass, maybe kill him, you go to jail. For what?"

"Sarge, the kid—"

"Yeah, yeah, I know—the kid. I've got kids, too." He backed me up against the wall. "There's always a better way. Think."

So I thought.

*   *   *

Kenny and I accompanied the ambulance to Bellevue. The girl was as yet officially unidentified, and we had a pile of paperwork to do. We needed a preliminary diagnosis from a doctor.

A young female intern, visibly shaken, met us in the hallway outside of the ER.

"Her insides are ripped apart. Multiple contusions, vaginal wall tears. Jesus, she's a mess. Someone apparently held her mouth open with a tool, might be pliers, and three of her teeth have been knocked out."

She talked; I wrote and kept quiet. I was formulating a plan, and the only person who was going to share in it was Kenny. "She gonna be okay, Doc?"

The intern snorted. "The vaginal damage was inflicted with something other than the male penis. We're still checking for further abuse. She'll make it—physically. I gotta get back."

I found a pay phone in the lobby and called the Angels' clubhouse on East Third Street.

Chuck Zito met with Kenny and me by Tompkins Square Park. He was on foot and alone, per my request. A thundering herd of Harleys wasn't conducive to keeping a low profile.

I told him the story.

After a few dozen expletives he finally said, "You believe this? My teenage daughter's name's Lisa. Fucking junkies—I hate 'em."

"Listen," I said, "we need a favor. What they did to that girl—"

Chuck held up a hand attached to a sinewy forearm. "Don't say anything; you'll be hearing from me." And with that he turned and left.

Two days later, Kenny and I were doing our last four-to-twelve. It was getting close to quitting time during what had been a particularly busy tour. Nothing like the approach of the holiday season to bring out the murderous inclinations of New Yorkers, at least in our little end of the city.

Our radio beeped three times. A dispatcher will utilize beeps only when the next job is serious and he needs to get everyone's attention. Immediately.

"Units in the Ninth Precinct, we've got a report of a gang fight on Thirteenth Street between Avenues C and D. At least five calls on this, reporting numerous bodies all over the street."

The Ninth Precinct is small. As soon as the call came over I heard blaring sirens, converging from all sectors in the command. Sector Adam was the first to respond. "We're going, Central." All other sectors that weren't out on jobs backed up.

"Nine Charlie's backing, too, Central," I said and flipped on the turret lights.

"Gee," Kenny said, "wonder what this could be?"

The street looked like a battle zone. There were fifteen unconscious men and women littering the gutter. All had taken bad beatings, some worse than others, but would live, if you can call going through life with two broken kneecaps living. The winners were nowhere to be found. These beatings were administered by professionals.

A thick-linked chain coupled by a padlock the size of a corn muffin secured the front of building number three-twelve.

"I guess these folks are the former tenants," I said.

Kenny shook his head. "The streets of Saigon looked better after Tet."

Ambulances were pouring into the block; cops were canvassing for witnesses. Across the street, Oric Bovar was in his usual spot on the sidewalk, this time without his can of paint.

"I gotta ask, Oric, you see anything?" I said.

He looked at me, unsmiling. "It pains me to witness such violence, Wags."

"That mean you saw something?"

"See what?"

The building stayed chained and vacant. The victims of the assault suffered amnesia as part of their injuries, undoubtedly induced by promises of things to come.

The police—that would be us—professionals that we were, established that four males wearing long leather dusters marched into the building and began throwing out the non-rent-paying residents shortly thereafter.

Rumors to the effect that members of the Hell's Angels had been involved in the massacre were proven to be unfounded. No one saw any motorcycles, and what self-respecting Angel would be without his bike or his colors?

So what became of those involved? Lisa Anderson was taken home by her family. Neither she nor her family ever contacted us, and Lisa was unable to identify her assailants. We weren't looking for thank-yous. We're cops. The last person to thank us did so after being shot only once, instead of a dozen times.

Later, Chuck Zito became an actor and could be seen playing the part of Pancamo in the hit HBO series *Oz*. He was a damn good actor, and there was talk of his getting his own television series. You could hear him occasionally on the Howard Stern show, too. He'd found his niche.

Big Vinny is no longer with us, having succumbed to a heart attack in the early '70s. He had one helluva send-off. The funeral was held at the Provenzano-Lanza Funeral Home on Second Avenue.

Over a thousand Hell's Angels from all over the world attended the funeral, and FDR Drive had to be closed from Houston Street to the Bronx to accommodate the mass of motorcycles.

Big Vinny's bike was driven right into the funeral home and parked next to his casket. A mural of Vinny, painted by Zito, adorned the wall of a tenement next to the Angels' clubhouse for years, until the building was demolished. A memorial beneath the painting read, *In memory of Big Vinny. When in doubt, knock 'em out.*

And Oric Bovar? He was to change my life dramatically.

16
The Black
Liberation Army

There have been many excellent books written about the rash of police killings in the 1970s committed by the Black Liberation Army (BLA). The best of the lot is *Target Blue,* an immensely readable book by Robert Daley, who served as the NYPD's Deputy Commissioner of Public Information during those troubled times. Daley was too popular with rank-and-file cops to last very long, and was the only DCPI I can recall who carried a gun and actually responded to radio runs.

His one year on The Job was a memorable one. The cops who are still around remember him as one of the few bosses who actually liked street cops. I highly recommend his book as an overall insider's view of the NYPD during those turbulent years.

What I will relate here is a microcosm of the entire BLA episode as it related to the Ninth Precinct, whose members were particularly affected by two of the terrorist group's more brutal slayings.

What occurred on the evening of January 27, 1972, would change our lives forever. This is that story from the eye of the storm.

It was open season on cops. Ten police officers were killed in the line of duty in 1971, tying a dubious record set in 1930.

Cops, however, weren't the only people getting bumped off in horrifying numbers. The homicide rate had increased more than thirty percent from the previous year. A shocking figure, to be sure, but tempered by the sobering statistic that almost seventy percent of those murders were committed by a family member or someone known to the victim. Small solace, I suppose, to the dead guy lying on his kitchen floor with an ax buried in his head, placed there by his loving wife.

The city would max out that year at 1,441 killings, a figure that would be surpassed by a few hundred during the crack years of the 1980s.

On May 19, 1971, two patrol officers from the Three-Two Precinct in Harlem—Waverly Jones, thirty-four, and Joseph Piagentini, twenty-eight—were gunned down ambush-style by two black youths as they left a housing project where they had responded to a radio run. They were the sixth and seventh officers to die in the line of duty that year.

These killings followed by two days the ambush of police officers Thomas Curry and Nicholas Benetti, both thirty-nine, as they chased a car that had driven past their radio car going the wrong way down a one-way street on the Upper West Side. When the officers pulled alongside the vehicle, a young black man stuck an automatic weapon out the rear window and fired, inflicting serious injuries to both cops. Fortunately they survived, although they retired on disability pensions due to the severity of their wounds.

Rumblings began within the ranks almost immediately. Rumors abounded, the foremost being that an organized group of black killers was hunting New York City cops.

The bosses at 1 Police Plaza quickly discounted the supposition. The following day, however, a package was delivered to the *New York Times* from a group calling itself the Black Liberation Army, claiming responsibility for both ambushes and declaring war on cops everywhere. Also contained in the *Times* package was the license plate of the vehicle Curry and Benetti had chased, and a .45-caliber bullet, the caliber of the submachine gun fired at the two cops.

This group was previously unknown to the NYPD, and while they were proficient killers, they weren't very bright when it came to forensics. A clean set of fingerprints was lifted from the package and identified as belonging to Richard Moore, twenty-six.

As the investigation progressed, assaults on police officers continued: a cop stabbed in the chest while sitting in his patrol car in Brooklyn, the attempted machine-gunning of a police sergeant in San Francisco, and the attempted murder of a police officer in Baltimore.

The cop in San Francisco was saved from certain death when the machine gun being wielded by the passenger in a stolen car jammed. After a brief car chase, Anthony Bottom, nineteen, and Albert Washington, thirty, were arrested.

In addition to the machine gun found in their car, a Smith & Wesson .38-caliber Model Ten revolver was recovered. A cop's gun. More specifically, police officer Waverly Jones's gun. A ballistics test was conducted on the machine gun. It was the same weapon used to ambush Curry and Benetti.

Both suspects denied involvement in the New York crimes, but bragged about their membership in the Black Liberation Army.

Evidence began falling into place. More names surfaced, specifically those of Twyman Myers, twenty, a hot-headed gunman, and Joanne Chesimard, twenty-four, known as the soul of the BLA.

New York City cops were on heightened alert. This highly mobile, nomadic group of killers could strike anywhere, but if you wanted to get headlines (and what terrorist organization didn't?), killing a New York City cop was a certain ticket to notoriety.

The Job was also getting information about the BLA from the very people the psycho killers were supposedly trying to liberate, black New Yorkers, who phoned in tips in record numbers after Piagentini and Jones were gunned down.

If this group of fanatics wasn't enough to worry about, cops were still being murdered and injured by the garden variety of felon so predominant on the streets of the city.

So many cops were getting killed, in fact, that by June 1971, I found myself attending at least one funeral a month.

One such funeral, the service for a Sergeant Tustin, gunned down as he attempted to thwart a robbery, had the department chaplain, Msgr. Joseph Dunne, so harried that he consistantly mispronounced the deceased cop's name as he spoke from the pulpit.

To be fair, Monsignor Dunne, normally a workaholic, now found himself ministering to so many families of dead and injured police officers that he was suffering from a constant state of exhaustion.

While eulogizing the departed Sergeant Tustin to a packed church on Northern Boulevard in Flushing, Queens, the good monsignor kept referring to the deceased as Sergeant *Mustin*.

The first time he did it, there was a polite rumbling from the flock. After the second time, there was some throat clearing, and after the third time, someone in the back shouted, "Tustin! It's Tustin, you idiot!" I saw the mayor and police commissioner cringe.

Monsignor Dunne wasn't very popular with the troops to begin with because he ran the Farm, an infamous treatment facility for alcoholic cops, located in upstate New York.

Members of the monsignor's goon squad, all former alcoholics, were famous for literally kidnapping suspected alcoholics right from their beds in the middle of the night and delivering them to the Farm for an extended, involuntary stay.

With this the general frame of mind, it didn't take the assembled cops at the sergeant's funeral service very long to get vocal, pissed off as they were at their helplessness as record numbers of their buddies were being slaughtered, and still feeling animosity toward the monsignor and his SS troops that had been festering for years.

Dunne, oblivious to it all, kept on mispronouncing the sergeant's name.

We never heard the shots.

Kenny and I were on a late meal break in Ya Ya's on Fourteenth Street. We were supposed to have eaten at eight P.M., but the radio was busy and our meal had been denied until ten.

It was an odd night. New York Januarys are a bitch, particularly at night when the temperature drops, the wind whips, and your best friend is the heater in the radio car.

Tonight, however, the weather was tranquil, the air wet and heavy with the promise of snow.

At 10:50 P.M. we were just finished eating and getting our gear together when the radio blared five sharp beeps.

When a cop hears those beeps his stomach drops to his knees. In a command where a serious job occurs damn near every minute, the beeps meant a catastrophe.

Central: "In the Ninth Precinct, I've got a report of two cops shot! That's two cops down on Eleventh Street and Avenue B! Units to respond!"

"Shit." I jumped up. "That's three blocks away."

Every radio in the division, which comprised six precincts, came to life. Literally within seconds, cops began pouring into the EVil from every command in lower Manhattan.

"Jesus," Kenny shouted, as we ran out the door, "who's on B, who's on B?"

My mind was racing. Mental pictures of every cop working the tour bounced through my brain as I slid behind the wheel of the car. The sound of approaching sirens grew louder. "I don't know—I think Foster and Laurie."

I fired up the engine. Five radio cars were screaming down Fourteenth Street. While my heart was pumping at a furious rate, I at least had the presence of mind to make certain we weren't wiped out by an approaching speeding sector car.

That's when I saw Oric Bovar.

He was standing on the corner beneath a street lamp wearing his signature sweater and khakis. Kenny spotted him, too. It was the first time either of us had seen him away from the front of his "church."

He smiled beatifically and pointed slowly to the sky.

His finger was still raised as I floored the car and flew past him, siren wailing, reflections from the turret lights bouncing eerily off a blur of passing tenements.

Kenny said, "It's a sign, it's a sign, man."

Kenny had never gotten over Bovar's "Death from Above" line, and now I sensed a shiver go through him as I skidded onto Avenue B.

We couldn't get any closer than a block to the corner of Eleventh Street. Radio cars were parked at odd angles, some on sidewalks, left abandoned, their doors wide-open. Cops were running on foot for the corner, guns drawn.

I was hyperventilating, my head swimming as I joined the mob of blue racing down the block. Streams of curses and the names Foster and Laurie were being shouted over and over again.

A group of uniforms had surrounded the corner and were looking toward the roofs, their guns drawn, pointing skyward, expecting an ambush.

Sergeant Reddy was already there, tears rolling down his face, walking around in tight circles, gun hanging at his side, his frustration evident.

"Sarge, what happened?" I said, then spotted more blood than I'd seen since the quadruple homicide in Staten Island in what seemed another lifetime. The blood had depth to it. A pile of blood. I realized then that the gore was a combination of blood and brains. I turned away.

"Greg and Rocco, slaughtered like animals." Reddy took off his hat and pulled at his hair. "Cops tossed them in radio cars, took 'em to Bellevue."

Bellevue had the best trauma unit on the face of the planet. If you had a life-threatening injury, the trauma teams at Bellevue stood the best chance of saving your life.

"Bad?"

"Greg's dead. Head shots, eyes shot out. Rocco's hanging on. They shot both of them in the back." He was holding back sobs, his voice cracking. But he was the ranking officer on the scene, at least for now. He began barking orders, instructing cops to canvass for witnesses, for others to preserve the crime scene.

I'd known Greg Foster and Rocco Laurie fairly well, but now I was wishing I'd known them better. Both were family men who went straight home after their tours, Rocco to Staten Island, Greg to the Bronx. Rocco was a star athlete in high school and was a big guy, in great shape, a nondrinker. Greg was quiet, both great cops. Rocco was white, Greg black, but we would soon discover that they were killed because of their common color: blue.

Bellevue was a madhouse. Radio and unmarked cars blocked the streets leading to the hospital. The neighborhood was eerily silent, the steady clicking of rotating turret lights and the barking of police radios the only sound.

It had just begun to snow as I arrived at the hospital. My radio car was hemmed into Eleventh Street, so I commandeered a gypsy cab for transportation. I lost Kenny somewhere along the way. Pandemonium reigned.

The scene outside the main entrance to the hospital was surreal. Uniformed cops were on their knees in the middle of the street praying. Others were just inside the main entrance crying and cursing.

Department brass arrived as I joined the throng of cops outside the ER. Commissioner Patrick Murphy, Chief Inspector Mike Codd, Chief of Detectives Al Seedman, and a myriad of pressed-out uniforms adorned with stars arrived within minutes of each other. Mayor John Lindsay, with an entourage of bodyguards, breezed by, followed by Deputy Commissioner Robert Daley.

Amid the confusion and chaos I managed to find Jim Liedy, who with his partner had transported Rocco to the hospital.

"What the hell happened?" This was a question I'd find myself asking for many days to come.

Liedy was a wreck, covered with blood and brain matter. His holster was empty (he would think he'd lost his gun, only to find it later on the front seat of his radio car).

"Jesus, they shot them in the back, both of them. A witness said two black guys—young guys—passed them on the street, whirled, and opened up. When Rocco and Greg went down, the two guys stood over them and pumped bullets into them. Greg's head came apart in my hands." He looked down at his blood-soaked hands, as if trying to will the gore away.

The room began to reel. I sought support against a wall. "Oh, God," I said, unable to fully grasp what I was hearing. Behind me I heard, "Death from Above." It was Kenny, ashen white, eyes as wide as beer coasters.

"I told you, Jimmy," Kenny said. "That fucking Bovar—Death from Above. They stood over them and shot them. He knew."

Liedy looked at Kenny for some kind of explanation. I grabbed my partner by the arm and got him outside.

"For crissakes, Kenny, get ahold of yourself, will you?" Despite the cold I was sweating a river. If there was ever a time in my life I needed a drink, it was now.

Kenny shook a finger at me, as if he were scolding a child. "I'm telling you, this guy knows something; he sees the future."

I guided him to a radio car and sat him down in the front seat. "Wait here," I told him. I feared that all the stress Kenny had been building up since his Vietnam experience and through three busted marriages was finally coming to a head. I considered taking his gun, but thought better of it. One day I'd be sorry I didn't.

I went back inside the hospital.

I saw that a lot of cops had gone from crying to muttering. Cliques were forming. Venom directed at police brass was the order of the day.

One cop said, "Cawley's saying that Rocco and Greg were on the take and got whacked by someone they knew." Chief of Patrol Cawley was about as unpopular as a boss on The Job could be, an effete blowhard who didn't think much of his own patrol force. Even so, I couldn't fathom a high-ranking supervisor making a statement like that minutes after arriving on the scene and not knowing anything about Foster or Laurie.

I was to find out, however, that it was true: Cawley had been denigrating both officers right out of the gate. While most everyone was logically linking the shootings to the Black Liberation Army, Cawley chose to jump to conclusions.

He wouldn't be the only one. Days later, Deputy Commissioner Ben Ward was still insisting that there was no conspiracy to kill cops, even after being shown overwhelming evidence. Finally he was forced to agree with the majority when a press conference was called to identify the individuals wanted in numerous police shootings across the country, including those of Piagentini and Jones the previous year, and later Foster and Laurie.

"We oughta frag the son of a bitch," a cop said, referring to Cawley and the practice some soldiers in Vietnam had of tossing grenades into the hooches of unpopular officers.

Such talk is just that—talk—but it reflected the enmity cops had that night for someone even suggesting that Foster and Laurie were crooks.

Rocco Laurie died at 4:35 A.M. that morning, a valiant fight for life lost to severe wounds and great odds. He was twenty-three. Foster was twenty-four.

When a cop, soldier, fireman, or someone in a hazardous job dies a violent death, the initial reaction of those who worked with the victim is one of relief: relief that it wasn't you who bought it. The second reaction is guilt, stemming from your first reaction. And you wonder why cops drink.

The police department was in a state of siege. While the largest manhunt in the history of the New York City Police Department was gearing up, cops were taking matters into their owns hands to stay safe.

In the days following the double assassination, cops began arming themselves with sophisticated weapons.

During the '70s the New York City Police Department didn't have the stringent rules it has today regarding what kinds of weapons its members could carry.

Today there are approved firearms that a cop may use on, and off duty. Back then, The Job's rules dictated that a member of the force (these days it's "a member of the service"; the word *force* is verboten) was obligated to carry a Smith & Wesson Model Ten, a Dan Wesson or Colt service revolver, all equipped with four-inch barrels, while on duty. Policewomen (the generic "police officer" would not appear for a few years) were permitted to carry service revolvers with three-inch barrels. Today there is no distinction as to barrel length.

Off-duty guns were optional and were generally two-inch-barrel versions of the service revolver.

What The Job didn't demand was that the aforementioned service revolvers be the *only* firearm carried. The carrying of a "backup" gun was encouraged, and a police officer could carry whatever he wanted as long as he also had an authorized weapon in his possession.

This led to a wide variety of backup guns being carried, but the general tendency was to carry small—a .25 semiauto or a Walther PPK .380, the theory being that small is easily concealable and more comfortable to hide.

Logic, however, went out the window during this rash of police murders, particularly after Foster and Laurie were killed and it was evident that New York City cops had become a priority target of the Black Liberation Army.

Most patrol officers purchased high-powered semiautomatic pistols as backups. One cop I worked with took to carrying a World War II Browning automatic rifle around in his radio car. A BAR is a heavy, cumbersome weapon, fired fully automatic, but held a small-capacity magazine. The thing was so long that this officer would be seen driving around the precinct with the barrel of the BAR sticking out the window. Great for community relations. No one said anything, however.

The public, surprisingly, was on our side and sympathized with our plight. While most New Yorkers don't necessarily like their cops, they're not crazy about people who shoot them. In addition, a scared cop is a trigger-happy cop. No self-respecting burglar wanted that.

Kenny, though, took the prize for exotic weaponry.

"What the hell is that?" I asked as Kenny slid a mean-looking rifle from a canvas bag. We had just turned out for a four-to-twelve tour the day after Foster and Laurie were killed.

"It's a CAR-15. Sent it back piece by piece from 'Nam. Pretty, no?" He stroked the short barrel and handed it to me.

The entire rifle couldn't have been more than eighteen inches long and resembled a miniature M-16, the grunt's weapon of issue in Vietnam. There was a nine-inch tube hanging under the barrel. "What's this?" I asked.

"Forty-millimeter grenade launcher."

"Don't tell me—"

Kenny held up a projectile that resembled a .45-caliber round on steroids. "Right here, big guy. Sent a few of these home, too. Never thought I'd need 'em when I got back to the world, though. Sorta like a souvenir." He ran down the nomenclature of the wicked little gun. "Selector switch right here, shoots either full or semiauto. Twelve hundred rounds a minute." He jiggled the canvas bag. "Nine magazines. Ready to rock 'n' roll."

I was more than a little concerned about Kenny. He'd been morose since his wife threw him out, and the thing with Bovar was unsettling, but now he was acting like he was back in the jungle hunting Vietcong.

"Hey, Kenny, you think maybe spraying a couple of hundred rounds in this city might hurt an innocent civilian?"

He looked at me like I was crazy. "Hey, man, this is Alphabet City; there are no innocent civilians."

He had a point.

Every cop in the city gave up their days off to provide security for marked radio cars by following them in their civilian autos during the tour. What surprised me was that this maneuver was actually sanctioned by headquarters. Normally, if it wasn't in the *Patrol Guide* (the bible of rules as thick as a cinder block that outlined procedures for every possible occurrence that could transpire on The Job), the commissioner wouldn't allow it. And I was certain that there was nothing that covered carloads of off-duty cops, armed to the teeth with automatic weapons, patrolling the streets of New York.

Rocco Laurie's and Gregory Foster's funerals were held jointly at St. Patrick's Cathedral in midtown Manhattan and were awesome in their scope.

A sea of blue stretched for ten city blocks in either direction from the church's main entrance. Cops came from all over the United States and beyond to pay their respects. I saw uniforms from England, Mexico, and Canada, in addition to military personnel and federal agents. All had shields affixed to their outermost garments, everyone's shield covered with a black band of mourning.

Due to the sheer size of the turnout, only a small fraction of those attending were permitted inside the church. Of course, this included members of the Ninth Precinct, brass, and politicians. The service was conducted by Francis Cardinal Spellman and moved everyone to tears.

Rocco Laurie's young wife collapsed inside the church. Behind the tears, cops masked their grief with vows of revenge, but did so quietly out of respect for the grieving families. But there was no doubt people would die for what they did, and it was a comfort to know that the urban terrorists who committed these crimes had vowed never to be taken alive. We would do everything within our power to grant them that wish.

Since I couldn't attend both burials, I chose to go to Laurie's because he lived in Staten Island. I felt a little ashamed that I had never really gotten to know him or Foster well, but being at the cemetery would assuage some guilt.

To comprehend the vast number of cops who showed up for the church service, consider the following example: When the funeral cortege left the church in midtown Manhattan for the trip to Staten Island, radio and private cars followed in an orderly line. By the time the hearse reached the cemetery in Staten Island, the last car hadn't yet departed the vicinity of the church in Manhattan.

I wondered who was watching the city. Every radio and unmarked car assigned to the NYPD seemed to be snaking its way onto FDR Drive as the cortege moved solemnly toward the Brooklyn Battery Tunnel.

Every car had its turret lights revolving and its siren wailing. Opposing traffic stopped dead, either out of respect or fear that they were witnessing a mass evacuation of the borough of Manhattan. I'm certain the cry of sirens could be heard into the outer boroughs of the city.

The quiet, residential Staten Island neighborhood adjacent to the cemetery was invaded by thousands of marked and unmarked cars. Legitimate parking spaces vanished quickly, and homeowners allowed cops to park their cars on private lawns, driveways, and sidewalks.

I had promised my father I'd meet him at the burial, but couldn't locate him in the mass of blue. I couldn't get to within two hundred yards of the graveside service, but it was still a day I'll never forget.

"Okay," Sergeant Reddy said, "listen up. These are the mutts we're looking for."

The muster room was jammed with the outgoing four-to-twelve platoon, which included my squad and two others, and an additional twenty-five off-duty cops who were going to follow us around in their private cars to prevent ambushes.

Aside from the fact that most cops owned similar civilian autos, I was wondering who was going to prevent our protectors from getting slaughtered. Carloads of white guys driving through the confines of the Ninth Precinct with rifle barrels protruding from windows would alert a dead man. There were definitely places I'd rather be.

Reddy passed out wanted flyers. "This first asshole is Twyman Myers, thought to be one of the most violent members of the BLA."

Myers looked like he was a born killer. Hooded eyes, furrowed brow, broken nose. This guy would scare babies, I thought. Myers was known to carry a hand grenade in his coat and a .25-caliber auto on a chain around his neck. If stopped and asked to assume the search position—hands on a wall, feet back and spread—his plan was to reach for the gun and shoot the cops from under his armpit while still in the frisk stance.

"Pictures two and three and four," Reddy said, "are Herman Bell, Albert Washington, and Joanne Chesimard."

"Chesimard would be the broad, right, Sarge?" Frank Moran asked. He was loaded, but spoke clearly. Frank had just left Cal's after two days of toasting Foster and Laurie.

Sergeant Reddy rolled his eyes. "Right, Frank. Anyway, Intelligence informs us that Bell may still be in the area, so watch your asses." Reddy looked right at Moran. "Got that, Frank? Herman Bell may still be around. Stay alert out there."

"Yeah, yeah, Sarge, I got it," Moran said listlessly.

An additional dozen flyers were distributed with the names and pedigrees of other known members and associates of the BLA.

Every cop in the city was skittish. Radical splinter groups were jumping into the fray. In the Bronx a plot was uncovered to assassinate cops from the Four-Four Precinct when they turned out for patrol. No specific group claimed credit for the plot, but it seemed like a copycat conspiracy.

The Four-Four Precinct station house is located practically on the eastern bank of the East River across from Manhattan. The plan was to have a sniper team armed with rifles fitted with high-powered telescopic sights on the Manhattan side of the river who would pick off the outgoing platoon as they left the precinct on the Bronx side.

Fortunately, an informant ratted on the plotters and their plan was foiled, but they weren't captured and were still roaming the city, heavily armed.

So it was with great trepidation that the uniformed contingent emerged from the Ninth Precinct station house that cold day in January. Cops had their hands on their guns and shot furtive glances every which way to make certain a reception committee wasn't waiting in ambush.

Kenny and I got in our radio car, me at the wheel, and got the hell off the block very quickly. As I drove down the street I was expecting a rooftop ambush or a well-placed grenade to be dropped into our laps.

Kenny had his CAR-15 in its canvas sack lying across his lap. "I'm ready for these motherfuckers." He showed me how fast he could get the rifle out of the case and ready to fire. "See that, three seconds at the most." He smiled.

Kenny had spoken very little since the killings. He stayed clear of Oric Bovar's street when he was driving and avoided looking at him when I drove down the church block.

Bovar wasn't his normal friendly self either. Whenever I passed him, he'd be out in front of his building but didn't acknowledge us. For two days he'd been there, paintbrush in hand, working on his creation, stopping only when the sun dropped behind the New Jersey skyline.

Coffee by the park was out. Too predictable. If someone wanted to shoot a cop, the park was a place where there would always be at least half a dozen at the beginning of a tour.

We found a secluded spot on an abandoned East River pier and backed the car precariously close to the end of the rotting structure. The only way psycho terrorist killers were going to get us now was by a frontal assault or if they had scuba gear.

We pulled Styrofoam cups from a paper sack and drank in silence. After ten minutes of staring into the darkness, I'd finally had enough.

"Hey, Kenny, you ever consider seeing someone about your problems?"

Kenny looked at me, a mystified expression on his face. "Problems? What problems?"

"Look, man, I've gotta work with you every day. My life depends on you having your head screwed on right and concentrating on what we're doing. You know—the here and now."

"Yeah? So?"

"So ever since your wife walked out on you, you've been acting weird. Then the Bovar thing—"

Kenny snorted.

"Now this brooding and arming yourself like the Vietcong are gonna attack the station house. It's a little upsetting. Look, I know you've been through a lot, but—"

"You bet your ass."

"But," I repeated, "if you're having a tough time coping, The Job's got people you can talk to."

"Hey, Jimmy, are you goddamn naive? I tell one of those shrinks that maybe I'm having a tough time sleeping nights and they put me in the Bow and Arrow Squad. No gun, no shield." He waved me off. "Tell you what, buddy. Maybe things haven't been rolling smooth with me the last few months, and maybe Rocco and Greg getting killed didn't help, but I'm coping. You can depend on me."

An illuminated billboard on the Queens side of the river cast an eerie glow inside the car. I looked at my partner and thought I saw tears in his eyes. Before I could say anything, the radio came to life.

"Nine foot post to Central, kay." It was Frank Moran speaking in a hushed voice.

"Central."

"I've got Herman Bell holed up in an apartment on Fifth Street between C and D. Requesting backup."

The coffee went out the window. "Oh, Christ," I muttered.

"Address, foot post?" Central responded.

There was a moment of silence; then Moran came back. "Seven-thirty-two. I'm in front of the building and"—a loud burp—"tell units no lights or sirens."

Kenny keyed the radio. "Charlie-Frank."

Another unit. "David."

Reddy came on board. "Nine, Sergeant."

We shot down the pier like we were being chased by Godzilla.

*   *   *

An armada of cops ringed East Fifth Street. In addition to every Ninth Precinct unit and the off-duty back-ups, three Emergency Service Unit trucks had responded. ESU cops wearing body armor were loading magazines into Stoner submachine guns when Kenny and I pulled up.

Sergeant Reddy was the ranking officer on the scene, although I was certain detective brass would soon arrive.

Reddy gathered us all in a circle.

"The building's halfway down the block. I want radio silence as we go down there. ESU will be first; we're following."

Jim Leidy said, "Shouldn't we wait for some brass, boss? You know someone's gonna be pissed if we go down there without a chief to take the glory."

"You've got a point, Jimmy," Reddy said, "but we've got a problem that requires we move out now."

Leidy looked perplexed. "What?"

"I can't find Moran."

Thirty-one cops snaked down the block like a spastic conga line. When we reached the front of the building, I spotted Frank Moran inside the vestibule. He opened the door a crack.

"Hey, Sarge," he whispered hoarsely, "c'mon up here."

We crouched against the building line while Sergeant Reddy went into the building, gun drawn. I saw Moran point to a wall, and then Reddy let loose with a string of curses. He threw the door open with such force that the glass shattered.

He stormed down the stairs and whipped out his portable. "Central, Nine patrol supervisor. East Fifth Street is unfounded; call off any responding units." He grabbed his driver, Andy Glover, by the arm. "C'mon, let's get out of here before the police commissioner shows up."

The ESU guys started back for their trucks, which left the Ninth Precinct grunts milling around with our proverbial phalluses in our hands.

"So what happened?" Kenny asked Sergeant Reddy.

I've never seen the sergeant so pissed. "Just go up and look." Then he mumbled, "Goddamn brain-damaged drunk," under his breath.

The lot of us ran up the stairs while the sergeant and Glover drove off. Moran was still in the vestibule, a shit-eating grin on his face.

"Hey, man, I thought I had the guy." He pointed to a row of mailboxes.

It was a typical array of minuscule tenement mailboxes with bells under each box. The years had turned the mailboxes and the bells one color, a dingy, rusty metallic gray, which made the buttons almost indistinguishable from the wall. The bells sort of blended in. One enterprising tenant chose to make life a little easier for any visitors and stuck a plastic label under his mailbox, right over the bell button, which read . . . BELL.

Frank Moran had thought Herman Bell lived in the apartment.

Within six months the entire BLA cadre was either arrested or killed. Twyman Myers was blown away in a shoot-out in the Bronx while attempting to escape from a regiment of cops. His body was brought to the Bellevue morgue. Kenny wanted to see the corpse.

"Aw, for crissakes, Kenny, what the hell for?" I asked.

"To make sure he's dead."

I humored him. We went.

When someone dies of gunshot wounds, six-inch sticks are placed into the entrance wounds to track the trajectory of incoming bullets.

Myers looked like a porcupine. There had to be fifteen sticks jutting in all directions. He was very dead.

"Satisfied?" I asked.

"Yeah, I suppose."

I heard later that a cop from the Ninth had smuggled a Polaroid camera into the morgue and taken a few pictures of Myers on a slab. Within days Myers's death photos were displayed prominently in every precinct in the city. It gave the cops a nice target to spit at.

Joanne Chesimard was locked up in New Jersey after she allegedly gunned down a state trooper. She escaped in short order, and rumor had it that she made it down to Cuba, via Algeria, and that Castro was hiding his fellow freedom fighter. She remains on the FBI's Ten Most Wanted List almost thirty years later and is the only active member of the BLA never brought to justice.

I thought of Chesimard throughout the years, living in relative safety and having no fear of paying for her crimes. While in custody, however briefly, she was impregnated by fellow BLA member Albert Washington in a holding cell. Her daughter is now older than Foster and Laurie were when they were cut down and is reportedly living with her mother in Cuba.

After I retired and became a private investigator, I handled a few cases that were international in scope. As a result, I acquired many sources within the intelligence and military communities of foreign countries.

In May 1999, I made contact through e-mail with Luis Lir Diegues (not his real name), a former (or active, I never found out which) Cuban intelligence officer who resides in Havana.

I told him who I was, making sure he was aware of my former police affiliation, and of my desire to contact Joanne Chesimard. He confirmed that Chesimard was in Cuba and that she had recently spoken at a rally. What was my purpose for contacting Chesimard? he asked.

"I'm a writer now," I told him (I was to send him a copy of my first book, *Jimmy the Wags: Street Stories of a Private Eye*), "and am interested in writing a book or at least a major magazine article about her."

Was I telling the truth? Would I manage to pull this off, and during the interview whip out a knife and cut her throat, or better yet, cuff her and deliver her to the Guantanamo Bay Naval Base?

My own motives confused me. Almost thirty years had passed since the BLA episode, the darkest period of the NYPD's glorious history.

Was Chesimard a genuine revolutionary or a bank-robbing, cop-killing thug? Is there a difference? She'd spent the last thirty years of her life in a country that's the last vestige of true communism left in the world. And she never left. Was this because she feared capture or she truly believed in the system? I wanted to find out, then make a decision as to what I would do, if anything, to bring her to justice.

Diegues told me that Chesimard didn't normally give interviews, which I did not find surprising, but he said he had influence and would see what he could do.

Months passed. Ground rules were set. I had to travel alone and be taken blindfolded to the meeting with Chesimard. No problem. I was getting closer.

I chose not to contact any law-enforcement agency, at least not yet.

Contact with Diegues continued until January 2000, when it abruptly ceased. My e-mails went unanswered. I had never spoken to, e-mailed, or otherwise had any contact with Chesimard. All the preliminaries were with Diegues. Or were they?

I never established who Diegues was or verified that he was aligned with the Cuban intelligence community. All I knew was what he told me and that he lived in Havana. After that, nothing. Were my inquiries being answered by Joanne Chesimard herself?

As of this writing I've heard nothing further from Diegues or anyone else in Cuba. Did Chesimard suspect a trap? Was Diegues a real Cuban spy? All unanswered questions.

I'm hoping to reestablish contact; until then, the killings of Gregory Foster and Rocco Laurie are never far from my conscious thought.

17

The Squad, Part III: Kenny Kenrick

One day Frank Moran vanished.

He had shown up straight from Cal's for a day tour, drunk but able to navigate. It seemed that the only time he wasn't drinking was when he was boxing. He would stay sober for two days prior to a bout, for which he didn't train. He would invariably lose, getting his brains further scrambled in the process. The last we saw of him that fateful morning, he was strolling toward Third Avenue to walk the foot post of his choice.

The prevailing attitude on The Job back then was to protect drunks as long as they weren't hurting themselves or anyone else. These days, if a cop shows up for work smelling of Listerine someone will turn him in.

But with Frank Moran, there was little the bosses wanted to do with him, other than protect his job. Sympathy for the death of his brother and how it had affected him had taken priority over their responsibility to the citizens of New York. Besides, cops and bosses from the Ninth stuck together. It was bad enough the rest of the world was trying to bump us off; at least we had each other.

Frank had been a damn good cop at one time and everyone liked him. Now that his retirement was but a few years away, no one saw the need to jam him up. If he was crying for help it would have been a different story, but he was content to survive day to day, wandering around the precinct on foot and handling minor street altercations.

Initially, it was thought that he was off on a bender somewhere, but when hours led to days and then to weeks, a natural alarm was sounded. Was there a new terrorist group out there targeting cops? Did they assassinate him? Kidnap him?

Kenny and I had our own theories. If Moran was a victim of BLA-like terrorists, whether as a murder or kidnap victim, someone most certainly would have claimed credit, because that's what terrorists do. To terrorize, one must publicize (thank you, Johnnie Cochran).

"He probably kept walking west and fell into the Hudson. Bet he washes up during the spring thaw," Kenny said. The emergence of spring invariably brought numerous bodies bobbing to the surface. You could set a watch by it.

"I think he just got fed up and took off," I said. "Enough is enough. Too much death in this precinct."

We were both partially right. After two weeks, the FBI got involved because of the possible terrorist angle. If it happened once with the BLA it could happen again.

They traced Moran to Cooperstown, in upstate New York. Turns out he headed north, as Kenny had predicted, and chose Cooperstown as his new home because the Baseball Hall of Fame is located there. It seems Moran was a fan. Enough *had* been enough, as I'd predicted, and he'd just boogied.

He was charged with being AWOL and quitting The Job without the permission of the police commissioner, both serious offenses. You can't take a piss on The Job without the PC's okay. Moran was fired, losing all pension rights.

Funny thing is, he could have fought the charges. His alcoholism and the death of his brother may have caused a mental breakdown, thereby resulting in his aberrant behavior. That angle would have at least saved his pension. But he chose not to have anything further to do with the NYPD, took his punishment, and settled into a new life upstate.

Kenny and I were the last of the original Sixth Squad. Of course, replacements were immediately assigned as our numbers dwindled, but we didn't get friendly with the new troops. This was a subtle, subconscious way of avoiding undue grief should something happen to them.

Kenny figured it out. "Did the same thing in Vietnam," he told me one night. "You've got your inner core of friends within an infantry squad, usually your assistant gunner and ammo bearer if you were a machine gunner like me, but you kept your distance from the rest of the platoon. If you don't know them that well, you can't be too broken up if they buy it."

Kenny was still struggling with his inner demons. His appearance, while by no means sloppy, was decidedly unmilitary. He still wore his jump boots, and they were always polished, but they didn't blind you with their usual spit-shine. His shirts were ironed, but without the razor creases he'd sported when I had first arrived in the command.

I don't subscribe to the Vietnam vet theory that was, and still is, popular in this country. Anytime a veteran of the Vietnam War begins to act weird, his troubles are usually automatically attributed to his combat experiences.

While any war recollections can be disturbing, I can name numerous friends who survived the Vietnam War, and its unpleasant memories, and went on to live normal, productive lives.

Kenny's funk, I believe, had more to do with the police department and what he'd seen on the mean streets of New York over an extended period of time. His street experiences had directly contributed to his failed marriages. His Vietnam memories, if anything, were a crutch on which he relied for escape from the frustrations of the present. Most cops get divorced, but most cops didn't fight in Vietnam. To Kenny, the military was a symbol of order, with clearly defined rules and authority. The streets of the EVil were just so much disarray.

One of the reasons a person becomes a police officer is because crime offends his or her sense of order, and the military is the quintessential orderly lifestyle. The inability to create order out of the chaos puts some cops over the edge, particularly those with a military background. Kenny followed that pattern.

On a brisk March night there was a break in the action.

"Pull over; I want to talk to this guy," Kenny said. He pointed to a skinny white male, about twenty-five, in jeans and an army field jacket, complete with buck sergeant's stripes, unit patch (First Infantry Division), and a Combat Infantry badge. He was unshaven, his hair was long and scraggly, and he carried a crudely scrawled cardboard sign that read, VIETNAM VET NEEDS FOOD AND SHELTER.

We'd seen this character standing on a corner near Tompkins Square Park for about a week. At his feet was an upended U.S. Army dress cap, an invitation to contribute money.

I pulled the car over. GI Joe threw back his shoulders and flipped us a sharp salute, but not before scooping a pile of bills out of his hat. "Evening, Officers." His eyes sparkled with a joviality that belied his appearance.

"Yeah, good evening," Kenny said. "You been to Vietnam?"

"Yes, sir. Big Red One, sixty-five to sixty-six. You guys, too?"

"Just me, First Cav. My partner's a draft dodger." Kenny and the former GI laughed. "Boonie humper?"

"Did my bit as an Eleven-B-Ten—rifleman with the Sixteenth Infantry."

"Hitting on hard times?" Kenny inquired.

"Some. You don't mind if I try to hustle up some dough, do you? Got nowhere to live; my wife threw me out. Need some seed money. You know what I mean?" He winked.

"Yeah," Kenny responded, "I know what you mean. You take it easy, okay?"

"Yes, sir." He got another highball salute, sharp and crisp.

We got back in the car and drove in silence for a while;

then Kenny said quietly, "Drive by the house, would you, Jimmy?"

"You feeling okay?"

"Yeah. I just want to test Sergeant Rock back there. Need to get something."

"You don't think he's on the level? He seemed to have all the right answers."

Kenny snorted. "He had the answers, but not the eyes."

"Meaning?"

We pulled in front of the station house. "Meaning the Thousand-Mile Stare. He don't have it."

The Thousand-Mile Stare is the look a combat veteran will get when he's seen too much death. It's a dull, vacant expression that extends outward from the eyes—the true definition of a poker face. I knew this because more than a few of the cops in the Ninth had that look. They could be recognized as cops from a considerable distance. I practiced in front of a mirror to avoid getting "the look," with only moderate success. I think I'm the proud owner of a Five-Hundred-Mile Stare, but I'm working on it. I still have it, even after ten years of retirement. Kenny had a Two-Thousand-Mile Stare.

Kenny went into the station house while I monitored the radio. The Ninth was backed up over ten jobs, and I was getting more than a little fidgety when Kenny finally emerged, carrying a piece of rolled-up cardboard.

"What's that?" I asked.

"Tell you later."

"C'mon," I said, "we've gotta take something; Adam's picking up our jobs."

"Okay," Kenny said, settling in. He keyed the radio and picked up a past burglary on Avenue B. "Back to our friend first. The burglar's long gone; the complainant can wait a few minutes."

I humored him and made for the park. The ex-soldier, or whoever he was, still stood on the same corner. We waved; he saluted. I pulled the radio car to the curb in front of him. We got another smile.

"Back so soon, Officers?" There was a wariness in his voice despite his outward conviviality.

Kenny unrolled the cardboard. With a felt-tip black marker he'd written, *I CORPS*. He turned it so that the panhandler could see it. "Tell me what this says."

The ex-soldier laughed nervously. "What's this all about?"

Kenny smiled, but I saw no humor in his eyes. "My partner and I are having a little disagreement. Maybe you can help us out. What's this say?" The last sentence was forceful, the friendliness gone.

The panhandler stepped back from the car and examined the sign, brows knit. He licked his lips. "Uh, it says, 'One Corp.'" He said it with a hard P.

Kenny turned to me. "See, numbnuts, I was right."

I played along, mystified. "When you're right, you're right."

The former soldier seemed to deflate. He smiled. Kenny smiled.

"You hang in there, buddy," Kenny said. "We gotta go."

We got another salute, and I pulled out.

"What the hell was that all about?"

"He failed the test." Kenny pointed down the street. "Stop around the corner and park."

"We're on the clock, Kenny . . . the past burglary."

"Fuck the past burglary; pull around the corner." There was fire in his eyes.

I was getting hot, too. "We're going to the goddamn job." I accelerated. He grabbed my arm.

His voice softened. "Jimmy, please, a few more minutes, okay?"

There was pleading in the request, an urgency. I pulled around the corner.

It was a little after ten o'clock. The streets around the park were dark and nearly deserted. Junkies don't like the cold. The few stragglers still out and about were waiting for a late delivery from Junkies R Us.

Kenny opened the door and looked at me, grinning.

"I'll be right back, dear; keep a light on." Manic. Panicked one second, jovial the next.

As I watched him walk away, curiosity got the better of me. I got out of the car and poked my head around the corner.

Kenny ambled up to the panhandler. They talked, but I couldn't hear what they were saying. Kenny pointed across the street to an alley and they both walked toward it. They had left my field of vision, so I crossed the street for a better angle.

Kenny backed the veteran into the mouth of the alley, out of the glare of the street's only lamppost. What the hell was Kenny doing?

Then I saw the gun.

Kenny had drawn his service revolver and stuck it in the soldier's gut. I looked around to see if anyone else had seen it. Other than a few nervous, strung-out, oblivious junkies looking for their connections, the block was empty.

The soldier was giving Kenny money, emptying his pockets in furious movements, while Kenny stuffed his pockets with cash. After what seemed like an eternity, the soldier held up his hands. Kenny reared back and laid the barrel of his Smith & Wesson across the panhandler's face.

Blood spattered from his nose and he went down. Kenny holstered his gun and started for the car. I ran across the street and cut him off, grabbed his shoulder, and spun him around.

"What the fuck did you do?"

Kenny's eyes were wild. "In the car, in the car." He broke loose, walked rapidly toward the radio car, and got in. I climbed in after him, envisioning a small army of bosses from Internal Affairs at my doorstep in the morning.

I left rubber and made for the East River, the past burglary we were supposed to be handling a distant memory.

We drove in silence. I slammed the car into park

after I backed onto a secluded, deserted pier. "Talk to me."

"The cocksucker was a liar." Kenny was breathing heavily, his eyes wide as hubcaps, his head nodding. "He's never been to Vietnam."

What was happening? "A liar . . . what liar? You held the son of a bitch up! At friggin' gunpoint!"

"The sign," Kenny said, calming down, "it says *Eye Corp,* like eyeball, and a soft P. Every soldier that ever passed through Vietnam knows that. It's the northern-most sector—"

"I don't give a fuck!" I was livid. "You stuck him up, for crissakes. We lock people up for that."

Kenny exploded.

"That motherfucker has no right! He has no right! Soldiers died; they died!" He spun in his seat, facing me. "Cops're dying, too, man; there's nobody left. That cocksucker is disgracing every cop and soldier who ever wore a uniform!"

I tried to be calm, the voice of reason. "Kenny, he's a con artist; the uniform's got nothing to do with it. Next week he'll be a priest or Ronald McDonald. You can't take this shit personally. You should know this by now."

"Oh, yeah? What happens if next week he's a fucking cop? What happens if next week he's wearing Rocco Laurie's fucking shield number? Huh? What then?"

Kenny was making absolutely no sense. At least not to me. A few seconds later he began pounding his fists on the dashboard. Tears came to his eyes; then they un-leashed in a flood—tears for every cop and soldier who was ever killed, tears for his inability to maintain a rela-tionship, tears for the hopelessness of it all.

I let him cry. After a while I put a hand on his shoul-der. I hoped that my presence wasn't embarrassing him. He didn't seem to notice.

We never handled that past burglary. Kenny had me drive to a church off Broadway, where he gave all the money he'd just stolen to an astonished priest. I put us out of service, drove to the station house, and Kenny went sick. He headed straight to the locker room to change while I checked in with Sergeant Reddy.

"What's wrong with your partner?" Reddy asked.

"Something he ate, Sarge. I've got some time on the books; can I follow him home, make sure he makes it?"

Being stupid is not one of the prerequisites for becoming a sergeant. Sergeant Reddy knew something wasn't right, but in the Ninth we stuck together.

"No problem. Call me if you need anything."

My calls to Kenny's apartment went unanswered. After two days I drove by his building and found his car parked around the corner. I debated knocking on his door and decided to come back later that day. After dinner I went back and found that his car had been moved to the front of the building. I went home.

Kenny stayed out for the rest of the set. He came back to work after the swing.

It was a new Kenny Kenrick who came through the door of the station house for our first day tour.

"Yo, Jimmy, how's it hanging?"

He was smiling from ear to ear. His formerly dead eyes sparkled.

"You high?" I asked, only half joking.

"Yeah, buddy, on life." And with that he bounded up the stairs toward the locker room, his uniform slung across his shoulder in a garment bag.

Kenny stood roll call like part of the honor guard for the Unknown Soldier. His boots were polished to an eye-tearing shine.

"How the hell do you do that?" Jim Liedy asked, admiring the best spit-shine I'd ever seen.

"Cotton balls, tap water, shoe polish, and six hours," Kenny said.

Liedy shook his head. "I think you gotta get laid more."

"Job's fucked me enough," Kenny said, and laughed. The military creases were back. Even his pistol belt, cuff case, and holster were spit-shined.

Kenny took some good-natured ribbing. Even Sergeant Reddy doled out a few shots.

"Wags, Kenrick, Sector Charlie, thirteen hundred meal. Kenny, *GQ*'s outside; they wanna do a spread."

Kenny grinned. "Spread this."

I was glad to see him back from the brink. Whatever transpired during the time he was out would forever remain a mystery. I didn't ask and he didn't volunteer any information.

Kenny was positively effervescent in the car. Shortly after the tour began, we found ourselves rolling down St. Marks Place. Kenny pointed to a garishly dressed hippie.

He beckoned him over to the car. This was a young kid, maybe nineteen, wearing blue-and-white bell-bottoms, an orange pirate-type shirt, and a tie-dyed denim jacket. His Mohawk " 'do" sported a red-and-purple dye job.

The kid was scared. "Yes, Officer?"

Kenny said, "I had sex with a parrot once, thought maybe you were my son."

I cracked up, the kid caught on and laughed nervously, and Kenny waved him off.

We were pulling off the block when we heard the familiar radio beeps. Five in a row. Trouble. I had my usual testicular tightening. "Oh, shit."

Central: "In the Ninth, we've got a jumper. Front of three-fifteen East Thirteenth Street. Units?"

Kenny keyed the radio. "Frank, central. Victim down or threatening?"

Central: "Off the roof, sidewalk in front of."

It took a moment for the address to register. It was Oric Bovar's building.

We'd seen Bovar in front of his church over the last few months, still painting his sidewalk. Kenny was nervous around him and steered clear when he was driving, and I managed to stay off the block entirely unless we had a job there.

"That's Bovar's—" I started.

"I know," Kenny said ominously.

An ambulance was already on the scene, a crowd just beginning to gather.

Oric Bovar's body, clothed in its usual attire, lay supine in the middle of the sidewalk. He seemed oddly intact, considering he'd made the leap from atop a five-story building.

His eyes were open, and he lay on his back, arms outstretched. Crucified without a cross. A small halo of blood was forming around his head.

"Anyone see this?" I asked the crowd.

Five people stepped forward. All described Bovar on the roof, seemingly praying before he did a swan dive toward the pavement, twisting in midair to land on his back.

I began moving the crowd back. Kenny was shaking his head.

"Jimmy, check this out."

I looked at the body, not realizing what he was referring to. Then I spotted it.

Bovar had landed smack in the middle of his artwork—a bull's-eye.

All those months he'd been painting a goddamn bull's-eye to jump into.

"Jesus Christ," I muttered. I heard more units responding, sirens screaming.

We finally got to see Bovar's church. Six of his "disciples," four men and two women, admitted us after Bovar's body had been carted to the morgue. No tears among the flock, just serenity and good fellowship.

"He had been planning this for months," a young woman with waist-length, raven-colored hair told us.

"He'll be back, you know," another said.

"Back where?" Kenny asked. He seemed to be taking the suicide pretty well. We hadn't been there fifteen minutes and he'd already come up with a lame Bovar joke. (It's a bird, it's a plane . . . !)

"He will rise from the dead," Raven Hair told us.

"Oh, yeah?" Kenny said. "When he comes back tell him to give me a call. I want to tell him he was right."

Now it was my turn. "Right about what?"

Kenny smirked. "Death from Above."

*   *   *

Old Oric turned out to be a pretty popular guy. He was laid out in a funeral home on Tenth Street, and it was standing room only. Of course, his followers attended, but a surprising number of politicians and celebrities showed up also. I recall seeing John Belushi and a few *Saturday Night Live* players, plus a few local musicians.

We passed the funeral parlor on the second day of the three-day wake.

"Wanna go in?" I asked Kenny.

"Nah, I'll catch him when he comes back."

Out of the mouths of cops . . .

Bovar did come back.

Bovar's body vanished from the funeral home the following night. We picked up the "missing body" job and went right to Bovar's church.

Sure enough, reposing in a makeshift coffin in an apartment on the top floor, basking in the glow of candlelight and surrounded by a dozen chanting devotees, was Oric Bovar, dead guy.

"Okay," Kenny announced, "you're all under arrest."

"What for?" one of them asked.

"Harboring a dead body," Kenny responded, sounding officious. "It's a misdemeanor."

"But he's not dead," a woman said (she actually looked worse than Oric). "He's in a state of transposition. He's returning."

"Good," I said, "then he'll be here when you get back."

We called the morgue wagon, booked the kooky cluster ("See," Kenny said, "smooth foreheads."), and repaired to Cal's for a few cocktails.

It was like old times. Kenny's return to being Kenny seemed like a permanent thing, and I couldn't have been more pleased. For a while there I'd begun to worry that he was losing his sanity.

The bar was packed with expectant cops—all expecting to get drunk and most well on their way.

I'd reached my two-drink limit. Kenny saw that I was getting restless.

"Looking to go home?"

"Yeah, Pat waits up on the four-to-twelves."

"You're lucky, you know. Got a wife, a kid—a little boy. Nice having someone to go home to," he said wistfully.

I wanted to break the mood. "You will, too, Kenny. Sometimes it takes time to find the right girl." I looked at my watch and stood. "Hey, gotta go." He grabbed my arm.

"One second, one second. I ever show you this?" He opened the top buttons of his shirt and pulled out a gold dog tag suspended around his neck on a thin golden chain.

"I've seen it in the locker room, sure."

"My most cherished thing in the world." He fingered it lovingly. "I melted down four eighteen-carat gold rings, made my own mold, and poured it myself. Used my real dog tag, imperfections and all. Had to take it to a jeweler to smooth it out, though. Didn't have the tools. Here, check it out." He removed the dog tag from his neck and handed it to me.

I felt odd touching it, like it was something real, alive, and it had seen much more than I ever had. What could anyone possibly buy in a jewelry store that would have more value than this flat piece of gold?

"It's beautiful, Kenny." I handed it back gingerly.

He looped it back around his neck. "Something happens to me, Wags, I want you to have it."

"What? Kenny, come on, nothing—"

He held up a hand. "Nothing's gonna happen? C'mon, this is the Ninth Precinct," he said with a laugh. Then quietly he said, "Anything could happen."

I left him at the bar. As I hit the street I heard his hearty laugh and a chorus of guffaws right behind it. Kenny Kenrick was working the room.

Kenny was late for our first day tour.

"Where's your partner?" Sergeant Reddy asked me as I stood by watching the rest of the platoon file out into the street.

"Hey, Sarge, I don't know. He was gonna be late he'd call. I—"

A clerk hollered from the desk. "Wags, Kenny's on three."

I smiled at the sergeant. "See, car probably on the fritz."

I picked up the phone and the clerk punched me through. I heard traffic noise.

"Wags?"

"Kenny? Where the hell are you?"

"Goddamn car broke down four blocks on the wrong side of the Brooklyn Bridge."

"You stay there; I'll pick you up."

"Nah, I'll grab a gypsy. Hey, there's one now." He yelled, "Over here!"

"Okay," I said, "I'll be out front picking up the jobs." I started to cradle the receiver.

"Yo, hey, Wags!"

"Yeah, Kenny?"

"Take care, okay?"

"I think I can manage for ten minutes." But he'd already hung up.

Five minutes after speaking with his partner, Police Officer James Wagner, on the telephone, Police Officer Kenneth Kenrick, while off-duty and on his way to work in a livery cab, asked the driver to stop in the middle of the Brooklyn Bridge. When the driver complied, Police Officer Kenrick exited the vehicle, placed his off-duty revolver to his head, and pulled the trigger, killing himself instantly.

—Excerpted from the official NYPD Unusual Report.

18
Suicide

In addition to being totally shocked and grief-stricken, I had a thousand questions.

Kenny's suicide came seemingly out of nowhere. He'd seemed so up, so animated. Did Bovar's suicide drive him over the edge? If it did, he'd disguised his true feelings pretty well.

A cop killing himself is not a rare event. Law enforcement professionals alternate with dentists as the top two jobs that provoke the most suicides. It's a rare cop who doesn't know someone who ate his or her gun. Kenny was the first of my friends to take that final drastic step, but by no means the last. While males lead the pack, the number of female cops who end it all is rapidly rising.

Although self-destruction is almost commonplace, The Job still stigmatizes the act. Often a suicide is disguised as an accidental death resulting from a gun-cleaning mishap, usually explained as a dropped pistol that landed on its hammer, thereby firing a round. This is virtually impossible because of the automatic safety bar that separates the hammer from the firing pin in police-issued firearms. The only way a cop's gun fires is when the trigger is pulled, and that takes thirteen pounds of pressure. Difficult to do accidentally.

Funerals of suicides are always guilt-ridden affairs. Everyone blames themselves for not seeing the signs, but the major guilt falls on the partner. In this case, me.

Kenny was in great spirits. What signs had been evident? The guilt was killing me. Why hadn't I seen *something*?

"It wasn't your fault, Wags," Sergeant Reddy said at the funeral.

Kenny's was not a line-of-duty death; there were no politicians in attendance, no brass, just the cops of the Ninth Precinct, reeling from yet another brother's violent end.

I took a week off. My dad and I took a ride upstate, just to get out of the city and look at the early spring scenery, away from the squalor and smell of death.

We stopped in a little town, Roscoe, in the Catskills and had lunch in a tiny diner. I hadn't mentioned Kenny for the entire two-hour ride. My father broke the ice.

"They're happiest when they know they're gonna do it, you know."

I was lost in thought, hands wrapped around a steaming cup of coffee. "Huh?"

"A suicide. Cops particularly. Once a cop makes the decision he's gonna kill himself, his whole attitude changes. He goes from morose to positively tickled."

"Really?" I said. I shook my head. "That makes no sense."

"Does if you think about it. Kenny wrestled with his demons, probably for a long time; you said so yourself."

"Yeah."

"He was melancholy, erratic—he *looked* like he was gonna eat his gun. Had you worried, remember?"

"So you're telling me once he made his mind up to do it, *that* put him in a good mood?"

"Sure. He'd fought the urge; now the fight was over. He was relieved."

"You've seen this?"

My father snorted. He looked a lot older than his forty-nine years. Over the last few months he'd dropped some weight ("No good places to eat anymore; Staten Island's going to hell."), and virtually quit drinking hard liquor. He still rode with Dave Ballantine, but they were dinosaurs, unable to comprehend the speed at which the world was changing. Their little fiefdom in Stapleton was being invaded by the marauding hordes, and they were overwhelmed. Still, they were fighting the good fight, although outgunned and branded pariahs by the people they served in a place where at one time they had been both loved and feared.

"Seen it? Jimmy, have I got stories for you."

A desk lieutenant, my dad told me, had signed himself out for meal, gone downstairs to the supervisor's locker room, opened up his locker, sat in it, pulled out his gun, and shot himself in the head.

"We heard the report. Loud as a son of a bitch. It was in Midtown South; Dave and I had a parade detail. Ran downstairs; there he was." He smiled ruefully. "I was about your age. It was the first time I'd ever seen a dead cop. What shocked me wasn't so much the suicide but how he got his fat ass in that locker." He spread his hands. "Ass as wide as the dashboard of a Buick—took the Jaws of Life to get him out."

I had to smile. Cops have an odd sense of humor. Keeps us going. Most of us.

"Why'd he do it?"

My dad shrugged. "I heard later he was named in a corruption case, but only as a witness. Real reason? His father was a chief, worked for the PC in the Puzzle Palace. Broke his son's balls, wanted him to be a superchief, continue the family legacy. The story around the precinct was that he never wanted to be a cop in the first place. Even if the kid was called before a grand jury for something he had nothing to do with, it's a career killer."

"That bothered him? Couple of years, it would have been forgotten; he would've been back on track."

"His old man didn't see it that way. The kid killed himself because he embarrassed his father."

We drove up what a city boy like me considered a mountain, meaning a hill higher than the escalator at Grand Central Station.

We followed a winding tree-lined road that meandered

past horse farms, a country club, and wooden firetrap resorts all named Something Manor or Lodge. After about twenty minutes the road widened, the trees thinned, and we found ourselves next to a lake.

"Remember this place?" Dad asked. "Tanana Lake?"

"No, should I?"

"I guess not. You were young, maybe five, six. We came up here one day with Dave. Went fishing."

It was an overcast day. Pillows of diaphanous fog settled over the lake. Summer cottages hugged the shoreline, abutting rotting piers suspended on rickety pilings. Nearby, off the main road, was a cluster of nursing homes. Some of the residents were in wheelchairs, blankets across their laps, facing the water, heads drooping, eyes unseeing, abandoned by their caregivers to enjoy the view. My father looked at them, then quickly turned away.

"Don't ever put me in one of these places, okay, Jimmy?" he said.

I felt myself flush. "Hey, Dad, I would never—"

"I hope not." He rubbed my shoulder. "Let's get off this grim subject and talk about something different." He smiled. "Wanna hear some more suicide stories?"

I did. Call it morbid fascination, but I had to know what drove a cop to kill himself. I wondered if what I feared most was that one day I'd be in a state of mind where I'd be pondering the ultimate solution.

The New York City Police Department Museum is recognized around the world as an achievement in recording the history not only of the NYPD but of the city itself.

Until the 1980s the museum was housed in the Police Academy (it was eventually moved to 1 Police Plaza) and run by one cop. Not a cop of high rank, just a patrolman (as police officers were known in the seventies) with a penchant for collecting NYPD memorabilia.

I'm specifically not naming the officers who committed suicide here. Their families have suffered enough. So call this cop Officer Al.

Officer Al was more an academician than a cop. He

was an extremely smart man in his thirties who collected, cataloged, and pampered artifacts from the earliest recorded period of The Job.

Officer Al spent a lot of his own money procuring NYPD memorabilia, items that he then altruistically donated to the museum.

He also gave enlightening guided tours of the museum to visiting politicians and dignitaries. His knowledge of the history of the NYPD was awe-inspiring. Yes, Officer Al was definitely a genius. But he had one failing.

"He couldn't pass a sergeant's test. He failed five of them," my dad recounted.

To get promoted in the NYPD, a cop has to pass civil service examinations. The only exception is promotion to the rank of detective. That is often a tenuous position where you serve at the discretion of the police commissioner. Besides, some cops aren't meant to be detectives. For them, it's the civil service route, sergeant being the first hurdle.

Officer Al, despite his superior intelligence, couldn't pass the damn test, and it bothered the hell out of him. It was all he talked about. To be fair, it's a difficult exam, and it's geared more toward the street cop rather than the academician.

One day, while tending to his trophies, Officer Al shot himself in the head. The cops who heard the shot raced to the scene to find the dead cop slumped over behind his desk, gun in hand.

"His death went down as an accident," Dad said. "An accidental discharge while cleaning his service gun. Oddly enough, the responding detectives found an open gun-cleaning kit on his desk." Dad snorted. "Gee, I wonder how it got there?"

"The cop was fighting with his wife," my dad was explaining. "He was the type who liked to do a four-to-four tour."

A four-to-four is Job parlance for a cop who goes to a bar after a four-to-twelve tour. Bars in New York close at four A.M. Do the math.

"So this goes on for months. Finally he trips home drunk for the umpteenth time, just as his bride is making breakfast. The kids are already on their way to school.

"Him and his wife get into a heated argument over the breakfast table, he flings a bowl of Cheerios to the floor, says something like, 'I'll show you, you cunt,' whips out his gun, and kills himself."

"He showed her, all right," I said, finding the whole thing hard to comprehend.

My father and I were in the middle of the lake in a rented rowboat. The fog had burned off and the sun reflected off the water. We had also obtained two beat-up fishing poles and a tin of worms from the old man who rented us the boat. So far no luck, but I was more interested in my father's stories than in fishing.

"Worked with a guy named Miller once. Quiet cop, bright guy, on the sergeant's list, single, kept mostly to himself. One day I'm off and I had this burning desire to see the movie *Al Capone* with Rod Steiger." Dad rubbed his chin. "I guess this was in 'fifty-seven, maybe 'fifty-eight.

"I'll never forget this as long as I live. So I take the ferry—this was a few years before the bridge—and two trains to the Victoria Theater on Broadway and Forty-seventh. The movie was only playing in Manhattan, no multiplexes back then.

"I just made the start, settled in with a bag of popcorn, and enjoyed the show. Afterward, the lights come on and who do I see but Miller, sitting by himself about six rows down. He spots me, all smiles. We leave the theater together, walk across the street to check out the pimp clothes in Leighton's, and wind up in Jack Dempsey's saloon for a few cocktails.

"We got a little fucked up, five drinks or so each. Miller turns out to be a regular guy, good sense of humor. Maybe the booze loosened him up a little, who knows.

"Anyway, I wanna get home in time for dinner and Miller wants to check out another movie. Okay, I leave." His pole was yanked into the calm lake water. "Hey, I got one!"

Dad landed a trout. We marveled at what a great fisherman he was and he threw it back. Live and let live.

"So what happened with Miller?"

"Oh, yeah." He baited the hook and tossed the line over the side. "Next day, I walk into the precinct and the whole place is buzzing. Miller wound up under a downtown A train an hour after I left him."

"Wow. Could've been an accident," I said. "He was drinking; maybe he fell."

My father turned to look at me; then his eyes grew distant, searching the past.

"Maybe."

We got off the subject. We called it a day after three hours in the boat, my father's trout the only score.

When we settled into the car he asked, "Want to grab something to eat?"

"Sure."

"I know a place."

The joint was the Skytop Lodge. I remember because it burned down the next day and the story made the *Daily News*.

We ate fresh grilled catfish and baked potatoes, washed down with a few beers. Over dessert and coffee my father said, "I've got a few more. Up for them?"

I knew what he meant. I could've heard a dozen more stories. "Yeah, sure."

He told me about a cop he'd worked with when he first came on The Job. Young guy, seemingly stable, good family man.

"His father dies, not unexpectedly, cancer or something. At the grave site, as they're lowering the casket into the ground, this cop pulls out his gun, shoots himself in the head, falls into the hole with his father's coffin."

"Jesus."

"Sergeant and his driver patrolling the Two-Six Precinct in Harlem. Sergeant was a friend of Dave's. A few hours into the tour the cop driving the boss needs to use the head. The closest place is a construction site with those portable johns. The cop wanders off into the site while the sergeant catches up on some paperwork in the car. After a while, still no cop. The sergeant gets concerned, goes looking for him. Finds him on the bowl, pants down, gun in his hand. Shot himself in the head. DOA."

He saw the concern on my face.

"Look, Jimmy, I know what you've gone through with Kenny and all. What I'm trying to tell you is that you or me could've been Kenny or any of these other guys."

I liked to think that I was a pretty stable person, and I conveyed that to my father.

"I bet Kenny thought he was a stable person, too," my dad said. "So'd all those other guys. What it is, is the availability of the gun."

I was listening.

"My theory, but I think a valid one: Firemen see much the same kind of shit we do, sometimes worse. How many firemen do you know who kill themselves? Almost unheard-of. Bet if they carried guns they'd be right up there with us."

"Not too easy to off yourself with a hose, huh?"

He smirked. "Exactly. It's a spur-of-the-moment thing. The world gets to be too much for a cop, the fancy hits him, he pulls out the gun, boom! He can't say then, 'Aw, shit, I didn't mean to do that.' "

We drove home in a sleek rain. Talk was kept to a minimum. What little we said was mostly commentary on the weather and traffic.

As we paid the toll on the Verrazano Bridge, I asked him if he wanted to come by my house to see Pat and my son.

"Not today—your mother's been cooking something special." He seemed pensive for a moment, lost in thought, perhaps pumping life into old ghosts.

"Jimmy, I want you to think about something, okay?"

"Yeah, sure, Dad. What?"

"Retirement."

I laughed. "Hey, Dad, I've got thirteen years to go before I pull the pin."

He touched my shoulder. "We live fast lives, Jimmy,

cops do. Twenty or more years of adrenaline racing on a day-to-day basis. Then you retire and it stops. We're not 'us' anymore, not a member of the fraternity. We're 'them,' part of the problem, a civilian."

This, he confided, was one of the reasons retirement scared him. How do you go from the excitement of police work, seeing all we see, to having to listen to your relatives bitching about crabgrass or the price of tomatoes?

"You know, who gives a fuck about this petty shit? I know I don't." He looked at me. "You don't either."

He was right. Time spent with someone who hadn't handled a quadruple homicide was like being with someone who lived in a bubble. I never took The Job home with me, never discussed it with anyone but my fellow cops, but I liked being *around* others who'd lived on the edge.

"It's worse for the war veterans who become cops," Dad said. "Years of maximum velocity to a dead stop. Some don't make it to retirement."

I thought of Kenny.

"The average cop has very little tolerance for civilians," he added. "Most haven't seen anything in their lives, and what's important to them bores the shit out of us. I don't really give a damn about my neighbor's tough day at the phone company. Can't relate. I dread the day when I gotta pull the pin."

"It's a while off yet," I said.

"Not too far off. You'll have that fear, too, that fear of being bored, of knowing exactly what you're gonna do every day." He shuddered. "Man, that's gotta be the worst feeling in the world." His eyes became distant again. "You know, a lot of guys leave The Job, sit home, and watch soap operas. Suicides happen more after retirement. You don't wanna hear about those."

We pulled up in front of his house, the home I grew up in. He got out of the car, leaned in the window, and kissed me on the cheek.

"You get out, Jimmy; go with something that won't make you bored. It's a death sentence. Plan for it now; think about the future." He smiled.

"What're you gonna do when you retire?"

He laughed and shrugged. "Who knows? But you can bet your ass it'll have some variety." I watched him walk into the house.

I think Oric Bovar's death was the last straw for Kenny. He was fragile to begin with, and Bovar represented a slim thread of reliability because Bovar knew what he wanted. While Kenny's world was crumbling around him, he saw in Bovar a man who believed in something, no matter how aberrant. Bovar believed in his own destiny and had the will to convince himself that he would return from the dead.

Kenny admired Bovar's strong beliefs in a world where he saw no order, no absolutes. While outwardly scoffing at Bovar's "church," he admired the man's conviction and inner strength.

If Oric Bovar could make the ultimate decision, take the ultimate step, so could Kenny Kenrick.

In the end, I couldn't take the dog tag.

Kenny had been wearing it when he shot himself. It went with him to the grave. Amidst all his pain, one of the few times I saw warmth in Kenny's eyes was that day in Cal's when he caressed that hunk of gold.

I wasn't going to deny him that.

19

Flight Attendant Abel

I was partnerless, and as such, subject to every crappy detail and fill-in assignment in the precinct.

I chose to go it alone while I decompressed. While I missed Kenny and wanted a partner, leaping into another close life-or-death relationship with another cop so soon after my partner's death wasn't advisable. I didn't want to act too soon after my loss and find that I wasn't compatible with my choice.

So I kept busy. Ever since my Academy days I'd been a physical-fitness buff. Not only did I not fall into a bottle like some cops, but I made almost daily trips to the gym, a habit I still adhere to today. However, sometimes it was tough to schedule workouts because of rotating shifts.

There were other cops of the same mind. Rather than drown their frustrations in booze, they would seek the solace and release of a few hours in the gym pumping iron. But between the difficult work schedule, court dates, and overtime, a cop desiring to hit the gym could go a week before finally getting there.

With the permission of the bosses, I began to solicit funds from local businesses to put together a gym in the station house. Local businesspeople recognized the value of a fit, happy cop, and in a short while I collected enough donations to launch a first-class gym with modern equipment.

While the Ninth was the first precinct in the city to have such a gym, within a few years, money for precinct gyms was allocated in the city budget. By the late eighties, every patrol command in the city had a modern workout facility.

While I cherished my role as the Arnold Schwarzenegger of the EVil and was appreciated for the work I was doing to get the command in shape, I was still a cop without a partner. I was still getting my share of shit details and training assignments.

In addition to a parking-ticket quota (yes, Virginia, there is a quota, despite vehement denials from politicians), commands were mandated to send cops to various training programs.

Precincts are obligated to maintain minimum manning—the absolute minimum number of cops that must be on hand to patrol a given command during a specific tour. Minimum manning is etched in stone. A precinct commander would sooner march through 1 Police Plaza wearing a sandwich board reading, THE POLICE COMMISSIONER SUCKS! than go below minimum manning in his command.

So rather than put a radio-car team out of service, cops without partners were the first to be sent to every inane training program in the NYPD.

I became the best-trained cop on The Job. I attended Radio School; Scooter School; the short-lived Black and White Police Dialogue, where black and white cops bullshitted each other for three days on how good race relations were within the NYPD; Advanced Weapons School; Crowd Control School; and the most useless training of all, Driver Training.

"But, Sarge," I whined, "I can drive a goddamn car, been doing it for years."

Sergeant Reddy was sympathetic. "Look, Wags, I know you're a regular Mario Andretti, but we're obligated to send one member of the command for a refresher. You're it." Then he smiled. "Of course, if you'd rather have me go . . ."

I went.

Floyd Bennett Field is located at the ass-end of Brooklyn, where Flatbush Avenue becomes a swamp, less than a mile from the ocean. A long, deserted airstrip, the air field was the embarkation point for Charles Lindbergh's historic transatlantic solo flight to Paris. It was also the launch point for the planes that killed King Kong at the end of the movie (the first one, not the remake no one saw). Right before the wrap party was also the last time anyone cut the grass.

In the middle of this weed-infested, garbage-strewn oasis of neglect was a beat-up hangar that housed the NYPD's Aviation Unit, which consisted of a bunch of cops who were smart enough to learn how to fly helicopters, some courtesy of the military. Those who survived Vietnam and joined The Job were cordially invited to become members of this elite unit, often credited with saving numerous lives and making a speedy response to numerous disasters.

Adjacent to the Aviation Unit hangar was a lone double-wide trailer that served as command headquarters for the Driver Training Unit.

June 24, 1975. I reported at nine A.M. for the one-day driver-refresher course as ordered. With me were ten other pissed-off cops from scattered commands. We were milling around bitching and complaining when a sergeant who hadn't seen the street since the Kennedy assassination bounced out of the trailer holding a clipboard.

"Good morning, men," he said cheerily.

This produced a few grumbles and muffled "Fuck yous." The sergeant rolled his eyes, resigned to the abuse he'd undoubtedly received many times in the past from seasoned cops who'd rather be locking up bad guys than driving through traffic cones for eight hours.

To be fair, the course wasn't a repeat of the one we'd had as rookies, where we spent hours learning how a siren worked and how to change a tire.

This time around we learned evasive maneuvers, my favorite being the bootleg turn. I'm sure you've seen it in the movies. A car speeding straight in one direction suddenly whips around to face the opposite way before driving off.

This is accomplished by getting up a sufficient amount of speed, locking the brakes, then, as the car begins to skid in a straight line, the driver cuts the steering wheel sharp left or right and releases the brake. The car whips around like it was hit by an artillery round. The driver then steps on the gas and gets the hell out of there, avoiding that nasty terrorist attack and looking cool in the process.

"Okay, men," our fearless leader said after demonstrating the move in a solo car, "let's try it a coupla dozen times."

We practiced on one of the abandoned runways. Three cops in the front, three in the back. Let me tell you, this is a real stomach-turner. As bad as it was for the cops in the front seat, it was ten times worse for the poor schmucks in the back. Unfortunately, we all got turns in the backseat.

After a half dozen spins I was ready to hurl, as were the rest of the guys in my car. The sergeant stood on the tarmac, smiling.

"Pretty good," he said after another pass. "Let's do it again." He grinned. This is how the son of a bitch got back at the cops who dissed him.

Another three passes. It was now my turn behind the wheel. I got the car up to sixty, then executed my turn. The world became a dizzying kaleidoscope of colors: green grass, black asphalt, blue sky, and pasty-faced cops.

"Lemme out! Lemme out!" a cop screamed from the backseat.

I screeched to a halt just in time for the poor bastard to stagger from the car and lose his breakfast. The four other cops were reeling, unsteady on their feet, making an effort to get far away from the officer who was projectile vomiting.

One cop, completely disoriented, said to no one in particular, "Where can I take a piss around here?"

The sergeant, enjoying the situation he'd created, pointed across the runway. "Portosan, over there."

The cop walked like a drunken sailor toward the bulletlike green plastic structure a mere fifteen yards away, situated alongside Flatbush Avenue, right in view of passing motorists. It took him about a minute to navigate the distance, falling once on the way.

When he got there he whipped out his dick and peed on the outside of the portable john, where every commuter could see him, really pissing off (pun intended) the sergeant.

The cop feigned confusion and the sergeant walked away still cursing. The Pisser, as he is now known in police lore, immediately straightened up once the boss was out of earshot, said, "Fuck him," and zipped up.

My sentiments exactly.

We went to lunch as a group (excluding the sergeant) to a bar on Avenue Z, about a mile from the training facility.

No one drank anything harder than soda. No surprise there; we were all still pretty nauseated from the bootleg turns.

While we were there, a few pilots from the Aviation Unit ambled in and joined us. We traded war stories for the next hour and returned to Floyd Bennett Field together, but not before I talked one of the cop-pilots into a tour of the Aviation Unit facility.

"Sure," he said, "come around after you're done."

I'll call the cop Bob, a pseudonym, used for reasons that will become evident shortly.

The day ended promptly at five and I went directly to the hangar. Officer Bob showed me around and let me climb into a shiny blue-and-white chopper.

"How cool is this?" I said, happy as a kid in Toys "R" Us.

"Wanna go for a ride?" Officer Bob asked.

"You're shitting me."

He shook his head. "Do it all the time. Cops come around with their kids, sometimes just want see what it's like themselves. Just as long as the bosses are gone. Gotta patrol Brooklyn North, anyway; glad to have company. You up for it?"

"You bet."

After Officer Bob made sure I knew enough not to mention my ride to anyone over the rank of patrolman, we were off.

The average street cop's entire world is wrapped up in his own precinct. As in the military, for every one cop on patrol there are two backing him or her who work in support units. Aviation is one of those units.

As we lifted off and swung north, I felt like I was on a different job. I was wearing a set of headphones that blared citywide radio runs. Bob would cut in every so often to point out something of interest or explain what we were going to do next.

"We're just beyond the Six-Seven Precinct now," he said as we descended a hundred feet. "While we're over downtown Brooklyn I like to maintain a lower altitude so the muggers and dope dealers can spot the 'copter." Crime deterrence, according to Officer Bob.

The weather was turning ominous to the east, with dark clouds forming over Queens.

"We going anywhere near those clouds?" I asked, cutting off a radio transmission, my nervousness evident.

He laughed. "Stupid I'm not. I didn't survive six months in a gunship flying over the delta only to be brought down by a raindrop in Queens. Besides, that's Kennedy Airport over there. We stay outta their airspace." Way off in the distance I could see planes circling, waiting their turn to land.

He banked the helicopter sharply and I grabbed the door handle.

"Relax," Bob said. "I haven't had a fender-bender since last Tuesday."

Funny.

As the chopper gained altitude, we put our back to the airport and headed toward Floyd Bennett Field. The ride was fun, but I wanted to get on solid ground again.

I was listening to jobs coming over the citywide band when three sharp beeps blasted through my headset.

"In the One-Thirteen Precinct we have a plane down,

repeat, numerous nine-one-one calls of a commercial aircraft down."

The radio was alive with responses, cops wanting to know the exact location. Before Central had a chance to answer, several units from the One-Thirteen began broadcasting at once, overlapping and cutting each other off. At the same time, Officer Bob swung the helicopter to the left at such an angle that I found myself looking down at the ground.

"Holy shit!" I began grabbing at everything that seemed solid.

As the helicopter leveled off, I could see Kennedy in the distance. To the left and rear of the runways I saw a huge cloud of black smoke.

Bob cut into the frantic radio transmissions, identified himself, and said, "We're responding to the scene, Central; will advise."

I keyed the intercom. "You gonna let me off first?"

"No time. Hold on."

We swooped down rapidly, but my testicles stayed at three thousand feet. Within a minute we were hovering over the northeastern end of the airport.

The plane, a big son of a bitch (I wouldn't know a 737 from a Piper Cub), was down in the middle of Rockaway Boulevard, a heavily traveled road connecting the airport to several major highways.

In the distance I could see the flashing turret lights of speeding radio cars and ambulances. There must have been fifty emergency vehicles racing to the scene.

"I'm setting down," Bob said, and eased the helicopter just off the road on the other side of a chain-link fence that the jumbo jet had reduced to twisted metal.

Parts of the plane were everywhere. I spotted the red lettering on three pieces of widely scattered fractured metal: *Eastern Airlines*. Smoke obliterated much of my vision, but I didn't see any flames. The chopper hovered for what seemed like minutes over a patch of grass and debris.

"Gotta take this easy; don't wanna put this thing down

on anything that's gonna go boom, or worse, on a person."

When we finally touched solid ground I began struggling with the door. The friggin' thing wouldn't open. Bob leaned across me and flipped the door lock. "This might help."

"Sorry." I grinned sheepishly. "Nervous."

"As well you should be."

I jumped to the ground and immediately lost Bob. He'd deplaned and disappeared into a cloud of oily smoke.

Pandemonium reigned. Rubble, luggage, and body parts—most looking like limbs from mannequins—littered the landscape as far as I could see.

Cops and EMS personnel were pouring into the area. No one had direction; the bosses were just as confused as the cops. The NYPD wasn't prepared for a holocaust of this proportion on a heavily trafficked street. No amount of training could prepare a cop for what I was seeing.

My first thought, unbelievably, was of Oric Bovar. *Death from Above.*

Soot-covered men and women were still strapped in their seats in pieces of the broken fuselage. Some were moaning. A goddamn miracle that anyone could have survived this, I thought.

A young female flight attendant on a stretcher was carried past me toward a waiting ambulance. She seemed in remarkably good shape. The only visible sign that she'd been in the crash was a grease-covered uniform, one sleeve ripped at the shoulder, and a cut lip. I was to find out later that she was strapped in a jumpseat in the far rear of the plane for the final approach, and that had saved her life.

Since that day, I always ride in the back of a plane, the portion of the aircraft that always seems to remain intact after a crash. My motto: Not too many planes back up into mountains.

The flight attendant and I made eye contact as she passed me on the litter. She had joined the ranks of those who possess the Thousand-Mile Stare. A slight smile formed on her bruised lips. She said, "Flight Attendant Abel," and kept repeating it as she was slid into the ambulance.

I was to find out later that "Flight Attendant Abel" was the term used by Eastern Airlines personnel to warn each other of an imminent crash without panicking the passengers.

The stench of human feces from truncated torsos, aviation fuel, oil, sweat, and burning rubber intermingled. Cops were bent over, retching. I heard a baby cry, or at least I thought I did, and went tripping through bodies and baggage looking for the kid. I never found it. For all I know, I was hallucinating.

I heard a helicopter engine revving and I turned to see Officer Bob's chopper lifting off the ground with shoeless feet protruding from an open door. The low-flying bird swung west, vanishing over the buildings.

I turned, distracted by screaming. These weren't the screams of people in pain. It sounded like *arguing*.

While I tried to draw a bead on what I was hearing, what I *saw* will forever stay with me.

Literally hundreds of people—civilians—were racing through the wreckage, rummaging through broken suitcases, stuffing their pockets with anything that they could get their hands on.

Cars had come to a halt along Rockaway Boulevard and more people were scampering onto the scene. I heard the arguing again.

Now I spotted two black males in a tug-of-war with an *arm*. Both had the tendon-trailing limb by the wrist. One guy was trying to yank a ring from a finger. The stream of curses from the men was animalistic, guttural.

I took my shield from my pocket and ran to them.

"Police!"

They didn't even glance at me, too intent on fighting over a massive diamond ring.

I grabbed the first guy I could reach around his neck and pulled. The man was smaller than me, but had fantastic strength and shrugged me off like I wasn't there.

I was propelled backward, tripping over something and falling flat on my ass.

I was pissed. I picked up the first thing I could lay my hands on, a flat metal tray, and, screaming like a maniac, attacked the two men with it.

I clipped the first guy with a sharp end behind the ear and his head opened up like a dropped watermelon. He went down.

The second man now had sole possession of the arm, and took off through a crowd of cops, civilians, and EMS people. He was laughing like a fool.

"Stop that man!" I screeched. A uniformed sergeant carrying a black attaché case turned just as the man with the arm reached him. The sergeant's eyes went wide when he saw what the man was carrying. He swung the attaché case at the man's head, striking him full in the face.

The man went down in a heap, still clutching the arm. The attaché case popped open and bundles of cash cascaded to the ground.

The sergeant and I stopped cold in our tracks, eyes wide as hubcaps, staring at the tumbling money. We weren't the only ones who saw it.

A small group of people—men, women, a couple of teenagers—stopped rummaging through debris and stared hungrily at the cash.

We drew our guns. The sergeant growled at the crowd, "Touch this fucking money and I'll kill the whole fucking lot of you miserable cocksuckers."

No denying sincerity. The crowd, which had grown, backed off.

The sergeant looked at me. "I'll take care of this. See if you can help some of the EMS people."

I turned and went back to hell.

There were certainly heroes that day. Many were civilians; most were service personnel. One civilian scooped up two survivors and took them to a hospital in his own car before the ambulances arrived, undoubtedly helping to save their lives.

The sergeant who found the money-stuffed attaché case turned it in. It came to a little over fifty thousand dollars. Would I have done that? Would you?

The plane that went down was Eastern Airlines Flight 66, a Boeing 727, carrying 124 souls. Nine survived.

During the final approach to runway 221, the aircraft was caught in a microburst-induced wind shear that caused a rapid decent. Having but a few feet of airspace, the aircraft slammed to the ground.

Now, twenty-five years after the incident, after seeing every form of fiendishness imaginable in my police career, the event still sticks in my mind as the worst example of man's inhumanity to man that I have ever witnessed.

Ordinary citizens, who moments before the crash were probably in the comfort of their homes enjoying dinner, or driving home from work, ceased being members of the human race when they debased and ravaged corpses for the valuables they possessed. Literally hundreds flocked to the disaster scene for the sole purpose of stripping corpses and looting baggage.

Arrests were made, but not many. Most of the cops on the scene were either too busy looking for survivors, caught up in crowd control, or too shell-shocked to react.

I wonder how those who stole from the dead are living with themselves, years after the crash. I wonder if they raised their kids to be upstanding human beings, just like them.

As the looters lie in their beds at night, experiencing those moments before sleep descends, when one's thoughts are at their purest, does the sound of an airplane engine jar them back to the day they abdicated their rights as human beings and stole the dignity from the dead?

I hope those still living in the area of the crash are reminded of what they did every time they hear a plane land. And for those who have moved, or were just passing through: You may have escaped the reminder of an aircraft's whining engines as it makes its final approach, but you're older now; life is slipping away. One day you'll join those whom you stripped of their honor.

They're waiting.

20
Ol' Blue Eyes Brings Tragic News

Three months passed. I was still the fill-in guy. Partner sick? On vacation? Indicted? New cop assigned to the Ninth? Hell, I'll work with you. Wags at your service.

I was riding with a variety of cops, and had only begun to think about hooking up with someone on a permanent basis. What better way to determine with whom I was compatible?

While I loved police work, what I really looked forward to was going home after the tour. I'm lucky; it's always been easy for me to leave The Job behind.

When my shift was over it was like it never happened. I could witness the worst that human nature had to offer and shrug it off. It all came down to understanding that no matter how many arrests you made, summonses you wrote, or lives you saved, nothing you did was going to change society one iota.

The cops who take The Job to heart are the ones who suffer. Alcoholism and divorce are the biggest disablers of cops. And of course there's suicide, the ultimate disabler. The number of cops hurt by bad guys pales in comparison.

At the end of a particularly tough night of rolling around on the ground with combative junkies, I would be comforted by knowing that I'd be home shortly, sleeping on clean sheets and in the company of my family.

If someone I locked up got off on minimal bail only to vanish, or was cut loose on a technicality, so what? I knew I'd done my job and didn't take the disappointments home with me.

Many cops I worked with, when slapped in the face by the criminal-justice system, gnashed their teeth, cursed, and headed straight to Cal's after work to commiserate with others of the same ilk.

As much as I cherished my wife, I realized one day that I hadn't taken her out for a really extravagant evening in a long while. The pressure of raising our young son, my hours, and my wife's job had taken time away from us as a couple.

So I began planning a spectacular night out for the two of us. But what started out as a magnificent evening ended in tragedy, with horrific news delivered by none other than Frank Sinatra.

My wife Pat and I are music fans, and enjoy all types of music. During the sixties and seventies we were mostly devoted to rock, and spent many nights in the Fillmore East listening to the legends. But we also liked jazz and popular artists.

Frank Sinatra, Count Basie, and Ella Fitzgerald were appearing at the Uris Theater (now the Gershwin Theater) on West Fifty-first Street.

All the shows were sold out well in advance. Tickets were being scalped for ten times their official value, but I was determined to get two and surprise Pat.

One good thing about being a New York City police officer (perhaps the only good thing) is that cops tend to think of The Job as one big family. If a member of the force (now referred to as a member of the *service*) needed something special, something unattainable, he or she needed only to turn to other cops. The term *networking* was unknown in 1975, but I bet it originated in the NYPD.

Within three days, some cop's brother-in-law from L.A. managed to score a pair of tickets for me at the advertised price: Row H, center orchestra, in the 1,900-seat theater.

September 16, 1975

We had dinner at Chez George, a little French restaurant on Fifty-sixth Street. The food was great; we had a couple of drinks, but the real thrill lay ahead. Pat and I were huge fans of Sinatra, and while we liked the music, the thought that we'd be witnessing history was also a thrill. When would these three icons get together again, if ever? And while the evening is forever etched in my memory, it remains there for reasons not related to the concert.

We had just settled into our seats as the houselights dimmed. Count Basie and his orchestra opened the show. The orchestra was on a movable stage. Basie led them from a fixed position near the pit while the musicians rotated around. The set lasted about fifteen minutes, after which Basie personally introduced Ella Fitzgerald.

Ella was wearing a tight-fitting ankle-length gown. She was a big woman, and the dress seemed to be constricting her movements as she made her way from the wings to center stage amid thunderous applause.

As she walked toward her mark, Pat leaned toward me and said, "She looks like she's going to crash into the band."

Sure enough, she collided with the movable stage and went down like a landlocked whale. Ella Fitzgerald, it seemed, was very nearsighted, almost blind. She was wearing thick glasses, which apparently did little to help her vision, or perhaps she was blinded by the stagelights.

The audience let out a collective gasp as Count Basie rushed to the fallen singer and tried to lift her up. No good. Basie was built solidly, but was smaller than Ella and couldn't budge her. Three members of the orchestra rushed over to help Basie, and between the four of them, they managed to hoist her to her feet.

With nothing more than a shrug and a smile, Ella began belting out a scat tune like nothing had happened. She brought the house down.

The rest of the evening was equally memorable, with Sinatra singing solo—and in great voice—accompanied by Basie's orchestra. He then sang a duet with Ella. Quite the historic evening.

Sinatra closed the show. He came onstage sans tuxedo jacket, with his tie loosened. The theater went totally dark except for a baby spotlight illuminating Ol' Blue Eyes. He sat on the stage, legs dangling over the side.

"I was informed," he began "that two New York City police officers were tragically gunned down in lower Manhattan not more than thirty minutes ago. This song is dedicated to those brave men." He went into a soulful rendition of his classic saloon song, "Quarter to Three."

It was everything I could do to restrain myself from jumping out of my seat and racing out of the theater. I felt that ominous gut-tightening fear that some cops call a sixth sense, the feeling you get when you know someone close to you has been killed. While there are thousands of cops assigned to lower Manhattan, I had a sense of foreboding that Sinatra was talking about Ninth Precinct cops.

A slow ballad, the song now seemed excruciatingly long, with Sinatra squeezing every nuance he could out of the lyrics. To this day I can't listen to that song.

When it was finally over I turned to Pat. I just looked at her, knowing anything I said would be drowned out by the roaring ovation Sinatra was receiving.

Pat was thinking the same thing I was; I could see it in her eyes. She squeezed my arm and said, "Go."

I kissed her cheek and handed her the car keys. A cop's wife. She knew.

I spent five frustrating minutes trying to find a working pay phone on the street. No luck.

I grabbed a cab and told the driver to switch his radio to 1010 WINS, the all-news station. We weren't three blocks from the theater when my worst fear was confirmed. A WINS reporter on the scene confirmed two cops shot on East Fifth Street, within the Ninth Precinct. Both were pronounced DOA at Bellevue. No names were released pending notification of next of kin.

Like a scene out of a bad movie I hung my arm over the front seat and flashed my tin in the driver's face.

"Police officer, step on it."

The station house block was jammed with cars. Radio cars, TV news trucks, and unmarked cars took up every inch of street and sidewalk space. I threw a ten at the cabdriver, jumped out of the taxi, and ran for the house.

My legs wouldn't work right. They felt rubbery, like my next step was going to be my last. I pushed through a mob of newspeople crowded near the building's entrance. I suppose because I was wearing a suit, some of the reporters assumed I was a boss and began hurling questions at me. I ignored them.

There was no more order inside the station house. The desk area was a sea of brass, all talking furiously among themselves, talking notes, and waiting for a chance at one of the three phones behind the desk.

I singled out a detective I knew well, spun him around, and said, "Who?"

He had tears in his eyes. "Reddy and Glover."

The sitting room during a tour is usually quiet and laid back, with cops leisurely eating sandwiches or reading as they take advantage of their hour meal period. Tonight the room was packed with cops, some crying, some cursing and pacing. Three years after Foster and Laurie were assassinated and I felt like I was reliving those horrific moments at Bellevue from that night.

In a corner, his shirt covered with blood and using the wall for support, was Steve Toth, a good cop with about four years on The Job. He and his partner Artie Cardaio worked Sector Adam.

"Steve, what the hell happened?"

He looked at me with the blankest, deadest eyes I'd ever seen. There wasn't a large enough number to put a distance on his stare.

The call came over a little after nine o'clock. Shots fired, Fifth Street, between avenues A and B. Steve and Artie were the first on the scene. Normally, within minutes of a shots-fired call, cars stream to the location. It's sometimes hard for radio cars to get near the reported location. But tonight Artie, the driver, decided to save precious time and drive against traffic on Fifth Street.

They found a crowd of civilians milling around a body in the gutter. When Steve pushed through the crowd, he saw Sergeant Reddy lying on his back in full uniform, his right hand clutching his service revolver. A large bloodstain soaked his shirt under his right arm. Steve didn't know whether the sergeant was dead or seriously wounded.

Sergeant Reddy's radio car, RMP 1286, was double-parked, the driver's door open. Steve took the revolver from the sergeant's hand, broke the cylinder open, discovered three spent shells, and jammed the gun into his waistband. With some effort, he carried Reddy to the radio car for the race to Bellevue.

"Wags, I couldn't believe what was happening," Steve told me later. "After I get Reddy in the car I ask Artie if he thinks the sergeant was okay. He told me he thought he was dead. He was like our father, for God's sake." Tears came to his eyes, but he remained composed.

Steve and Artie hadn't searched for Andy Glover.

They didn't look because Sergeant Reddy had decided to drive himself that night. Glover had been assigned to a foot post in Tompkins Square Park. Reddy, it was later assumed, had decided sometime during the tour to pick up Glover, but no one was aware of it at the time.

As Steve and Artie were pulling out for the mad dash to Bellevue, a civilian ran up to the car and pointed to the space between Reddy's double-parked radio car and a legally parked auto and said, "Hey, Officer, there's one over here."

Steve and Artie thought that the civilian was referring to someone Sergeant Reddy had shot before he was killed.

"The last thing we wanted to do was waste our time bringing a perp to the hospital," Steve said. "Reddy was our primary concern." They started for the hospital as other radio cars spilled into the block.

Sergeant Reddy was dead on arrival at Bellevue. He was shot once under the right armpit, the bullet piercing his aorta, presumably as he raised his revolver to fire at the shooter. Sergeant Frederick Reddy, Shield 1258, was fifty years old, the father of six, and had twenty-eight years on The Job.

As Steve Toth and Artie Cardaio were speeding to Bellevue with the mortally wounded Sergeant Reddy, Police officers Charles Hall and Mel Ashe from Sector Charlie rolled onto the block. It was this team who discovered Andy Glover's body wedged between the sergeant's car and the other car parked against the curb. His service revolver was missing.

Andy Glover had been shot twice in the face and once in the heart. He appeared to be dead, but Ashe and Hall rushed him to Bellevue anyway. There's always hope. He was pronounced dead on arrival at the hospital.

Police Officer Andrew Glover, Shield 14007, was thirty-four years old, married with one child, and had seven years on The Job.

It took a few hours for detectives to piece together what had happened. As was apparent, Sergeant Reddy picked up Glover during the tour. No one was able to establish what time this occurred, and it really didn't matter.

Sergeant Reddy was driving. While a sergeant is assigned a chauffeur and is under no obligation to get behind the wheel, Reddy liked to drive and was often seen chauffeuring Andy Glover around the precinct.

A 1967 red Plymouth convertible was double-parked on East Fifth Street. There were two Hispanic males in the front seat. Sergeant Reddy, violating department policy, pulled the radio car *in front* of the illegally parked vehicle before attempting to question the occupants.

Department rules dictate that when making a car stop, the operator of the radio car is to pull the car behind and a little to the left of the subject vehicle. This gives the cops a tactical advantage because the occupants of the stopped vehicle have to turn around to confront the cops. If someone in the car starts shooting, the radio-car team can take cover behind their vehicle, and the protruding radio car protects the cops from getting side-swiped by oncoming traffic while they're talking to the people in the stopped vehicle.

In this case, Glover walked toward the stopped car from the front passenger side. Unbeknownst to Reddy and Glover, the two men inside were wanted for numerous armed robberies.

When Glover reached the passenger window, he was shot and killed. Reddy may or may not have been outside the radio car at the time. What is known is that when the gunfight began, Reddy drew his revolver and fired three shots at the driver. At the same time, the driver fired one shot at the sergeant, killing him instantly.

Both suspects were captured within two weeks and are still in jail. There were, however, serious ramifications after the killings.

Racial tensions had begun to emerge within The Job during the seventies, particularly in Brooklyn, where fistfights occurred between black and white cops.

Despite what was going on in the rest of the city, the Ninth Precinct remained free of racial strife. As in any combat zone where your life depends on your fellow soldiers, in the EVil the cops were extremely tight. The only color that mattered was blue.

But when Andy Glover was left in the street while Sergeant Reddy was rushed to Bellevue, rumors circulated that he was left behind because a white cop's life was deemed more valuable than that of a black cop.

Remarks were exchanged between black and white cops in the locker room, but there was never any associated violence. After it was understood that Toth and Cardaio had had no idea that Glover had been present, that it was assumed Sergeant Reddy rode alone that night, the tensions subsided.

Andy Glover's funeral was held in the Bronx, Sergeant Reddy's on Long Island. Because of the considerable distance between the two places, the Ninth was provided with motorcoach buses to ferry the troops between the services.

Other commands were sent to the Ninth to take over the patrol function while we attended both funerals. The mood was somber as we gathered in front of the station house and filed quietly into the buses.

Ruthie, our resident nut, was on my bus, along with her dog, Shep. This would be the first and last time any of us would see Ruthie wearing makeup. She had made a valiant attempt, but her face looked like a taped-together ransom note. The dog normally wore a red bandanna around his neck. The day of the funeral the bandanna had been replaced with a black one.

Ruthie had loved Sergeant Reddy and was a basket case. She must have cried for weeks. Long after Reddy was killed, the mere mention of his name would reduce poor Ruthie to tears.

This day she was on her best behavior, and no one had to shield their groins as she made her way down the aisle to the back of the bus.

As we drove uptown toward the Bronx, radio cars from other precincts stopped traffic and saluted us as we passed by. The cops in my bus barely noticed the tribute. The ride was silent except for occasional sobs from Ruthie.

Glover's funeral was a blur. I'd been to so many over the years, and this one, while a carbon copy of the others, complete with politicians touting gun control and grieving family members leaning on each other for support, was different because it was one of our own.

After the service, we piled back onto the buses and headed for Long Island to Sergeant Reddy's funeral. Fate and a low bridge were to intervene, and I never did make it.

The Grand Central Parkway begins in Queens, and as it snakes east it becomes the Northern State Parkway. Commercial vehicles are not permitted on either the Grand Central or the Northern State because of the narrow lanes and low overpasses.

However, because the shortest route to Sergeant Reddy's funeral was via these two roads, the boss in charge of the entourage, Inspector Robert Houlihan, decided we'd take them.

"If we stick to the middle lane where the overpasses are highest," he'd said, "the buses'll clear them."

Famous last words.

I was one of eighty cops (plus Ruthie) in the second bus, driving down the center lane of the Northern State, closely behind the first bus. A passenger car in the left lane signaled and pulled over into our lane in front of us.

The car was moving slowly and the first bus was pulling far ahead. Our driver, seeing no overpass, decided to pass the car on the left.

He executed the maneuver on a curve, and as the bus entered the left lane, an overpass materialized in front of us.

I was in one of the front seats, saw the danger immediately, and brought my legs up to my chest. Had I had the time, I would have kissed my ass good-bye; this looked like it was going to be a bad one.

The driver jammed on the brakes, sending the cops sitting on armrests talking to each other cascading into the aisles.

Within seconds I was riding in a convertible. The top of the bus struck the overpass, which sheared off the roof. Twisted metal crashed onto the highway behind us. Fortunately there was no traffic to our rear, and no other vehicles were involved. We swerved off the road and came to a screeching stop on the shoulder.

Almost the entire busload of cops was injured, some so severely that they subsequently retired on disability pensions. Because I had braced for the collision I was virtually unhurt. Ruthie had a bump on her head. Her dog slid the length of the bus on the floor, but was otherwise unhurt.

We never made it to the funeral. By the time ambulances carted off the more severely injured, and we had filled out witness statements, Sergeant Reddy was already in his final resting place.

I got a ride back to the city with an off-duty Nassau County cop. The last thing I remember seeing that day was Ruthie standing by the side of the road, crying.

21
Joe Friday Helps a Fellow Cop

I had a new partner. Richie Innes was my age (thirty) and had been in the Ninth for a few years. At six-four and thin as a zipper, with curly brown hair, he was a double for the Chicago Bulls coach Phil Jackson. Richie's previous partner had been transferred, so we were both orphans. We hit it off after riding together for a few tours, and requested that the arrangement be made permanent.

Richie was a great cop, and better yet, the closest he'd ever gotten to a war was watching reruns of *Combat* on television. While I revered Kenny's memory, I was looking for someone stable, with one wife and no intentions of trading her in. Aside from a sick sense of humor, Richie was (and still is) a cop's cop. Today he's a lieutenant in Queens.

Richie's humor is legendary. One time a cabdriver flagged down our radio car while we were cruising down Third Avenue during a day tour. We pulled over (*behind* the taxi) and the driver bounded out in an extreme state of agitation.

The cabbie spoke little English (a prerequisite for becoming a New York City cabdriver). He was waving his arms frantically.

"Officer, passenger took shit in backseat of cab!" he howled, justifiably indignant.

Richie, calm as could be, said, "Well, sir, if the turd remains unclaimed for thirty days, it's yours." He tipped his hat, smiled, and pulled away, leaving a dumbfounded hackie standing in the middle of the street scratching his head.

Another time we responded to a two-car collision on FDR Drive. A car had broken down in the far right lane and a second car had plowed right into it, killing the driver, a middle-aged woman. This might have been a run-of-the-mill car crash except the dead woman had a *poodle* imbedded in her chest. The dog was also DOA.

As near as we could figure, the pulverized pup was riding on the deceased's lap when she probably became distracted by the dog, didn't see the stalled car in front of her, and rammed right into it. There were no skid marks indicating that the driver had tried to stop. The steering wheel pushed the dog into the dead lady's chest. The squished poodle bled like, well, a squished poodle. The woman looked like she'd taken a direct hit with an artillery round.

The Accident Investigation Unit estimated that she was doing at least fifty when she was killed. Fortunately the driver of the first car was outside his vehicle awaiting a tow truck, and was unharmed.

Soon traffic came to a halt in both directions. Morbid curiosity mandated that everyone take a turn looking at the corpse, which was hanging outside of the car.

A passing news van stopped and set up video as a knockout blond reporter stood within arm's length of the body, and fixed her hair before she went on the air. Ambulances drove on the road's shoulder to reach the mangled car, and several NYPD bosses showed up to get their mugs on the six o'clock news.

In the middle of all this were Richie and me. We were responsible for the paperwork and keeping Central apprised of what was going on.

The radio barked. "Central to Nine Sector Charlie."

Richie keyed the radio. "Charlie."

"Any fatalities, Charlie?"

Now, standing in the midst of cops directing traffic, department brass, EMS personnel, and a TV reporter, Richie said, "We've got a woman down here DOA, Central, lying in a *poodle* of blood."

The cops and EMS people, naturally, cracked up. There was a captain standing not more than three feet away from Richie. He turned and walked away like he didn't hear anything. The reporter, however, was ruffled.

"Officer," she said to Richie, "isn't that a bit insensitive?"

Richie looked like a deer caught in approaching headlights. "Huh? Me? What?" He denied that he'd said anything other than *puddle*. Fortunately, after Richie sweet-talked her, she wasn't sure what she'd heard and didn't make a big deal of it. I'm just glad his remark wasn't picked up by a mike.

Richie was a good talker. One time we responded to a past burglary in a gynecologist's office. The office was a mess. My guess was that the culprit was a junkie looking for drugs.

The female doctor was justifiably upset. Richie tipped his hat and said, "Officer Innes, Doctor, at your cervix."

It took him five minutes to convince the doctor that she had heard wrong.

Richie and I studied like madmen for the sergeant's exam. Not only would promotion to sergeant merit a hefty pay increase, but it would take us out of the daily drudgery of handling radio runs.

We threw questions at each other for hours on end and attended a tutorial course designed to help us pass the test. Only one out of ten cops ever makes boss on The Job, and we were determined to be members of that select few. While the test was about a year away, there was enough material to keep us busy.

It was during these marathon study sessions that Richie noticed something was wrong with his eyesight. He complained of seeing "sparklers" constantly. Within a few weeks, he was diagnosed with pars planitis, a rare disease that could cause permanent blindness.

Richie's eyesight got so bad that he could no longer drive; I became the permanent operator. Richie was the steady recorder and handled the paperwork with a magnifying glass the size of a tennis racket.

Richie couldn't tell The Job about his disability. Since he was almost one year short of ten years with the NYPD, he didn't qualify for a pension. If he was forced out on a disability, he'd lose everything, and he had a family to support. So we faked it for a year until the day he had his ten, and then he went sick.

Richie had a delicate eye operation, and while he needs very thick glasses to see, he's still on The Job, albeit not on the street.

While all this was going on, my dad decided to pull the pin.

"I'm retiring, Jimmy; enough's enough." He had twenty-five years on The Job.

To me, Dad had always been a cop; I couldn't remember him any other way. His announcement came as a shock out of nowhere.

"It'll happen the same way with you, Jimmy," he told me. "Little things will begin to annoy you, and one day you'll retire on the spur of the moment." He was right, of course, but with me it would be those little things plus one big one to end my police career.

Dad went to work for the New York Giants football organization as an assistant locker room manager. His two brothers, Patty and Whitey, and Whitey's son, Edward, also worked for the Giants, so it seemed a natural transition.

My father was in charge of the coaches' uniforms for all the home games. It was a good job with many perks, the best one being able to stand on the fifty-yard line during a game.

Dad acclimated very well, sometimes a hard thing for a cop to do after spending almost half a lifetime chasing bad guys. It was a welcome change that brought steady hours, which made my mother happy. Plus, I don't recall the last time an assistant locker room manager was assassinated.

After Dad was with the Giants a while he asked me if I'd like to work the games with him on my days off.

"As what?" I asked.

He shrugged. "Sort of an assistant to the assistant. You'd basically be a glorified gofer. Whatever the players need, you get."

Me being an avid football fan, I figured this was the next best thing to being drafted by the NFL. "Count me in."

"Don't you want to know how much you get paid?"

"You mean they pay me, too?"

What a racket.

After being on The Job for ten years, I was unaware that there was real money to be made in the outside world. There were all kinds of ways to make an extra legitimate buck. These scams—I mean entrepreneurial endeavors—were legal, just in violation of the Giants organization's rules, so care had to be exercised or I'd wind up canned.

My primary job was to make sure the players had towels, Gatorade, ice, etc. I became friendly not only with most of the Giants, but with the visitors as well. Dealing with the visiting team was where the extra money could be made.

All NFL players are given four tickets per game for personal use. If a player was at home, it was fairly easy to get rid of his extra tickets. Most sold them; some gave them away.

For the visitors, it was a bit tougher to sell the tickets because they weren't on their home turf and usually didn't know anyone. This is where I'd come in.

I'd take the four tickets and give them to the Wackenhut Security guard. He would scalp them, and he and I would split the profit. I'd give the face value of the tickets to the player, usually twenty-five bucks a ticket. Players were forbidden to sell their tickets for more than the printed value.

This went on for quite a while, and I was making a few extra bucks. One day, Ronnie Lott, a defensive end for the San Francisco Forty-Niners, gave me two tickets to sell for him.

"See me after the game with the fifty," he told me.

"Not a problem." I did the usual, passed them to the guard, and we whacked up the money at the end of the game.

Somehow Lott and I never hooked up. I got sidetracked, and he had to be on the bus on the way to the airport within ninety minutes of the completion of the game. When I finally had time to look for him and give him his fifty dollars he was long gone. So I forgot about it.

Meanwhile, Lott was on the plane back to California bitching and moaning that I never gave him the money for the tickets. The word eventually got back to my uncle Whitey, who was the locker room manager and my boss.

Whitey chewed me out for selling tickets and fired me. My own uncle. As pissed off as I was at my uncle, I was even more aggravated with Ronnie Lott. The guy had to be making two million dollars a year and he bitched about a lousy fifty bucks. Go figure.

But between the Lott incident and my getting canned, I was involved in the Hot Dog Caper.

Ezra Johnson, a defensive end for the Green Bay Packers, had a hot dog jones. He was once fined a few thousand dollars for glomming a hot dog from a fan and eating it on the sidelines.

The NFL fed both teams a gargantuan breakfast before the game—steak, eggs, cereal, anything the players wanted. Johnson, it seemed, was a late sleeper and always missed breakfast. By halftime he was ravenous. During one game he sought me out.

"Hey, Wags, could you get me a few dogs with everything on them?"

"Yeah, sure, but if someone sees you eating them . . ."

He put his arm around me, turned me around, and walked us away from the sideline cameras. "This is what you do." He was whispering like we were planning the Kennedy assassination. "Buy the dogs, wrap 'em, and put 'em behind a commode in the locker room john."

I looked at him like he'd grown an extra head. "You gotta be kidding."

"No, man, I'm starving. Have 'em there at halftime."

So I entered into the Great Sabrett's Conspiracy. I had just managed to stuff the two carefully wrapped hot dogs behind the commode in the locker room when Johnson burst in.

"Where are they?" He looked desperate.

I pointed to a stall.

"I owe you, man."

With all his gear on he was barely able to squeeze into the stall. I left him sitting on the bowl, a huge grin on his faced, stuffing hot dogs into his mouth. He later gave me a hundred dollars.

Dad continued with the Giants. Since he was full-time, he went on the road with the team. One day, while at a summer practice session at Pace University in Pleasantville, New York, he went into convulsions and began throwing up blood.

He was eventually diagnosed with colon cancer, had surgery, and for a year seemed to improve. Then, in late 1981, the cancer returned with a vengeance and spread to his brain.

I never considered the possibility of my parents' deaths. My mother was healthy, as was Dad until the cancer hit him. Even after his surgery, his doctors gave him a good prognosis.

I thought my dad was invincible. As I watched him wasting away, I was drawn back to those hot summer childhood days when he and Dave Ballantine would come home for a quick lunch, and would entertain me with war stories. He seemed so big and strong, as most fathers do in the eyes of their kids. As I got older, joined the NYPD, and worked with him in the same command, I realized how tough he actually was, and how much he was revered in the community because of that toughness.

"I want to die at home," Dad told us.

And so we granted his wish. We had a minihospital set up in the living room, complete with bed, visiting nurses, IVs, a steady supply of painkillers, and something hospitals couldn't provide—love and attention.

At night, when the rest of the family had either left or gone to bed, I'd sit at my father's bedside and watch him sleep, his labored breathing becoming more pronounced as time marched on.

He talked a lot in his sleep, often recalling happier times with the family and recounting endless war stories. I'd be nodding off on a recliner by his bed when I'd be jolted awake by a burst of words. He'd start out strong, loud enough to be heard in the next room, but would gradually peter out and slip back into a drug-induced sleep.

He had his good days when he seemed strong, but he'd soon grow weak and exhausted, falling into a melancholy drift, smiling at something he'd recalled.

One day I was reading the morning newspaper to him when he said, "Hey, Jimmy, remember when you were a kid? When we used to listen to *Dragnet* on the radio?" He smiled. "Life was so much goddamn simpler then, wasn't it?"

"Sure was, Dad. I think that was when I decided to be a cop, just like Sergeant Joe Friday." I hastily added, "And you, of course."

He laughed. "That's okay. I always wanted to be a cop like Joe Friday, too." He paused, taking a breath, conserving his energy. "I wonder if they ever put those shows on tape. I'd love to hear some of them again."

I stayed with him until my mother returned from shopping and then shot home quickly to change and get ready for work. All that night I thought about what my father had said about the old *Dragnet* shows, and I set out the next day to find audio copies—if in fact they still existed.

In the early eighties we were still several years away from the ease of the Internet, so I had to research old-time radio (OTR) at the local library.

It took me a few days, but I found two dealers, Ed Carr and Ted Davenport, both of whom had extensive inventories of *Dragnet*. I ordered thirty half-hour shows from each of them, explaining my Dad's love of the show and why I needed the tapes in a hurry. ("Yesterday would be nice.")

Both men messengered the cassettes. I never got a bill from either of them, and never forgot their kindness. I tracked them down when I began writing this book. Today Ted's got an OTR Web page ("Radio Memories") and Ed has a home-based OTR business in Boyertown, Pennsylvania. Fine people.

The story you have just heard is true; only the names were changed to protect the innocent. On February eighth trial was held in Superior Court, Department 92, city and county of Los Angeles. In a moment the results of that trial.

We'd been listening to the tapes for about a week, mostly at night after Mom went to bed and visitors departed. It was a father-son thing, my dad reliving memories of us sitting together on the couch, and the hold that The Job had on both of us.

By mid-December, Dad would drift during the shows and reminisce about when he was a young cop. A lot of what he said didn't make much sense, but I knew he cherished those years when he was treated like a king in our Stapleton neighborhood.

One night, as he rambled, I slipped down to the basement to a cedar chest he'd used for years to store his old uniforms and other police memorabilia.

Neatly folded on top was his uniform winter blouse, known as a choker, because it fastened tight around the neck. Chokers were the sharpest uniforms the NYPD ever had, but generally only looked good on the younger cops because as cops aged, the neck portion of the uniform usually wouldn't close (too many doughnuts). The choker was replaced by a leather jacket in the early seventies.

I put the blouse on and it fit like a glove (I was never a doughnut man), and I now realized that six days a week in the gym over the course of fifteen years had done me some good.

His hat, with chromed cap device (Shield 8206), was clean and blocked. My dad always took pride in his appearance. I put it on, adjusting it in a mirror.

The gun belt was just as I remembered it as a kid. It still smelled of gun oil and was polished to a dull sheen. I strapped it on. It fit a little better than when I was nine. I went back upstairs.

The room was dark. Joe Friday's prisoner had since been sentenced and the deck had automatically stopped at the end of the tape.

The stillness of the room made my dad's breathing seem that much louder. As I stood over his frail figure, I yearned to be nine years old again, cuddled up next to him on the couch, learning from Joe Friday how to be a cop.

"Daddy," I whispered. No response. "Daddy." Louder this time.

He opened his eyes and smiled. I grasped his hand and squeezed. "Someday I wanna be a cop just like you, Daddy." At that moment I was nine again. Maybe we'd throw a ball around after dinner.

He looked me up and down, licked his lips, and grinned. "You're such a good kid, Jimmy." Then he fell asleep.

He died two days before Christmas.

After the funeral, we discovered that my mother wasn't eligible to receive any part of my father's pension. He had chosen Option Two as his retirement package, which meant that he received the highest pension payout allowable by law every month, but the money died when he did.

This option is usually taken by younger retirees because their life expectancy is long and more money can be made over the course of a lifetime. Older retirees take Option One, which reduces the monthly payout, but the benefits are passed on to the beneficiary upon the pensioner's death.

Our family had been so caught up in treating my father's illness that we never thought of changing the pension option to make certain my mother was taken care of after my father died. The retiree has at least a year until the pension is "finalized," and can change the option at any time. So my mom was left without a livable income.

When Wellington Mara, the owner of the Giants, heard about my mother's predicament, he called and told me that he'd just found a $100,000 life insurance policy that my dad had taken out through the Giants organization, listing my mom as beneficiary. Just happened to find it lying around his office.

Don't say anything bad about the Giants around me.

22
No Such Unit

I was promoted to sergeant in November 1985. The time spent hitting the books had paid off. The good news was that I received a substantial pay increase, no longer had to handle radio runs, and got a driver and a nifty set of stripes. The bad news was that I was transferred out of the Ninth Precinct.

The Job had a rule that a cop couldn't stay in the same command when he was promoted. A logical rule, really. How much authority could a new sergeant have if yesterday he was one of the guys?

A few hundred cops were promoted with me. The ceremony was held in the auditorium in 1 Police Plaza. We all got to shake the police commissioner's hand and listen to Mayor Koch tell us what bright people we were.

After the ceremony, we filed upstairs to the shield desk to get our new gold shields. As we were standing on line, some pencil pusher stood on a table and announced that if any of us had a preference for a certain shield number, we could request it when we reached the desk.

When it was my turn I said, "Is shield seven-fourteen available?"

The bored clerk looked up at me. "That sounds familiar."

"Yeah, it was Joe Friday's shield. You know, *Dragnet*."

"Hold on; I'll look." He fingered through a few hundred shields neatly arranged in envelopes and then referred to a computer printout.

"Nah, that shield was retired in 1982. Says so right here."

He handed me the printout. Sure enough, the number was retired, never to be issued again. Later I found out that The Job retired it when Jack Webb died in homage to all he'd done to improve the image of cops everywhere.

"What's the closest number you've got?" I asked.

More rummaging. "How does shield seven-seventeen sound?"

"Sold." I wore the shield proudly until the day I retired, and always thought of my dad when I pinned it on.

I was assigned to the newly established Neighborhood Stabilization Unit (NSU) in Manhattan South. The NSU mission was to put as many uniformed cops on the street as possible. These cops were fresh out of the Academy, and their time in the NSU was to serve as a breaking-in period before going on to precinct-level commands.

It's been said that one of the scariest times in life is driving a new car home from the showroom. Whoever originally said that never walked into a new command as a rookie sergeant.

One day you're one of the guys; the next day you're a boss. Cops who would pal around with you the day before now avoided you like you had diphtheria.

So it was with great trepidation that I reported to the Seventh Precinct, home of the Manhattan South NSU, to meet and greet my new rookies. At least it would be easier dealing with kids straight out of the Academy than supervising battle-weary veterans who knew the score.

I stood in front of the desk and addressed the lieutenant.

"Police Off— I mean, Sergeant Wagner reporting, Loo." It didn't matter if I had stripes sewn on my arms; I still felt like a cop.

"Oh, yeah, Wagner," the lieutenant said, and referred to a clipboard. "You've got the Thanksgiving Day Parade. There's a busload of cops outside waiting for you.

The bus'll take you guys to where the parade starts, somewhere uptown."

"I'm assigned to NSU, Loo," I said.

"You start there tomorrow. Today you've got the parade detail."

The parade is an easy gig. Once it's over, the assigned cops get an early dismissal and an early start on their family bird. It's also a laid-back day. Everyone's in a festive mood, and the worst that can happen is you get stuck with a lost kid. I wasn't expecting any trouble for my first day as a boss.

Right.

The bus was loaded with seasoned cops; they all knew that I was a new boss. The NYPD is like a jailhouse grapevine in that respect. Word filters down to the cops, much the same way it does to the cons when a new kid arrives on the (cell) block. I was the new kid, and I was sure that I was going to be tested.

I took the roll call, happy to see that everyone was present, settled into a front seat, and told the driver, "Eighty-sixth Street and Central Park West."

On the ride uptown there was a lot of laughing and kidding around, which is normal when a bunch of cops get together. What wasn't normal was the gunshot that exploded from the back of the bus as we exited FDR Drive at Ninety-sixth Street.

I turned to see a cloud of smoke and smelled the accompanying cordite as I ran back up the aisle.

There I found a cop holding his side crumpled in his seat. He was bleeding profusely from the stomach. The cop next to him held his service revolver in his hand and was staring at it incredulously. "The fucking gun," he said, "it just went off."

I smelled alcohol, but I figured I'd deal with that later.

I grabbed the gun and jammed it into my waistband. Most of the other cops had left their seats and were crowding me, trying to get a better look at what was happening.

"Everybody sit down!" I bellowed. They sat. To the bus driver I said, "Where's the nearest hospital?"

He was wild-eyed, panicked. "Uh, I dunno . . . maybe St. Clare's."

A cop standing next to me said, "No, go to Metropolitan; it's right up the friggin' block."

We were two blocks away. While I held my hand over the cop's wound to stop the blood flow, the bus made it there in what seemed like seconds. The wounded officer never lost consciousness, but the cop who shot him looked like he was going to faint.

Needless to say, we missed the parade. By the time the duty captain arrived and took statements, I'd also missed Thanksgiving dinner with my family.

The two cops (shooter and shootee) had been out all night after a four-to-twelve and showed up for the parade detail drunk. For some reason, they decided to compare service revolvers, with one wounded cop the result.

The injured officer lost his spleen. The cop who shot him lost his job. I wonder who fared worse.

I finally made it home a little before midnight. I figured that since I'd had a bitch of a first day as a sergeant, it had to get better.

I renamed NSU No Such Unit because no police organization could exist for any period of time with the bunch of misfits I had in that squad.

Instead of dealing with the savvy cops I knew in the Ninth, I was wet-nursing a bunch of kids. I'm not saying that *all* the cops were in need of Mr. Rogers, but a goodly number should never have become cops in the first place.

The era of military veterans entering The Job was over. Not one of my twenty charges had had military service. Most had never been to the big, bad city until they showed up at the Police Academy that first day to get sworn in. I had a platoon of suburbanites.

I remember once having to draw a map to the U.N. building for a group of my rookies who were flying there for a demonstration. New York City was a foreign country to most of them.

A normal part of a cop's job is to provide directions

to anyone who asks. Not only is it good public relations for a cop whose shield says *City of New York* to know where the hell the Empire State Building is, but it makes the entire NYPD look less than competent when a uniformed cop has to get on his radio and ask if the Lincoln Tunnel is located on the east or the west side of Manhattan. Believe me, it's happened.

While I was entitled to a driver, I chose to drive myself. I'd have been better off being driven by a Pakistani cabdriver with limited language skills than by most of the rookies who worked for me.

Part of a sergeant's job is to make certain he knows where his cops are at all times. To accomplish this, the sergeant makes the rounds in his car to the various foot posts (NSU was all foot posts; no one rode in a marked radio car) and signs the officers' memo books.

If a cop can't be found on his or her assigned post, the sergeant gets on the radio and ascertains a location. Usually the foot cop is off handling a call for service, or in the bathroom, and will respond with a location.

The world's smallest cop was assigned to my NSU. She stood less than five feet, and weighed about a hundred pounds. The nightstick on her pistol belt dragged along the pavement when she walked. The Job had abolished height requirements, and lowered the age to nineteen to take the entrance exam. We had our own version of Don't ask, don't tell. Technically I could have a unit comprised of midget cops who couldn't drink in a bar, and were members of the George Michael Fan Club.

One day I drove up and down her post three times and couldn't find her. Finally I tried the radio.

"Post Three, location?"

She came right back. "Avenue C and Second Street, Sarge."

I'd just driven by that location and she wasn't there. I drove by again. Still no midget cop.

I pulled to the curb.

"Post Three," I said, "I'm on C and Two. Where are you?"

She stepped from behind a mailbox right next to my car. "Right here, Sarge," she called out, all smiles and wearing the brightest, reddest lipstick I'd seen since I was locking up hookers on the Bowery. She was actually shorter than the mailbox.

"Ten-thirteen! Ten-thirteen! Avenue B and Fifth! Ten-thirteen."

I swung the car around, flipped on the siren, and sped the three blocks to the cop in trouble.

When I slid to the curb I saw a sight I'll never forget. The male rookie who had called in the Thirteen had a pit bull attached to his back.

The dog had a death grip on the middle of his jacket and was off the ground, growling and thrashing. The cop was running down the block like—well, like he had a pit bull on his back.

I chased the cop to the corner and had to grab him by the collar to stop him. The dog held on.

"Stop, goddammit!" I yelled.

"Get him off! Get him off!" The cop was in a panic, whimpering and screaming. A crowd was gathering. How embarrassing.

The pit bull was wearing a chain collar. I grabbed it and pulled. Nothing.

"Owww!" the cop screamed.

"Shut up. For crissakes, I'm trying to get the friggin' thing off!" The dog's neck was like a piece of timber, and strangling it was doing no good. I took out my Mace and gave him a squirt right in the eyes. It just pissed him off and he dug in harder.

I couldn't shoot the dog for fear of hitting the twenty or so civilians who had gathered to make fun of us, even though I was sorely tempted.

I pulled out my unauthorized spring-loaded lead sap, and proceeded to play a tune on the dog's head. Occasionally I'd miss and hit the cop—purely unintentionally.

After the six or seventh swing, the dog had had enough, released his grip, and went scampering up the block. The cop, who was approaching hysteria, tried to explain how he'd become so intimately acquainted with a pit bull.

"Sarge, I—"

"I don't wanna hear it." I got in my car and pulled away.

One of the cops assigned to No Such Unit was a former police commissioner's granddaughter. A sorrier, more hapless individual you'll never meet. She was constantly apologizing for her actions.

"Sarge, I'm sorry I dropped the cat off the roof."

"Sarge, I'm sorry I didn't know where Brooklyn was."

"Sarge, I'm sorry I had makeup in my handcuff case."

You get the idea. Because of her propensity to say she was sorry for everything except the current state of unrest in the Middle East, I called her Officer Mea Culpa. Her real name was Maria. She didn't understand New York-ese very well, having been raised in Levittown, so she never caught the implication.

After turning out the troops one day I pulled her aside and said, "Listen, Mea, your post is First Street and First Avenue. You know what condition we have over there?" It was like talking to my nine-year-old son.

Brow knit, she searched her underutilized gray cells for an answer. "Uh, no, Sarge, sorry."

"There's a steady crap game in the park. I drive by, I don't want to see it in full swing, got it?"

"Yeah, Sarge, sorry."

I rolled my eyes. "Take your post."

About two hours later, I drove by the park on First Avenue. Sure enough, there's the crap game going full tilt. There must have been ten guys hunched over the dice, and a sidewalk full of money.

I pulled in by a hydrant on the corner. "NSU sergeant to Post Nine."

The lilting voice of Mea Culpa responded. "Post Nine, Sarge."

"Ten-eighty-five me on First Avenue and Avenue A." She was there in two minutes.

"Did you tell those mooks over by the park to break up the game?"

She looked like she was caught in the Oval Office making nice to the president. "Uh, I told them to move along, but they wouldn't listen to me. Sorry."

Now I was pissed. "Get in the car."

We drove to the park. A few of the shooters glanced our way and went back to the game. Why not? They had carte blanche from the foot post.

I strode up to the guy handling the dice and slapped him full across the face. No one moved, including Officer Culpa. I scooped up the dice, grabbed the first guy I could lay my hands on, and shoved the cubes into his mouth.

"Now get the fuck outta here!" I hollered. They scattered like roaches after the kitchen light has been turned on. If you're outnumbered, make the opposition think you're crazy. Works every time. I turned to Mea.

"Now that's how it's done. You've got a gun, a shield, and a nightstick. Use the goddamn things. If you feel you're outnumbered, call for backup, but never let these mutts get the upper hand. If you do, you're dead. Got it?"

She burst into tears right in the middle of the street.

In full uniform.

She said, "Sorry."

You certainly are, I thought, you certainly are.

The Police Academy was scaring the recruits. For six months they pumped into the rookies' heads that if you used excessive force, the least that would happen to you was that you'd lose The Job; the worst was that you'd be indicted.

Instructors also made it sound as if recruits so much as accepted a free cup of coffee, they'd do life without parole.

So what we got on the street upon graduation was a bunch of rookies who were afraid of their own shadows. This attitude led one cop to behave so cautiously that he was nearly beaten to death by a bunch of street punks.

Knowing that he who hesitates is lost, I would constantly pound into my cops' heads when to use deadly physical force.

"Bottom line: If your life or someone else's life is in danger, shoot the son of a bitch."

A hand was raised in the back of the room. It was Officer What-If, a cop who would question everything and come up with dozens of hypothetical "what-if" questions.

"Sarge, what if you shoot the guy and it turns out he only had a fake gun?"

"Well, shame on him," I said. "You've only gotta be reasonable; you don't have to be right."

"Yeah, but what if you're not sure . . . what if—"

"Don't hesitate. Make a decision and act. It could save your life."

Officer What-If looked perplexed. "But what if—"

"Take your posts."

A few hours later I was enjoying a cup of coffee (the free kind) when my radio keyed.

"Hey, man, can anyone hear this fucking thing?"

I grabbed my portable. "Unit, identify yourself."

A few seconds passed. "I grabbed this cop's radio, man. He's out cold on Stanton Street, man. I think maybe you should come here."

Oh, shit. I tossed the coffee. "Stanton and where?" He told me. I was on my way, light and siren. In the distance, I heard more units racing to the scene.

Officer What-If was laid out cold in the middle of Stanton Street with five Hispanic males circled around him. One of them had police radio clutched in his hand. He ran up to the car when he saw me.

"Six guys, man. The cop told them to break it up and they started pushing him around. He just, like, stood there, man. They beat the shit outta him. I grabbed the radio, man, called for help."

I got out of the car and pointed to my name tag. "See this name? Wagner. You get in a jam you call me, okay?"

"Yeah, man, thanks."

An ambulance rushed the injured cop to Bellevue, where he remained for a week. I visited him when he was able to talk.

"What happened?"

"I was jumped."

"Yeah, I know. Six guys? Why didn't you shoot?"

He looked down at the sheets. "I didn't think I could. I thought I'd get in trouble."

I couldn't believe what I was hearing. Rather than chew him out, I just wished him well and left. He was going to need all the good wishes he could get in his career.

After I retired, I read in the newspaper of a sergeant who was gunned down in Brooklyn. It was Officer What-If. Really makes you think.

23

Pig of the Month

NSU cops came and went. When a new class graduated from the Police Academy, I'd lose my old crew to permanent commands and start all over again with new rookies.

During the late eighties the city was in the midst of a crack epidemic. Because it was so cheap, crack became the drug of choice for the economically deprived. A very potent form of cocaine, crack led to violent outbursts, and an insatiable desire to do as much of the drug as the wallet and the heart would allow. The stuff was instantly addictive, right from the first pipeful. As a result, the homicide rate went through the roof, topping out at over two thousand murders a year, along with a rapid rise in burglaries and robberies.

Police Commissioner Ben Ward, with support from federal law enforcement agencies and a pile of government money, inaugurated Operation Pressure Point on the Lower East Side. The idea was to saturate a neighborhood with cops, and make arrests for drug possession and sale. Gee, what a unique concept.

The EVil was so bad that some street corners had literally hundreds of people milling around making buys. Any cop who turned out of a lower Manhattan precinct at 3:30 could easily have a collar by 3:31. If cops locked up everyone they saw with drugs, by four o'clock there'd be no radio cars left in Manhattan South for patrol. To prevent this I instituted "The Wags Doctrine of Selective Enforcement."

Avenue B and Third Street was one of the worst corners

in our area of responsibility. On an average four-to-twelve tour, hundreds of people from all over the tristate area would gravitate to that corner to buy drugs.

I'd mount the sidewalk with my radio car on Avenue B and push junkies like a snowplow to the other end of the block, where my crew would funnel them into a receiving line, search them, and confiscate drugs. Only those with large quantities of drugs would get arrested; the others would get a beating and be sent on their way. Their stashes would be deposited in a sewer.

I especially liked to target the yuppies from New Jersey in their BMWs. While I'm not a fan of junkies of any social strata, the white professionals who came to the EVil to score, and then drove back to their comfortable little towns complaining about what a cesspool New York was, particularly pissed me off. A few nights sharing a cell with a guy named Angry Black always gave these folks well-needed attitude adjustments. Somehow some of their cars (amazingly only the assholes who gave us a hard time, or told us who they knew) would wind up in the river, although I was never able to figure out how they got there. When they got out of the can, and their cars were fished out of the drink, they'd find the slogan *Just Say No* scratched into the hoods.

In addition to my NSU team, every available cop in the city, plus agents from the Federal Drug Enforcement Agency (DEA) and Alcohol Tobacco and Firearms (ATF), were pumped into the target area. The Ninth Precinct and the northern portion of the Seventh Precinct were ground zero. There were literally hundreds of cops, in and out of uniform, jammed into a one-square-mile area.

Over five hundred arrests were made every day, a booking nightmare. A special area was set aside in the Seventh Precinct to accommodate the traffic and process the prisoners.

In addition to ridding lower Manhattan of junkies, it gave the rookies a fast baptism by fire. The average cop would go from NSU to his or her permanent command with over thirty arrests. I know some cops who spent twenty years on The Job who didn't have that many.

Many drug dealers aren't stupid, a trait they don't share with their customers. So while we were locking up a huge number of users, the daily dealer tally kept diminishing. Some simply moved to other precincts, but many dealers hunkered down and elected to stay, because the EVil was where the money was.

To decrease their chances of getting arrested, the dealers came up with some ingenious plans. Barricading themselves in tenements was one of them. The street was where the cops were, they figured, so if they stayed indoors, there would be less chance of getting caught, or so the theory went.

A few buildings in both precincts were impenetrable. The dealers would cement themselves inside an apartment using cinder blocks and bricks. Deals would be made through a shoe box–size opening in the wall. Money in, state your order, the drugs came out. During the night, dealers would slip out of the buildings through steel-reinforced doors and a series of excavated subterranean catacombs, to be replaced by a new crew. Some drug gangs even booby-trapped the hallways with spring-loaded bear traps beneath flimsy floorboards, like the punji-stake holes in Vietnam Kenny had once told me about. Step on one of those and it was instant amputation. These drug dens were twenty-four-seven operations, with nameless, faceless people running them.

Some bureaucrat suggested we obtain a warrant and bust our way in. It would take a crane to break through those walls, I countered, and by that time the drugs would be destroyed. Besides, we'd probably have to take the entire building down to get to the dealers. Then one day I had an idea.

I bought a few cans of red spray paint and distributed them to my troops.

"Okay, now go and place orders. As soon as someone asks for money, spray them through the holes."

It was a coordinated attack on six fortresses. Later that night, we locked up any red guy we saw on the street. This worked for about two days until the word got out, and the dealers stopped putting their faces close to the holes.

"What now, Sarge?" I was asked by a rookie.

"We go to Plan B."

"What's Plan B?"

"I don't know; I'll make one up."

I decided on chemical warfare. This time around I bought spray bottles, ammonia, and bleach. I was making a serious monetary contribution to New York City's war on drugs.

I mixed the ammonia and bleach, and dumped the caustic fluid into the spray bottles. Then I gathered the troops.

"Okay, I need six volunteers." Twenty-seven hands shot up. "The paint guys put your hands down; let someone else have the fun."

It was another coordinated raid. We wound up temporarily blinding a bunch of pushers. Screams could be heard throughout the neighborhood.

As I drove down Avenue C, a legitimate citizen rushed over to the car.

"Sergeant, there's screams coming from that building." He pointed across the street.

Someone was hollering at the top of his lungs, just as two of my cops came strolling out of the building carrying spray bottles. They smiled. I waved.

I know that my measures were crude, illegal, and worst of all temporary, but we were in a war to take back the streets, and there were no rules.

I knew that as soon as the pain subsided, or the paint faded, the dealers would be right back at it. My satisfaction came from knowing that the drug pushers knew we didn't play by the rules, and anything was possible.

I was reminded of what Kenny used to tell me about the Vietnam War. "Wags," he'd say, "I can't tell you how many operations we went on where we'd take a fucking hill or a village, kill a bunch of the enemy, and lose some of our own men, then leave the goddamn hill by chopper and be forty feet in the air, only to see the VC coming out of the jungle to reclaim their territory."

"So what was the purpose?" I'd ask.

"We killed some of their soldiers, burned down their hooches, put them out of business for a while. It hurts morale when you lose a lot of small battles."

We were winning the small battles, but losing the war.

*   *   *

Operation Pressure Point slowly petered out. While the Lower East Side became safer than Vatican City, the dealers branched out to the outer boroughs, and there weren't enough cops to police the entire island.

Now we had other problems, and they came in the form of squatters.

The late eighties might have been part of the Reagan boom years, but there was still a lot of poverty in the EVil. Homeless people had commandeered a bunch of abandoned city-owned buildings throughout lower Manhattan. After a while, City Hall gave the order to move them out, and if they didn't go peacefully force was to be used.

There were hundreds of squatters living rent-free in fifteen buildings. When the time came to get them out, we met with major resistance.

The squatters were professional agitators. Prior to making a last stand in the abandoned buildings, these people were the driving force behind a series of riots in Tompkins Square Park that claimed many casualties and made national headlines. At that time they were protesting the closing of the park at night. They shouted that the park belonged to "the people," and tried to reclaim it. They lost, but only after a week of pitched hand-to-hand battles with the police.

Now they were in fortified structures, and it would be exceedingly difficult to get them out.

I was in charge of about forty cops. Our mission was to stage a frontal assault on one building at a time, extract the squatters, and arrest them. Easier said than done.

We were bused to a location at Avenue B and Fourth Street, where we were met by at least three hundred squatter/protesters, and a huge bonfire blazing in the intersection. Wooden police barriers were being used as fuel. We were attacked as soon as we got off the bus.

The first casualty was my hat. Someone grabbed it and tossed it into the bonfire. I was lucky I wasn't attached to it. These were some violent people.

They were very organized. I gave the order to

charge, and we waded into the crowd with flailing nightsticks, spraying everything that moved with streams of Mace, including each other.

The original throng of protesters retreated into the block, luring us into an ambush. We were laying out people in the mob like we were swatting flies, but they didn't care. Once we were in the middle of the block, the trap was sprung and everything that wasn't nailed down came off the roofs. These items included milk cartons full of urine, bags of feces, bricks, bottles, Molotov cocktails, bags of Sheetrock, you name it.

Cops began to go down. I lost it. While I was doing my share of swinging, as the boss I was in more of a support mode, keeping everyone in line and shouting orders. Once I saw my troops falling, I stopped being Mr. Nice Guy, pushed my way up front, and started aiming for heads.

Cops are taught to swing their nightsticks low, to go for the torso or limbs. There are two reasons for this: 1) a head shot could kill someone—those nightsticks (or batons, as the politically correct choose to call them) are solid cocobolo wood, and 2) it's poor public relations when a photo is taken of a cop winding up to slug some civilian like he's Roger Clemens.

But I didn't give a damn. For me it was survival. We were outnumbered and trapped. Screw the politically correct and the media. I was out for blood.

Unfortunately, the late eighties was the dawning of the video age, and I was captured by more than one camera, batting my way through the crowd like a mad Mexican in a room full of piñatas.

We prevailed, although at a great price. The squatters were removed, but I lost most of my cops to injuries, some serious. I was a little banged up (and hatless), but otherwise okay.

I was, however, a celebrity. The next day, plastered on tenement walls, lampposts, and under car windshields, was a picture of me bringing a nightstick down on someone's head. The squatters, who had their own neighborhood newspaper, had the picture on their front page, and had proclaimed me Pig of the Month.

I fully expected that I'd be made a scapegoat to appease the liberal sector, but nothing came of it. After things quieted down, and the buildings were demolished to make way for new housing, I went back to being an anonymous boss in a sea of blue.

I was battle-weary, and tiring of being a man without a country. The NSU had no permanent base and no permanent cops, and we were constantly flying to various commands to bring them up to minimum manning and to control the burgeoning crack-fueled crime wave. There was no end in sight to the madness. It was about this time that I started thinking about my eventual retirement.

It was the late eighties, and the AIDS scare was gripping the city. The mayor was on a campaign to close down all gay bathhouses and clubs where members practiced unsafe sex. The gay community was being beaten into legal submission and they weren't about to sit still for very long.

ACT UP was an organization that sprang up in the midst of the chaos. This was a group of militant gays who at first tried to protest peacefully, but when that didn't get them anywhere, they resorted to more aggressive forms of activism.

To be fair, the group had legitimate complaints. Discrimination against AIDS victims in housing and the job market, and the high cost of medication, had brought organized demonstrators to the streets in record numbers. The gay community was dying off by the thousands, and ACT UP wanted satisfaction, and they wanted it immediately.

The demonstrations were becoming increasingly violent, and a reinforced police presence was required. The Pig of the Month to the rescue.

We were assigned to a particularly noisy demonstration in front of Trinity Church, in the financial district

of lower Manhattan, one rainy November afternoon.
With five hundred demonstrators protesting a drug company's limited access to an experimental AIDS drug, we
were outnumbered two to one. This was par for the
course in a city where the mayor's office was concerned
with the show of force.

The demonstrators were lying in the street blocking
traffic. A beefy chief with a bullhorn gave them one minute to pack up and disperse. When they didn't comply,
he issued the order.

"Okay, men, lock 'em up!"

Our leader.

The protesters were divided into two groups, the sitters, who sat in the middle of the street and wouldn't
budge off their asses, and the walkers, who basically co-
operated and got up and walked to a waiting city bus
for the drive to jail.

I was given two cops, who had to carry the sitters to
the bus, while I escorted the walkers. Rank has its privi-
leges. After a while I grabbed another cop and helped
carry the sitters. The cops were struggling by themselves.

It was a chore. It took us about an hour to jam
seventy-seven bodies into the bus, a decidedly tight fit.
It should be noted that because the media was all over
the place, someone had given the order that the prisoners
were not to be handcuffed, lest the public think we were
mistreating the poor souls.

The first thing you learn in the Academy is that *all*
prisoners get cuffed. No exceptions. Lock up an eighty-
six-year-old grandmother for shoplifting? She gets cuffed.
Just shoot a bank robber four times in the head? He gets
cuffed. I'm sure you get the idea.

Today, however, the rule was out the window. So there
I was, on a bus with seventy-seven *uncuffed,* highly
pissed-off prisoners, on our way to the Thirteenth Precinct for booking. Don't think the city didn't provide me
with all the help I needed (or they said I needed). This
translated to two cops. One was a policewoman who
made Dr. Ruth look like Sheena, Queen of the Jungle,

and the other was a male cop who was so skinny he almost disappeared when he turned sideways.

The bus wasn't out of first gear before trouble started. All seventy-seven prisoners decided to make a break for it. They were going to do it by trampling me and my cops, then fleeing out the front door.

The crowd surged forward, pinning me against the fare machine. Several prisoners were jammed into the bus driver's foot well and were pressing on the accelerator. The bus driver, a civilian employee of the Transit Authority, panicked.

The vehicle veered crazily down Third Avenue with the driver screaming, "We're gonna fucking die!" At the same time I was fighting a losing battle trying to keep from being crushed against the windshield. I lost the two cops who were with me. They were somewhere on the floor getting trampled.

Finally I realized that if I didn't do something drastic, I might be killed. Shooting was out of the question, mainly because I couldn't reach my gun, but also because I didn't think it would sit well with the grand jurors I was sure to face should I let loose with six rounds.

One of the prisoners had his back pressed against me. I was able to grab him by the ears and twist. He let out a piercing scream, and the crowd began to retreat to the rear of the bus, or as far back as their sheer numbers would allow. The two cops were battered and stuffed into the space between the first bench seat and the driver. They were useless.

I maintained my grip on the guy's ears, and got him to his knees. "I'll rip his ears right off his head if you don't quiet down and stay still!" I hollered.

Most complied, but a few agitators began to goad the mob. "Fuck him; he's only one cop!"

The bus driver pulled over, opened the door, and started to leave.

"Where the fuck do you think you're going?" I demanded.

He was middle-aged, white, overfed, and scared. The

closest he'd ever come to a riot was probably trying to get the last bet in at OTB on payday. He stammered something, and I ordered him back into his seat. All this time I was maintaining a death grip on my prisoner's ears.

By the time we got to the Thirteenth Precinct booking facility I had practically twisted the guy's ears all the way around. His ears were now facing backward.

This caused quite a stir among the cops in the precinct. "Hey, look at the guy with the Mr. Spock ears!" An ambulance was called. It arrived at the same time as an ACT UP lawyer.

"Where's the guy with the bent ears?" he asked the desk officer. Word had gotten out quickly.

"The prisoners are in the cells, but you can't go back—"

The lawyer was gone, headed for the cell area before anyone could stop him. I caught up with him as he was walking down the cell block.

"Okay," I said, "get out. I'll bring the prisoner to the interrogation room."

He looked at me. He was about a hundred and fifty pounds, all attitude. "You can't tell me what to do. I represent an injured prisoner. A victim of police brutality! I demand—"

"You're under arrest," I said, then spun him around and slapped handcuffs on him.

The prisoners in the packed cells jeered and cursed me. The lawyer sputtered, "I'm a lawyer; you can't do this to me. What's the charge?"

"Criminal trespass."

He was the only prisoner whose charge stuck.

I received seventy-seven civilian complaints for brutality. All were eventually dismissed as unsubstantiated, but this was another episode that was making me increasingly disgruntled with The Job. The crowning touch would come shortly, and I would end my career.

24
End of Tour

After five years in NSU, I was transferred back to the Ninth Precinct as a patrol supervisor. Now, with twenty-one years on The Job, I was one of the old-timers.

Not much had changed. A lot of the cops I'd worked with had either retired, been promoted, or left The Job on some sort of line-of-duty disability, but the physical presence of the EVil remained the same.

Gentrification was still years away, and the squalor that was the Ninth Precinct greeted me like a long-lost relative.

The only thing that was different was the homicide rate. It actually went down. At this point there were about fifty murders a year in the smallest command in the New York City Police Department, down from an average of sixty when I was originally assigned there.

The caliber of cops had also changed. The Vietnam War vets were replaced by suburbanites who had to learn the ways of the mean streets quickly or perish. The Ninth Precinct cops were still a cohesive group, set apart from others on The Job because of the conditions in which they worked, but they lacked the character and verve of the cops I'd worked with during the seventies.

I kept pretty much to myself. I worked out every day in the precinct gym I'd created ten years before, and while I was entitled to a driver, I chose to drive myself most of the time. I had the reputation of being a tough but fair boss, and a cop should expect nothing else from a supervisor.

It was around this time that I began to toy with the idea of retiring. My physical condition notwithstanding (I was in better shape than most men half my age), this was a young man's job.

I couldn't make up my mind. My wife, of course, wanted me to go. By this time we had three kids, all of school age. Pat figured I was pressing my luck if I stayed any longer.

But it was difficult to separate myself from the only job I'd ever had. Police work was as much a part of me as my role as husband and father. During this time of indecision, two incidents occurred that convinced me to finally give it up.

I was asleep. Normally that's what I do at three A.M. I had just completed my last four-to-twelve tour and was looking forward to a three-day swing. I was out like a baby.

It was Pat who heard the noise. I felt an elbow in the ribs.

"Jimmy," she whispered.

"Uh." Alert, ready for action, that's me.

She shook me. "Jimmy, wake up. I think there's someone downstairs."

That got my attention. I sat bolt upright in bed, closed my eyes, and concentrated. There it was! I heard it, too. It sounded like someone was rattling the blinds in the living room. You had to be inside the house to do that.

I swung my legs out of bed. "Wait here." As soon as I spoke I saw a light go on in the hallway outside our bedroom. I heard the intruder stop right outside our door.

I froze. My gun was downstairs. Any cop who has kids goes to extraordinary lengths to secure his guns. My off-duty Smith & Wesson .38 was in a bowl on top of a china cabinet, the cylinder open with a padlock through the frame. If someone attacked our place settings for twelve, I was ready.

As for the present, I was screwed. I made a quick

decision and got back in bed. I whispered to Pat, "Be still."

We huddled under the covers. The door opened slowly. Pat was jammed up against me, shaking ever so slightly. I had the blanket pulled to my nose and was squinting out of one eye.

A black man, well over six feet tall with spiked hair sticking up at least eight inches, walked to the foot of our bed and stared down at us.

We didn't move. He stood stock-still for at least three minutes, just looking at us, then turned and quietly left the room, closing the door behind him.

I sprang out of bed, went to the door, and saw the man creeping down the stairs. My first thought was of my kids, who were all asleep in bedrooms down the hall. I checked on them. They were okay. But what if this guy came back upstairs? I went back to our bedroom and said to Pat, "Call nine-one-one."

She reached for the phone. "Where are you going?" she whispered.

"Hunting." As I left the room I heard her telling an emergency operator that her husband was a cop and someone had just broken into our house.

I stood at the top of the stairs and tried to think of something I could use for a weapon. I went into a hallway closet and grabbed a metal vacuum cleaner attachment. It was about three feet long and had some heft. I'd Electrolux the son of a bitch if I had to.

I heard unidentifiable noises from downstairs. I had to be standing there for ten minutes. Where the hell were the cops? I went back into the bedroom.

"Where's the goddamn police?" I asked my wife.

She shook her head, eyes wide, fear palpable. "They're supposed to be on the way. Did you check on the kids?"

"The guy's still downstairs; kids are asleep." I grabbed the phone and called 911 again.

After whispering our problem to another operator, I went by the window and waited. Seven minutes later a radio car pulled up in front of the house.

"They're here," I said.

"Thank God." Pat got out of bed and stood with me by the window.

It was the middle of summer, so the window was open. I could hear a cop talking on the radio.

"One-two-two Nora at the location, Central. There's nothing here, the house is locked up, no lights on. Make it unfounded."

Unfounded? I was livid. The two lazy bastards in the car never even got out to check on us. The radio car slipped into gear, cruised about forty feet up the street, and stopped. The interior light went on. The cops were either catching up on their paperwork or having coffee.

I stuck my head out the window and, talking as loudly as possible without alerting the burglar, said, "Hey, up here! There's a man in the house, downstairs." No response.

"What are they doing?" Pat asked, the panic returning to her voice.

"Goofing off, that's what."

I took the screen off the window and sailed the thing like a Frisbee across our lawn. It landed with a crash right on the windshield of the radio car. That got their attention. Both cops jumped out of the car.

No more whispering. "I'm on The Job; there's a man in my house!" With that, I rushed downstairs. On the way down I heard my oldest kid, Jimmy, call out from the hallway, "What's going on?"

I took the stairs three at a time.

The living room was dark, which was the way I wanted it. I knew the layout of my house and could have done pirouettes around the furniture blindfolded.

The intruder was hiding behind a curtain by the sliding-glass doors he'd broken through. I was on him in a nanosecond, beating him with everything I had. I must have hit him forty times with the metal pipe before the two cops dragged me off him.

I was struggling with the cops, trying to get at the burglar, who looked like he'd been dipped in a barrel of blood. I'd opened up his head and pounded his nose to mush. He was unconscious.

One of the cops jammed me up against the wall while his partner handcuffed the prisoner.

"Daddy, what's going on?" My five-year-old daughter, Patricia, was standing at the bottom of the stairs with her sister and brother. She was crying.

Pat rushed downstairs, enveloped the kids in loving arms, and gently ushered them back upstairs.

I was hot and hyperventilating, cursing a blue streak. One cop stood between me and the prisoner, while his partner flipped the man onto his back.

"He's in bad shape," he said to his partner.

"What's your name?" the cop who was holding me asked. I shook him loose and told him who I was and where I worked.

"You know, Sarge," he said, "you gotta take this collar. We're not touching him."

I looked at the cop's name tag. Partega. A name I'll never forget. "What?"

"This guy's beaten to a pulp. You tuned him up; you lock him up." Partega was young, about twenty-five. His partner—the name tag read Locascio—was a few years older.

I wasn't about to start an argument with these guys. "Call your boss."

A sergeant responded within five minutes. An older man, he looked like he'd been around the block a few times. He wanted to talk with me privately. As we went to the kitchen, I heard the unmistakable siren of an ambulance rapidly approaching.

"What do you want to do?" the sergeant asked me.

I was puzzled. "About what?"

He tossed his head. "Shithead inside. You want him arrested?"

I was stunned. "Of course I want the cocksucker arrested! He broke into my house; he could've killed my kids!"

"He have a weapon?"

I was getting hot all over again. "How the fuck am I supposed to know? I've got a houseful of weapons." I waved an arm around the kitchen. "Jesus, there's knives in here. He could've grabbed anything."

Partega poked his head into the kitchen. "Sarge?"

The sergeant excused himself and walked into the living room. He was back in a flash. "Your guy out there is an escaped prisoner from South Beach Psychiatric Center. Just came over the radio." He shook his head. "We're gonna psycho him, bring him back to the hospital. No collar."

We argued for ten minutes. I insisted he leave the decision whether or not to recommit him to a judge. "Lock the son of a bitch up," I said. "He was sane enough to make it here from the hospital. It's five goddamn miles. He was sane enough to break into my house."

No amount of persuasion worked, and the prisoner was returned to South Beach. I went sick with a line-of-duty injury to my hand, which was beginning to swell. But I was by no means through with the two cops who failed to do their jobs by calling in my emergency call as "unfounded."

I did some investigating on my own and found out that Partega and Locascio worked steady late tours (midnight to eight in the morning) because they had full-time day jobs. They didn't want to get involved in a possible arrest situation where they'd have to miss their moonlighting jobs, so they blew off my 911 call by saying everything was okay at my house.

I was more than pissed. To my way of thinking, these cops shouldn't have been on The Job. They were disgracing the uniform by pretending to be real police officers.

I contacted Sgt. Larry Ernst, a Sergeants Benevolent Association trustee, and told him my story. He listened to the entire tale and said one word, "Unbelievable," after which he personally took me to the borough commander, a one-star chief.

The chief soaked in the tale, and was even more pissed than I was.

"Sergeant Wagner," he said, "I'm ordering you to file civilian complaints against those two officers."

Since I was off duty when the incident occurred, filing civilian complaints was the accepted procedure. I drove to the One-Two-Two Precinct and filled out the forms.

A few weeks passed. While I awaited the results of the investigation, I checked on the disposition of the mutt who'd broken into my house.

After receiving numerous stitches, he'd been returned to South Beach Psychiatric Center, where he remained. I was still determined to pursue my goal of having him arrested for burglary.

I went to the One-Two-Two to speak to a boss, any boss. A duty captain read me the section of the New York State penal law that defines burglary.

"'A person enters or remains in a dwelling with the *intent* to commit a crime therein.'" He closed the book. "It's our feeling that in his psychological state, he couldn't form intent."

I was thinking that I could form intent right then and there and introduce this asshole captain to the same vacuum cleaner attachment that I'd used on the burglar. However, while I may be a little crazy, I'm not stupid. I left the captain's office and went to my favorite backup strategy—the always reliable Plan B.

I looked for any former Ninth Precinct cop assigned on Staten Island who would have the testicular fortitude to do the right thing.

Det. Bobby Edwards fit the bill. Formerly a patrol cop assigned to the EVil, Bobby had been transferred to the Crimes against Persons Squad on Staten Island when he was promoted to detective. I remembered Bobby as a super cop with a long memory.

I went to his office cold, no preemptive phone call. He was at his desk, almost hidden behind a pile of paper.

"Hey, remember me?" I said.

It took him a second, but his face lit up when the lightbulb went on. "Hey, Wags! Man, come on in, sit." He pulled out a chair.

We reminisced for a few minutes, but he knew I'd

stopped by for a reason. I related the story. He was quiet, took some notes. When I was finished he threw down his pen.

"Fuck him; he's going to jail." And off he went with a few uniforms to South Beach and placed the man who'd broken into my home under arrest.

Would anyone ever wonder why I revere the cops from the Ninth Precinct? Those guys were a breed apart, cops who remembered that our lives depended on each other, who would risk being called on the carpet to help someone with whom they shared their time in hell.

I was sitting in the Integrity Control Officer's (ICO) office in the One-Two-Two Precinct. The ICO, Lieutenant Murphy, had been assigned to investigate my civilian complaints against Officers (and I use the term grudgingly) Partega and Locascio. It had taken three months to complete the investigation. Today was judgment day.

"They're each losing a vacation day," the lieutenant said.

I remained under control, pissed off though I was. "A day? What kind of punishment is that? These guys shouldn't even be cops. They're more concerned about their day jobs than they are about doing police work. And they knew I was on The Job, for God's sake."

"We feel it's a just punishment, Sergeant. Let's get this behind us, shall we?"

What choice did I have? I was so disgusted with what The Job had become I just didn't give a damn. "Yeah, sure," I said, as I got up and started for the door. No handshake, no "Thanks, Loo." I just wanted to get the hell out of there.

"Oh, hold up a minute, Sergeant Wagner; we're not finished."

I turned. "Huh?"

"You're getting a written reprimand in your folder."

I was dumbstruck, almost speechless. "What?" I couldn't be hearing him correctly. "A reprimand? For what?"

"For using vulgar language to the responding officers and the sergeant."

Un-fucking-believable.

About a month later, my wife found a steak knife with a taped handle that had been shoved under the carpet behind the couch in the living room, near where I'd tackled the nut the night he'd broken into my home. The presence of the knife would qualify as intent, but by that time the case had wound its way through the system. After spending a few months in jail awaiting a disposition, our psycho/burglar was returned to South Beach Psychiatric Center.

If there was a more disgusted, depressed cop on The Job than I was, you'd be hard-pressed to find him. And while I was close to calling it a career, the proverbial straw would come in the form of a chance meeting.

"Yeah, c'mon, I'll give you a ride," I said to the young rookie who was looking for transportation to the Seventh Precinct for a crowd-control detail.

The Staten Island Nut Incident was still fresh in my mind even though it had happened eight months ago. Every day I woke up in a different frame of mind. If I'd had a particularly frustrating tour the day before, I'd ruminate about retiring. A decent tour had me in a better mood. There were more of the former.

After dropping the officer off at the Seventh Precinct station house, I went inside to use the men's room. On the way out of the building I passed a group of young cops milling around, part of the crowd-control detail, waiting for direction from a boss.

There had to be fifty cops scattered around, doing what cops do best: waiting. For some inexplicable reason, I glanced down at the shield of one of the cops as I approached my radio car.

He was wearing my old shield!

I did a double-take and stopped. My old weathered tin, number 28725, was adorning the chest of a twenty-something Hispanic cop. His name tag read Rodriguez.

I stopped directly in front of him. "Well, will you look at this," I said, and smiled.

Rodriguez stiffened, tension evident. Sergeants do that to cops, especially the young ones.

"My shield," I said, "you're wearing my shield. How long've you been on The Job?"

"Uh, eighty-seven, Sarge, gonna be three years," he said, his unlined baby face a mask of confusion.

He'd been given my shield after I'd made boss.

"Man, I wore that thing for fifteen years," I said, immediately flashing back to my days on patrol with Kenny.

"Uh, okay, yeah, sure," Rodriguez said, and turned to walk away.

I grabbed his arm. I wanted to tell him the history behind the shield, where it had been, and that he should be proud to wear it.

"I was in the Ninth almost my whole time with that shield. It's been through a lot."

He looked at me blankly.

"You know," I said, "Foster and Laurie . . . Reddy . . . Glover."

I could see that Rodriguez had no idea what I was talking about. He just stared at me, uncaring.

I should explain that to a police officer, a shield is a living, breathing object. That small piece of tin represents the honor and tradition of the New York City Police Department. It goes everywhere with you for your entire career. The only time you're separated from it is when you're asleep, in a shower, or having sex (and sometimes not even then—Maureen the nun liked to . . . Ah, what's the point; that was ancient history). I was the first to wear my shield; it was brand-spanking-new when it was issued to me.

The majority of shields have been handed down from cop to cop for years. Rookies with generations of cops in their families request their relatives' shields when being sworn in. The request is always granted, as steeped in tradition as The Job is, providing the shield hasn't been reissued to someone else.

Cops make crusades out of researching the history of

the shields they wear, often visiting the families of members of the force who wore their shield before them. At least that was what the cops I knew did.

Rodriguez, apparently, was part of the new breed.

"You don't know who Foster and Laurie were?" I asked, hoping this rookie would come out of his fog and snap to. "Reddy and Glover?"

"Uh, no, Sarge. Who were they?"

"The BLA. The Black Liberation Army?"

He shook his head. "Uh-uh. Sorry, Sarge."

I felt like crying. "Look," I said softly, "you wear that tin proudly, okay?" I put my hand on his shoulder, gave a squeeze, got in my car, and keyed the radio.

"Nine Sergeant. Time check, Central."

"Okay, Sarge. It's twenty-three-oh-five hours, KEA-837, First Division radio. Tour's over, boss. Safe home."

I aimed the car toward the Ninth. Yeah, safe home.

Epilogue

I retired on April 19, 1990. In twenty-two years, I compiled over four hundred arrests and forty medals, including the New York State Medal of Valor.

My family was thrilled that I was out. I was apprehensive, as most cops are when they leave the blue cocoon.

My life took a dramatic turn after I left The Job, as I recounted in my first book, *Jimmy the Wags: Street Stories of a Private Eye* (William Morrow, 1999). The paperback came out in 2000, and somewhere in between, a movie deal was made.

I have a new life and a new career as a writer and public speaker. My Web site, www.jimmythewags.com, is visited daily by the curious from all over the world. Best of all, I'm safe. I know that barring an act of God, I'll be around to see my grandchildren grow up. With any luck I'll be a cranky old man, as is my right, and die in bed at an advanced age.

Still, I miss The Job. Even more than The Job, I miss the Ninth Precinct. Oddly enough, I stayed away from the retirement rackets (parties, to you civilians) and the annual precinct reunions.

I wanted to remember the EVil on my own terms, not sit around with a bunch of flabby, retired cops and embellish our war stories. My memories are special to me.

When my coauthor, Patrick Picciarelli, and I were discussing writing this book, I thought it mandatory that we walk the Ninth Precinct. For me, to recall portions of my past that could be jarred loose by seeing a certain tenement, a particular corner. For Paddy, a retired lieutenant from The Job, to familiarize himself with a precinct he worked in only sporadically while a member of the elite Tactical Patrol Force.

We walked the grid, starting at Tompkins Square Park, east to the river, south to Houston Street, and north to Fourteenth Street.

Along the way we talked to store owners and tourists. Yes, tourists. The precinct is now a mecca for visiting suburbanites as well as out-of-towners who visit some of the many exotic restaurants that are now scattered throughout the precinct. Twenty years ago I took my life in my hands every time I ate in what passed for a restaurant in the Ninth. Today the EVil is a gourmet capital.

I found an old foot cop who remembered me. He told me that Ruthie died two years before. She was still grabbing crotches right up until the end. Ruthie was part of The Job's history. May she rest in peace. Watch your hands, Ruthie, wherever you are.

We checked current crime stats. There were *two* reported homicides in the Ninth Precinct in the year 2000. In the early seventies, at the height of the crack epidemic, we'd average fifty to sixty murders a year. The EVil is now downright safe.

New housing abounds. Alphabet City is currently one of the more desirable neighborhoods in the city. In my day, Alphabet City looked like Sarajevo after a U.S. bombing run.

The people are the best thing: white, black, Hispanic, Asian, and some I couldn't put a label on. Families now walk and play together in Tompkins Square Park. Mommies pushing strollers are a common sight everywhere in the Ninth, as are kids playing in the street. These same kids are safely in their homes at night at a reasonable hour. Gone are the days when I'd see three-years-olds wandering the streets unsupervised at midnight.

When we turned up Fourteenth Street, I grabbed Paddy by the arm. "Hey, Paddy, mind if I walk this alone?" After twenty years on The Job, he'd seen a lot, too. It took a cop to read between the lines.

"Yeah, Jimmy, no problem. I'll meet you back at the car." He wandered back in the same direction we'd come from.

I wanted to go to Ya Ya's, the coffee shop where Kenny and I were the night Foster and Laurie were killed. The urge to sit in the same booth, to order the same greasy hamburger, to smell the smells, feel the tension, trade stares with the junkies, was overwhelming.

But Ya Ya's was no longer. It had morphed into an upscale coffee shop packed mostly with white kids, each hovering over a $4 latte.

I walked north on Avenue B to Eleventh Street. On the corner where Greg Foster and Rocco Laurie died, a bunch of white, black, and Hispanic kids played together. I examined the spot where both cops went down, looking for bloodstains, a sign that part of them still lived. Short of spraying the pavement with Lumenal to bring out minute blood particles, all I could see was clean pavement. Time and the elements had washed away the telltale signs of the double assassination that had enveloped the NYPD in a cloak of fear for more than a year. I wondered how many cops today knew the names Foster and Laurie. I knew at least one in the Seventh Precinct who didn't have a clue. And he had my shield.

I went on to Fifth Street, between Avenues A and B. Halfway down the block a few cars were double-parked, in about the same spot where Sergeant Reddy and Andy Glover were gunned down. No kids playing here, just a couple of folks on their way home from work, striding purposefully over the spot where two men gave their lives for the city of New York.

Paddy was waiting for me in the car.

"You okay?"

I shrugged. "A stroll down memory lane. Hungry?"

"Sure."

We stopped at an Italian restaurant on the Brooklyn side of the Battery Tunnel. Paddy had brought a tape recorder and a yellow legal pad with him.

I had a story to tell.